TOC

MANAGING CORPORATE CULTURE

To all my final year
Business Studies students at
City University Business School, 1988

MANAGING CORPORATE CULTURE

RONNIE LESSEM

Gower

Published by
Gower Publishing Company Ltd
Gower House
Croft Road
Aldershot
Hants GU11 3HR
England

Gower Publishing Company
Old Post Road
Brookfield
Vermont 05036
USA

British Library Cataloguing in Publication Data
Lessem, Ronnie
    Managing corporate culture.
    1. Business firms. Management
    I. Title
    658

ISBN 0 566 02774 7

Printed in Great Britain by
Billing & Sons Ltd, Worcester

Contents

Acknowledgements vi

1 Introducing corporate culture 1

2 Uncovering fertile British grounds 13

3 The primal way 32

4 The rational way 46

5 The developmental way 78

6 The metaphysical way 108

7 The primal approach to corporate culture 137

8 A rational diagnosis of corporate culture 149

9 The story of Psion 168

10 The metaphysical approach to cultural transformation 191

11 Managing cultural change 215

Index 227

Acknowledgements

My special thanks go to Michael Hollands, Ben Stoddart and Michael Ron; to Chad Tan, Audra Schneiderjon, Michael McNeil and Jeremy Monk; to Angela Clark, Andrew Gilbert, Andrew Lemonofides and Sally Rowland, for their excellent research work into living corporate cultures. I would also like to thank my good friend David Potter of Psion, and Frances Schultz of JMS Seed Company. Academically, I owe a particular debt to Terry Deal and Allen Kennedy, to Edgar Schein and Harrison Owen. Finally, I'd like to thank Malcolm Stern, Sarah Sutton and Kathryn Harvey at Gower, for their encouragement and editorial assistance.

1 Introducing Corporate Culture

BEING INTRODUCED TO CORPORATE CULTURE

What is culture?

Technical, social and religious culture

As a practising manager, or even as a student of management, you have undoubtedly come across that much bandied about term, 'corporate culture'. After all, those redoubtable students of business excellence, Peters and Waterman, have stressed how important a subject it is. 'Without exception, the dominance and coherence of culture proved to be an essential quality of the excellent companies.'[1]

The problem is, of course, that few of us know what 'culture' actually is. In fact, if you are not an anthropologist by background, you may be in for a surprise.

> CULTURE DEFINED
>
> . . . an integral whole consisting of implements and consumer goods, of constitutional charters . . . of human ideas and crafts, beliefs and customs . . . a vast apparatus, partly *material*, partly *human*, and partly *spiritual*, by which man is able to cope with the concrete, specific problems that face him.[2]
>
> Every culture . . . has three fundamental aspects . . . the *technological*, the *sociological*, and the *ideological* . . . The technological is concerned with tools, materials, technique and machines. The sociological aspect involves the relationships into which men enter . . . The ideological aspect comprises beliefs, rituals, art, ethics, religious practices and myths.[3]

As you can see, there is much more to culture than first meets the management eye. There are material and technological, as well as

1

ideological and spiritual aspects to it. So techniques and products, relationships and charters, customs and religious practices all have their place.

The concept of 'culture' therefore cuts across the traditional business disciplines of production and marketing, finance and human resources.

Corporate culture as shared values

'Corporate culture', in other words, is not the exclusive preserve of the personnel or general manager. It has much more wide-ranging scope and implications. In the course of this book we aim to uncover these, and then to help you create the right corporate culture for your purposes.

But why, we must first ask, has the concept conventionally, and recently, acquired more limited connotations? To answer this question we need to return to Peters and Waterman who, in recent years, have become the high priests of business management.

CORPORATE CULTURE DEFINED

As we worked on research of our excellent companies, we were struck by the dominant use of story, slogan, and legend as people tried to explain the characteristics of their own great institutions. All the companies we interviewed, from Boeing to Macdonald's, were quite *simply rich tapestries of anecdote, myth and fairy tale.*

And we do mean fairy tale. The vast majority of people who tell stories about T.J. Watson of I.B.M. have never met the man or had direct experience of the original more mundane reality . . . Nevertheless, in an organizational sense, these *stories, myths, and legends* appear to be important, because they *convey the organization's shared values, or culture.*[4]

We can see that the two Americans have taken us down a particular cultural track in which the sociological and ideological eclipse the technological.

Moreover, for many managers one step removed from Peters and Waterman's original insights, the simpler and singular concept of 'shared values' (sociological) overtakes the more complex and interwoven idea (ideological) of story, myth and legend.

Thus 'culture' and 'shared values' become interchangeable. The rich cultural diet – with its material, human and spiritual ingredients – is reduced to a poor, and ill-nourished equivalent. It is my intention, in this book, to offer a rich diet rather than a poor one. I only hope that in the process I do not give you indigestion!

To establish a context for this rich cultural diet, I shall go through the major reasons why corporate culture has risen to managerial prominence.

Why corporate culture?

Almost overnight, or so it seems, 'corporate culture' has become a byword in management circles.

In the fifties and sixties MBO – management by objectives – was the order of the manager's day. In the sixties and seventies OD – organization development and the management of change – exercised progressive managers' minds.

In the eighties and nineties it seems likely that *corporate culture* will play a dominating role in general management thinking. Why should this be?

There are, in fact, four main reasons:

1. Management has become *progressively more human.*
2. There has been a recent move *back to basics.*
3. Managers, today, have become *'cultivators of meaning'.*
4. *Myth and ritual* have now entered the management arena.

As we examine each in turn we shall discover that 'corporate culture', in its essence if not in current terms, has been evolving over at least fifty years.

Why?

YOU HAVE BECOME PROGRESSIVELY MORE HUMAN

'Culture is the total pattern of human behaviour dependent on man's capacity for *learning* and transmitting *knowledge* to succeeding generations through the use of systems of *abstract thought.'* (*Webster's New International Dictionary*)

Through the emergence of the behavioural sciences

Culture, as the anthropologists tell us, is what *distinguishes rational man from instinctive animal.* Over the past fifty years, business enterprise in particular, and the management of organizations in general, have become more rational and also more human.

As life, at least in the industrialized world, has become 'less brutish and short' so the softer qualities have begun to gain precedence over the harder survival-oriented ones. The same process of evolution has affected the theory and practice of management.

Whereas traditional (classical) approaches to both enterprise and organization have been economic and administrative, contemporary management theory and practice is more social, 'behavioural' and humanistic in its orientation. However, even as hardened an engineer and administrative theorist as Henri Fayol[5] referred in the 1920s to 'esprit de corps' as a vital constituent of an organization's functioning.

Twenty years later, in his seminal work on 'Leadership and Administration', the American sociologist Philip Selznick outlined his views on the properly functioning organization. People like Selznick paved the way for the emergence of the behavioural sciences.

CRITERIA FOR ORGANIZATIONAL HEALTH

1. *Security* of the organization as a whole in relation to the social forces in its environment.
2. The stability of the *lines of authority* and communication.
3. The stability of *informal relations* within the organization.
4. The *continuity of policy* and of the sources of its determination.
5. *A homogeneity of outlook* with respect to the meaning and role of the organization.[6]

A leading advocate of the so-called behavioural sciences has been the American organizational psychologist, Warren Bennis. In the sixties he wrote his treatise on what he called 'organizational health'.[7] In fact, organizational health, organizational climate and the role of values and ethics in management predated the concept of 'corporate culture'.

For Bennis, mental health – within the individual or the organization – resulted from a 'scientific' outlook on life. It included a spirit of inquiry, a desire to experiment, and an adaptative personality. It depended on a certain behavioural or cultural attitude rather than on a set of depersonalized, albeit 'scientific' procedures.

Establishing a rationally based culture

Bennis' concept of the fully functioning organization, like that of his academic predecessor, Philip Selznick, predates that of 'corporate culture' by a full generation. Both men have been advocates of a scientific and behaviourally oriented approach to management that anticipates the approach to corporate culture that Edgar Schein[8] of M.I.T. has taken (see Chapter 2).

This *rationally based corporate culture*, then, *includes enduring and adaptable relations with social forces inside and outside the company*, both *formally and informally constituted, reinforced by continuity of learning and policy making and by homogeneity of outlook.*

The rationally based culture is therefore represented by:

- the company's definition of its business
- prevailing values, attitudes and beliefs
- the shape of its formal and informal structures
- the business' primary knowledge base.

No sooner, though, had management entered the age of reason than its very rationality was knocked on the head. Unfortunately amongst practising managers, or so it seemed, the hard, procedural side of rational management – rigorous and methodical, had eclipsed Bennis' soft, behavioural side – curious and adaptable.

'Professionalism in management is regularly equated with hard headed rationality . . . It doesn't show how strongly workers can identify with the work if we give them a little say-so . . . It doesn't show that good managers make meanings for people, as well as money.'[9]

YOU HAVE GONE BACK TO MANAGEMENT BASICS

'Culture is that *body of customary beliefs*, social forms, and material traits constituting a distinct *complex of tradition* of a racial, religious, or social group.' (*Webster's New International Dictionary*)

Through the emergence of anthropology in management

Secondly, and ironically then, corporate culture has grown out of a *back to basics* movement in management. It is thereby rooted not in the contemporary behavioural sciences, but in that traditional discipline, imbedded in the primitive world, anthropology.

'Culture', in this primal context, is not a reflection of management's sophistication, but of its most basic, customary, and visible activities and sentiments.

Peters and Waterman, in their search for excellence amongst American companies, discovered that the best ones, above all else, were 'Hands-On, Value Driven'.

FIGURE OUT YOUR VALUE SYSTEM

Let us suppose that that we were asked for one all-purpose bit of advice for management, one truth that we were able to distil from the excellent company research. We might be tempted to reply, *figure out your value system*.

Decide what your company stands for. What does your enterprise do that gives everyone the most pride? Put yourself out ten or twenty years in the future: what would you look back on with greatest satisfaction?[10]

The two Americans rejected the sophisticated concepts of their academic predecessors, and concluded that plain and simple *shared values are the major source of excellence*. Those shared values, in turn, emerge out of a cohesive corporate culture.

Yet why, you might well ask, did the notion of shared values lead to the concept of corporate culture, in particular?

Establishing a 'primally' based culture

For Peters and Waterman 'culture' not only had a primal ring to it, but it was also a simpler and more telling concept than, say, 'organizational health' or 'organizational functioning'. Moreover, as highlighted in Tom Peters' second book,[11] the concept of culture – unlike behavioural theory – was as much concerned with product as with people, and with customer as with worker.

This primal approach to culture is best articulated by those other two American analysts, Deal and Kennedy[12] (see Chapter 3).

Their *corporate culture represents* a return, then, to *the primordial unity of a closeknit community, where producer and consumer, art and artifact are tightly integrated and are personally as well as visibly directed.*

Such a primal culture is therefore represented in:

- immediately impactful stories, fairy tales and legends
- tangible products, services and mission statements
- business heroes and a cultural network of characters
- management by wandering about and a bias for action.

However, Pascale and Athos' ideas, if not Peters and Waterman's, also represented a departure from a nationally circumscribed concept of management, towards a globally based one.

YOU HAVE BECOME MAKERS OF MEANING

'Culture is the *art* or practice *of cultivating*; the *act of developing* through education, discipline or social experience; the enlightenment and excellence of *taste* acquired through *aesthetic* and intellectual training.' (*Webster's New International Dictionary*)

Through the emergence of Japanese management

Twenty years ago the managerial workshop of the world was located, indisputably, in the USA. Although a few management theories originated from Europe, the vast majority were based on American concepts and applications.

The resulting stranglehold was not broken until the early eighties, when Pascale and Athos, themselves American, uncovered 'The Art of Japanese Management'. Because the Japanese had by this time made such heavy inroads into the American and European economies, the managerial world was eager to discover how the Japanese did it.

Pascale and Athos revealed that *managerial reality*, in the first instance, is not an absolute. Rather it is *socially and culturally determined*. In other words, it is cultivated in particular cultural soils. That is why the Japanese approach to management, rooted in one set of historical and geographical conditions, is so different from the American one, rooted in another.

Secondly, Pascale and Athos concluded that all great companies, wherever they are based, have to *make meaning* for their stakeholders inside the organization and out, by recognizing their maintenance and development needs. Similarly, they have to *cultivate meaningful products* and services for their individual customers and collective markets.

THE ART OF MANAGEMENT

In management, as in music, there is a bass clef as well as a treble. The treble generally carries the melody in music, and melody's equivalent in management is the manager's style. A manager's style – the way he focusses his attention and interacts with people – sets the 'tune' for his subordinates . . .

Beneath these messages is a deeper rhythm that communicates more fundamentally. The bass in music – whether hard rock or a classical symphony – often contains much of what moves the listener. So, too, the 'bass' of management conveys meanings at a deeper level and communicates what management really cares about. These messages can influence an organization profoundly.

In Japanese organizations, a great deal of managerial attention is devoted to ensuring the continuity and consistency of these 'bass clef' messages.[13]

Similarly, the Japanese devote underlying attention to the quality
and consistency of product development, manufacturing and distribution. The analogy of *cultivation*, with its rearing and nurturing
associations, is a very appropriate one in this developmental and
cultural context. It *draws more on ecology or biology than on
behavioural science or anthropology*.

Establishing a 'developmental' culture

Within an Eastern management context, then, the two American
organizational psychologists, Pascale and Athos, have highlighted
the significance of an aesthetic awareness for the quality conscious,
and harmoniously oriented Japanese manager. This form of awareness affects both the material and the social fabric of the organization. This is portrayed in my own book 'The Roots of Excellence'[14]
(see Chapter 4).

Such a *corporate culture*, therefore, *has to cultivate a humanly
fulfilling context – in space and time – within which the production
and consumption of needed, worthwhile, and quality products and
services can take place.*

This *'developmental' culture* is represented through:

- the history, and evolution of the company and its people
- the social/economic/cultural contexts in which it evolved
- the quality/meaning/significance of its products/services
- the design and 'quality of life' of its working environments.

Commonplace understanding of corporate culture is restricted to
the rational, primal and developmental domains with which we
have now become familiar. They comfortably span the technological
and social, but not the ideological aspects of culture (see note 3
above). In other words, in terms of Malinowski's initial definition,
we have given scant attention to the 'spritual' attributes of culture.
It is to these that we now turn.

MYTH AND RITUAL HAVE ENTERED YOUR WORLD

'Culture is that complex whole that includes knowledge, *belief,
superstition, morals, religion*, law, customs and art.' (*Webster's
New International Dictionary*)

Through the emergence of a new management spirit

Until very recently few managers, management teachers or students, would have acknowledged that myths, rituals and seemingly *religious* practices had a place within the mainstream of business enterprise. While business ethics surely had its place it was always a peripheral one.

Pascale and Athos, initially, challenged the prevailing wisdom by comparing and contrasting Eastern with Western approaches to management and organization.

CULTURE AND SPIRIT

The large organization began to emerge as a dominant organization in society around the turn of the century. As the West tended to lead the rest of the world in spawning such enterprises it is not surprising that so-called 'modern' management, as we know it, is largely a Western creation.

The scope of activity of these large and diverse enterprises required tiers of management and delegation of authority. But how could those without ownership be trusted? Nearly half a century was needed for the concept of professional management to establish itself.

How could these new 'professionals' manage? The principal problems facing them were and are (1) how to organize efficiently and delegate responsibilities, and (2) how to reward and control employees, as well as how to control resources and ensure results. The way in which management solves these problems in society is a measure of itself.

The principal differences between Eastern institutions and those in *the West* is that ours *turned to organizational structure and formal systems* to cope with these challenges. In contrast, *Eastern institutions*, while until recently advancing more slowly in thinking about organizational forms and formal systems, *paid much more attention to* social and *spiritual means*.[15]

In the last two or three years, in particular, the role of 'spirit' in organizational life has suddenly gained a new prominence in management circles. The student of corporate culture who has done most to promote what might be termed a 'metaphysical' approach to management is Harrison Owen.

His major source of influence is neither anthropology, ecology nor behavioural science, but what is termed the *phenomenology of religion*. In other words, Owen draws on the language – of myth and ritual, covenant and liturgy – that is common to all religions.

Moreover, as a management consultant and lay preacher, Harrison Owen has taken a particular interest in the spirit of an

organization, including the ways in which it is created and transformed. His starting point is myth. This 'spirit' is contained within
the seminal stories of an organization's being.

Establishing 'metaphysically' based management

Myth is the story which represents an organization's past, present
and prospective future. Ritual is the tangible, and social means
whereby this myth is regularly re-enacted. For example, there is the
story of Michael Marks, the founder of Marks and Spencer, who set
up his market stall in the 1880s, pricing every item at one penny.
This was, in embryo, the first self-service supermarket in Great
Britain.

Today this vast retailer is converting all its cash tills to an
electronically controlled, integrated information system. In telling
the story of this latest information processing revolution, the company is re-enacting, through an appropriate communication
medium, the creation of the first penny bazaar. In the course of it
M & S is enabling its staff to relive, in their imaginations, the
creative process that Michael Marks initiated.

CULTURE AND TRANSFORMATION

Myth and ritual is the image and channel for Spirit. As image, mythos
– myth and ritual combined – gives us the 'picture' of the shape and
quality of Spirit. Mythos is therefore simultaneously representational
and formative.

Our intent is not that organizations become more spiritual, but rather
that we might *recognize that organizations, in their essence, are spirit*,
and then get on with the important business of caring intelligently and
intentionally for this most critical and essential of elements.[16]

Harrison Owen, in fact, has done more than anyone else to uncover
the metaphysical aspects of corporate culture (see Chapter 5).

The metaphysically based culture, then, *encompasses the spirit
of an organization, thereby covering its myths and rituals, including
those stories of creation and of resurrection through which vision is
turned into action, and vice versa.*

It is represented by:

- the creation stories and their ritualistic re-enactment
- the creative vision behind the acts of business foundation
- the technological and cultural soil in which the products and
  services are deeply imbedded
- the profound art or science underlying the business activity.

CONCLUDING YOUR CULTURAL INITIATION

You re-visit corporate culture as a whole

Corporate culture, though apparently a new concept on the management horizon, actually draws on a longstanding tradition of theory and practice. If that extended tradition is not taken into account then you, as a manager, will lose the power and richness of the concept, and its application.

Table 1.1 outlines the key features of corporate culture, drawing on its full breadth – technical, social and spiritual, and depth – primal, rational, developmental and metaphysical.

Table 1.1   Corporate culture as a whole

Breadth	Technical	Social	Ideological
Depth			
Primal	Physical impact	Shared values	Stories, fairy tales, legends
Rational	Product concept	Formal/informal relationships	Attitudes, beliefs, ethics, values
Developmental	Product quality and significance	Quality of working life	Cultural context and business evolution
Metaphysical	Artistic/scientific origin – destiny	Shared creation	Myth and ritual; spirit and vision

These will be spelt out in much more detail, both in theory and in practice, in the chapters that follow.

Planning your corporate culture

The plan of this book is as follows. Chapter 1, the *introduction*, outlines the breadth and depth of corporate culture; Chapter 2 sets out the European and British context in which most of this book's business applications are set.

Secondly, the section on *Theory* lays the theoretical foundations

(Chapters 3, 4, 5 and 6), from the primal surface to the metaphysical depths. Thirdly, the largest section on *Practice* (Chapters 7, 8, 9 and 10), represents each of the four cultural domains, through the appropriate companies and their cultures.

Finally, the *Conclusion* (Chapter 11) on managing cultural change encourages you to relate theory and practice with the help of a cultural inventory which you are able to apply.

REFERENCES

1 Peters, T., and Waterman, R., *In Search of Excellence*, Harper & Row, 1982, p. 75.
2 Malinowski, Bronislaw, *A Scientific Theory of Culture*, Oxford University Press, 1948.
3 Lewis, John, *Anthropology Made Simple*, W.H. Allen, 1969.
4 Peters and Waterman, op. cit., p. 75.
5 Fayol, Henri, *Industrial and General Administration*, International Management Institute, 1930.
6 Selznick, Philip, *Foundations of the Theory of Organizations*, American Sociology Review, vol. 13, 1948, pp. 25-35.
7 Bennis, Warren, *Changing Organizations*, McGraw-Hill, 1968, p. 34.
8 Schein, Edgar, *Organisational Culture and Leadership*, Jossey Bass, 1986.
9 Peters and Waterman, op. cit., p. 279.
10 Peters and Waterman, op. cit., p. 29.
11 Peters, T., and Austin, N., *A Passion for Excellence*, Collins, 1986.
12 Deal, T., and Kennedy, A., *Corporate Cultures*, Addison Wesley, 1983.
13 Pascale, R., and Athos, A., *The Art of Japanese Management*, Penguin, 1982, p. 177.
14 Lessem, Ronnie, *The Roots of Excellence*, Fontana, 1986.
15 Pascale and Athos, op. cit., p. 24.
16 Owen, Harrison, *Spirit, Transformation and Development in Organizations*, Abbott Publishing, 1987.

2 Uncovering Fertile British Grounds

UNCOVERING THE GROUNDS FOR BUSINESS

The global balancing act

ADAPTABILITY AND HARMONY

In my book *The Global Business*[1] I identified particular cultural dilemmas that had to be resolved by each of the four quarters of the globe. It was, and is, my opinion that although, for example, the Chinese and the Japanese in the East are very different from one another, as are the British and the French in the North, there are underlying cultural attributes that each holds in common.

As a result the four quarters of the globe have different points of orientation, affecting their economies and societies, as they evolve.

More specifically, as they evolve and develop, countries in the East have to achieve a balance between *adaptability* and *harmony*. It is in such combined cultural grounds, therefore, that Japanese or Chinese companies have to be nurtured and developed.

ENTERPRISE AND COMMUNITY

The West, that is the United States of America in particular, is built upon very different grounds. The fundamental issue facing the American nation is that of balancing *enterprise* and *community*. It is from such cultural grounds, therefore, that the American pursuit of business excellence has emerged.

VISION AND ACTION

It is the developing countries in the South that have made least impact, to date, on global business development. The indigenous cultures of African and Latin American countries have, until very recently, been dominated by colonial masters to the extent that their own innate identity has remained largely underdeveloped. From what I have observed and experienced, though, I suspect that the

13

critical balance to be secured, in Southern grounds, is between dreams or *vision*, and reality, or *action*.

Now I want to uncover those Northern grounds upon which this book is being written. In other words I want to look at Europe in general, and at Great Britain in particular. The unique balancing act that has to be accomplished in a Northern setting is that of combining *freedom*, on the one hand, with *order*, on the other.

Balancing freedom and order

Fertile grounds for *order*, in a British setting, are found in two places. The one contains a spirit of *tolerance*, and the other an orientation towards *quality*. Thus fertile grounds for organizational order do not lie in regimented and class-based authority but in a sense of fairness and justice (tolerance), coupled with a sense of aesthetic balance and appreciation (quality).

Similarly, fertile grounds for individual *freedom* in Britain are to be found in two other places. The one contains a spirit of *creativity* and the other a love of *recreation*. Thus fertile grounds for personal freedom lie not in 'bucking the system' for its own sake, nor even in 'making your pile'. Rather it lies in a combination of subtle humour, scientific inventiveness and artistic illumination (creativity), coupled with a sense of fun and a love of play (recreation).

Let me now investigate each of these in turn.

YOU NEED, ON THE ONE HAND, ORDER

The most fertile grounds for organizational order, in Great Britain in particular if not in Europe in general, combine the pursuit of quality with a spirit of tolerance. Similarly unfertile business grounds, derived from the same cultural source, would combine overdue product orientation with a spirit of apathy or indifference.

The pursuit of quality

Productivity is higher in New York, Dusseldorf, Paris and Stockholm. There is a nervous intensity in these towns; crowds hustle along city streets, heads down, business-like. People in London streets tend to amble round, move more slowly. This hurts the growth rate, but it may ease the psyche.[2]

The ideal businessman

The above quotation from a correspondent with the *Washington Post*, Bernard Nossiter, may be less applicable to Thatcherite Britain than in the sixties and seventies, but a strong grain of truth remains. John Ruskin, the nineteenth-century English writer and philosopher, described his ideal businessman as one dedicated to a code of honour instead of a calculus of advantage, and 'taking as his duty the enhancement of the *quality, not* the *quantity of life*'.

J.A. Hobson, the economic historian, followed Ruskin in arguing that the true value of a thing is neither the price paid for it, nor the amount of present satisfaction it yields to the customer, but the intrinsic service it is capable of yielding by its right use. *Those goods that have a capacity for satisfying wholesome human wants provide 'wealth'*, whereas those that are detrimental to man he called 'ilth'.

A.H. Marshall, the influential economist of the late nineteenth century, suggested that *money should be incidental to the task of doing a job well*. He hoped to encourage the spread of such 'economic chivalry' amongst the nation's business elite. In fact, just before he died he wished he had devoted his life to psychology rather than to economics.

The emergence of cottage industry

To trace the emergence of this quality consciousness we need to go back to the fifteenth century. By that time the feudal manor had been broken up, and the serfs had been given their freedom.

In fact, the fifteenth-century modern village was a society of wealthy farmers, village craftsmen, and free, but landless, labourers drifting into the towns. *Every village had its carpenters, spinners, weavers, smiths, millers and bakers.* These crafts, or trades, gradually became grouped into 'guilds'. The guild members were 'small men' together, *a proud fraternity of skilled men of the trade*.

Though each was divided between master and apprentice, there was no division of authority based on class or inheritance. The guild movement was an egalitarian one, with cultural, religious and educational activities blending with one another. The centre of productive activity was the rural cottage, where women played their part alongside the men. In fact, a cotton worker's cottage was a miniature factory, with the whole family working together.

The demise of quality

The guild system, however, was not favourable to capital accumulation. As Britain entered an age of commercial expansion, in the seventeenth and eighteenth centuries, the merchant capitalist rose to prominence. As this occurred, the guild craftsmen began to occupy a position that was subservient to the middleman and trader.

Whereas in the seventeenth and eighteenth centuries, the cottage remained the source of supply for the dominant industries, that is wool and cotton, by the nineteenth century the town and factory began to gain prominence. In the in-between stage, as rural industry declined and urban centres were established, there was much unemployment and misery for women. And once they became factory hands, while the women gained a certain independence, they lost many of the best things in life.

> In the 1790s the modern English slum town grew up to meet the momentary needs of the new type of employer. *A rampant individualism*, inspired by no idea beyond quick monetary returns, *set up a cheap and nasty model of modern industrial life*. While the ruling class enjoyed its pleasant life apart, what happened was that . . . Man acquired formidable tools for refashioning his life before he had given the least thought to the question of what sort of life it might be well for him to fashion. (Trevelyan[3])

Although Trevelyan's view is a little one-sided, in essence it is correct. The era of cottage industry, from the fourteenth to the seventeenth centuries, was one of comparative order and equilibrium. Moreover, certainly when compared with the preceding feudal system, and the succeeding urban desolation, it offered men and women in England, on the whole, a comparatively good quality of life. Yet, without the industrial revolution, we could never have had the additional material progress that we see today.

Before we enter into the spirit of the industrial revolution, though, and into the era of creative freedom that fuelled it, I want to investigate the spirit of tolerance in Great Britain. For it is this British tolerance of diversity, alongside the nation's pursuit of quality, which provides inherently fertile grounds for its industrial and social order.

Exercising a spirit of tolerance

'The country has never been torn apart by prolonged bloody

revolution; its rulers have accommodated themselves to change and reform'.[4]

We're a Mixed Lot!

As a refugee from an oppressive regime in the country of my birth, I can vouch for the fact that British society is a relatively tolerant one. The nature and extent of this tolerance has only become apparent to me through a study of history.

It came as a complete eye-opener to me when I picked up Toynbee's monumental *Study of History*[5] and discovered Great Britain's real roots. I have reproduced his diagram (see Figure 2.1) as an indication of how cosmopolitan this nation really is.

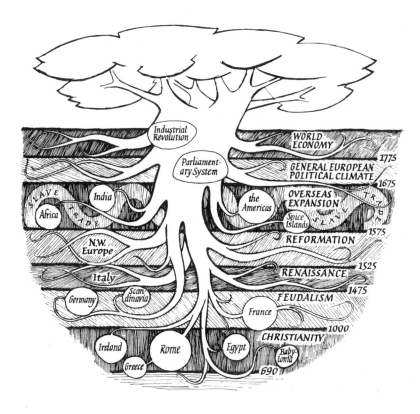

Figure 2.1 Britain's roots in the cultures of the world

Learning to live and let live

English, if not British history, concerns a people who, 500 years before the birth of Christ, first settled on an island off the coast of continental Europe. Our island was created by an Atlantic flood which, eight thousand years ago, cut it off from the European mainland. Like the rest of Europe, Great Britain, after the ending of glacial times, was settled by perhaps three ethnic stocks: Nordic, Alpine and Mediterranean. Then, around 500 BC, the relatively recent settlers followed from France, Germany, Holland and Scandinavia: 'Refugees from the mainland, they were from the beginning a mixed lot, and their story is a standing refutation of all theories that claim racial purity to be a recipe for national success.'[6]

Unable to find sufficient food to maintain themselves, the immigrants sought richer soil. Many of them were Celts whose forebears, in prehistoric times, had spread from the steppes of Southern Russia into Central Europe. In classical times the Celts had been warlike, for in 390 BC they sacked Rome, but by 100 BC they had settled down, to mingle with the native population.

They learnt, as a result of bitter struggle and difficulty, to live with and tolerate other peoples. Successive invasions of Romans, Jutes, Angles and Saxons, Danes, Norwegians and Normans never ultimately broke this pattern of tolerance for diversity:

> The survival of racial minorities, defying yet ultimately intermingling with the predominant majority, together with the island climate and situation, shaped English history. Long tall and broad, short build and tall, dark pigmentation and blonde . . . such intermixture in so small an island helped to make its people many-sided and versatile.[7]

So much diversity among neighbours was a constant stimulus and education. Yet England was fortunate in that the invasions which gave her so mixed an ancestry were separated by long periods. This enabled *each new influence* to be *digested*, and saved the island from either anarchy, at one extreme, or complacency on the other. Moreover, left to themselves the Anglo-Saxons of a thousand years ago might have settled down to a sluggish torpor.

But they were harried by the Danes and Norsemen, and subsequently conquered by the Normans. In the face of these powerful minorities the Anglo-Saxons had to struggle for centuries to retain their customs, institutions and language. Moreover, behind their well ploughed shires, lurked the vibrant and artistic Celts.

The immigrants kept on coming

After the Norman conquest of 1066, the steady stream of immigrants continued, no longer invaders, but refugees flying to England's shores from poverty and persecution. Flemings came in the fourteenth and sixteenth centuries, Huguenots in the seventeenth, Jews in the eighteenth, and West Indians and Pakistanis in our own day. Added to these have been, in recent times, more than a sprinkling of immigrants, from the old colonies and America, who have been attracted to Great Britain by the liberal atmosphere and cultural stimulus.

With the advent of international business, particularly in the City of London, *a mix of faces and cultures from all over the globe have descended on the British Isles*. The fact that English is an international language has reinforced this tendency, also providing educational opportunities that foreigners take up here.

Value in diversity

Over 2500 years, *each* of the invading or immigrant populations *brought something distinctive*, which has never been lost. The Celts were a vibrant and artistic nation, who treated their women as equals – a trait which has only recently begun to return to modern civilizations. The Romans built the first roads, aqueducts and solidly constructed buildings. The Anglo-Saxons were the early farmers, and the Normans were the great advocates of law and order. It was the Danes, however, who introduced the first juries, and these Viking colonists were the early sailors, adventurers and tradesmen.

They, in fact, taught the Anglo-Saxons much in the line of trade, a field of activity which has been strongly developed by the Jews and Asians more recently. The West Indians, in their turn, have brought with them music, and a sporting prowess, which is gradually spreading into many fields of physical and prospectively commercial endeavour. Interestingly enough, the Caribbean community has stepped upon fertile soil.

For the record of British inventiveness in sport, according to Anthony Glyn who wrote *The Blood of a Britishman*, is 'astonishing'. It was the British who gave the world football, cricket, golf, skiing, mountaineering, whist and darts. This will bring us on, as we shall discover (see p. 20), to the love of recreation.

Mingling with the foreign populace

Anthony Glyn has also pointed out that Britain, long before the discovery of America, was 'the America of Europe'. As the furthest European point West, men were driven into these isles by invaders from the East. This tendency has since continued and been combined with yet another British phenomenon:

> The large majority of those whose *wanderlust has taken them abroad* wish to identify closely with the people with whom they have chosen, or happen by chance to live.[8]

T.E. Lawrence is perhaps the best example. I can remember, in Rhodesia, the extent to which the British became Africanized, even if maintaining themselves apart from the black community. It is also notable how many British novels, or short stories, are based on countries other than this one: 'The authors are trying not only to describe the life of a foreign person, but to enter his mind and often his speech as well.'[9]

Attaining order through disorder

The *fertile, orderly grounds* within British culture are, therefore, distinctive. They *involve a blend of craftsmanship and aesthetic appreciation with accommodation of diversity in people and things.* This qualitative order is best represented not within established industrial organizations but in the picturesque rural landscapes, throughout the United Kingdom.

What has always struck me about the countryside in the UK is its extraordinary patchwork structure. It combines, in the most fascinating way, unconventional order with conventional disorder. I was therefore intrigued to discover that the basic principle of an English garden is that 'it must be carefully planned', according to Glyn, 'to look as unplanned and natural as possible'.[10] There must be no formal symmetry. The object is to make the garden appear as if it were part of the natural landscape and not an artificial pattern imposed by man. *Nature must be given*, or seen to be given *its head*, and not cut down to size.

Within this framework, which is instinctive rather than theoretical, an immense amount of variety is possible. Along with this variety comes a balance of shape, timing and form (whereby the heights of various flowers and shrubs, and the different times at which they will flower, are taken into account). The same might apply to an organization structured along those innate lines.

YOU HAVE, ON THE OTHER HAND, FREEDOM

Whereas the pursuit of quality and a spirit of tolerance constitute the fertile grounds for order, a love of *recreation* and a spirit of *creativity* constitute the grounds for freedom – of the most fertile variety.

The love of recreation

The preference for leisure over goods applies chiefly to those toiling in mines or on assembly lines, labouring at routine tasks in huge white-collar bureaucracies, public and private. This work cannot, does not, enlarge personality; quite the contrary. It diminishes it. They work because they must, to earn enough to support themselves and their families. It is these workers who have decided there are limits to how long and hard they will labour for extra goods. Britons, in short, appear to be the first citizens of the post-industrial age who are choosing leisure over goods on a large scale . . . It *reflects* an attitude, *a lifestyle, a choice* . . .[11]

A sense of fun, the pursuit of hobbies, a love of play, and a spirit of adventure, is innate to the British. 'Play', in this context, is not the American variety, involving lots of physical exertion, nor the Mediterranean version, involving a lot of social activity. The British version is more reflective and introverted in character. Moreover, as Nossiter has indicated, it affects working life as well as leisure.

Generalizing from this, Anthony Glyn has gone so far as to say that the Britisher gets more satisfaction from his unpaid work than from his job. This is because, Glyn believes, Britons are such rugged individualists.

Rugged individualism

The more frustrated the British become working for some bureaucratic department, the more energy they put into DIY, community work, gardening, the local computer users' club, or some such recreation. Yonedi Masuda has extrapolated this trend a stage further. As a Japanese futurist who has written a book on *The Information Society*, he claims that:

If the goal of industrial society is represented by volume consumption of durable consumer goods or realisation of heavy mass consumption, the information society may be termed one of highly intellectual creativity where people may draw future designs on an invisible canvas, and *pursue and release individual lives worth living.*[12]

Glyn maintains that the object of work to the average Britisher is to do something, produce something, repair something, complete something. The *work is a means to an end*, not an end in itself. One of the reasons that so many mindless bureaucrats occupy certain positions of mediocrity, in certain large establishments, is because, deep down, they cannot see the purpose in what they do.

This is of course different from the attitude of many Germans, Japanese or Swiss, who may be drawn towards work for its own sake, or on behalf of their organization and community. Such a British attitude to work parallels that of the 'gifted amateur' who becomes involved through innate interest in what he is doing, rather than as a result of professional training.

The cult of the gifted amateur

There is, perhaps, no better known example of 'Britishness', in this recreational context, than the cult of the gifted amateur. One of the earliest and most illustrious cases in point was William Caxton, who brought the printing press to this country in 1477:

> Caxton was an early and prominent example of a well known modern type . . . the individualistic Englishman following out his own hobbies . . . As a successful merchant he made enough money during 30 years to devote his later life to the literary pursuits he loved.[13]

Caxton provides us with a good example of an individual making best possible use of the mature phase of his life. Professor Charles Handy refers to that phase as the 'third age',[14] an age of development and recreation:

> Caxton began by translating French books into English. While so engaged, he fell in love with the mystery of printing with moveable types. In 1474 he produced abroad two of his own translations, the first books to be printed in our language. Then in 1477 he brought over his press to England, set it up at Westminster, and there *during the remaining 14 years of his life*, under royal and noble patronage, *he poured out nearly a hundred books*. His diligence and success as translator, printer and publisher, did much to lay the foundations of literary English.[15]

In turning his recreation into work and vice versa, William Caxton has had a profound effect on this country's destiny. The same applies to the Reverend Doctor Edmund Cartwright, the inventor of the power loom at the end of the eighteenth century. Here is an excerpt from Cartwright's own correspondence: 'Happening to be at Matlock in the summer of 1784 I fell in company with some gentlemen of Manchester, when the conversation turned on Arkwright's spinning machinery.'[16]

One of the company observed that by the time Arkwright's patent had expired, many more mills had been erected, and cotton spun, than there were hands to weave it. Something had to be done about the situation, perhaps involving Arkwright in the invention of a weaving mill. But the Manchester gentlemen agreed that this was impractical:

> . . . addressing arguments I was certainly incompetent to answer or

even comprehend, being totally ignorant of the subject, I contro-
verted, however, the impracticability of their arguments by comment-
ing that there had lately been exhibited in London an automaton
figure that played chess. Full of ideas I employed a carpenter and a
smith . . .[17]

By the following year Cartwright had taken out a patent on a power
loom which he had invented – the clergyman had turned technologist.

Another prominent example of such gifted amateurism is represented in the group of industrialists, scientists, artists and craftsmen
who met in Birmingham – at more or less the same period as
Cartwright's gentlemen from Manchester – and conspired to change
the world.

They established a network of connections, in their so-called
'Lunar Society', by friendship or self-interest second to none. The
society included such people as Wedgwood, Watt, Benjamin
Franklin and Joseph Priestley. And the reason, for example, that
Wedgwood initially joined was to pursue his interests in canals
rather than in pottery or industry. As far as these 'lunatics' were
concerned, their work and recreation were inseparable.

Even for us mortals, we have it on the Anglo-German economist,
E.F. Schumacher's, authority: 'that *work and leisure are comple-*
mentary parts of the same living process and cannot be separated
without destroying the joy of work and the bliss of leisure'.[18]

The Englishman's garden

The archetypal representation of this balance lies in the Englishman's *garden, as a source of recreation* and replenishment from
'work'.

> . . . deep in British hearts is a feeling for the soil and the countryside,
> from which they came less than 200 years ago, and by tending a small
> area of suburban garden, they are trying, perhaps unconsciously to
> keep the link with the soil alive.[19]

The Britisher, according to Anthony Glyn, has chosen to spend his
time and energy in the garden because, above and beyond his sense
of social obligation to the community, his wish to impress his
neighbours, his longing to win prizes at flower shows, 'his garden
is an expression of his creative personality'.

I shall never forget my ride, with a chauffeur employed by ICI
Pharmaceuticals, through a picturesque part of the north of
England. I was particularly struck by the man's apparent state of
contentment with life. Surely the lot of a chauffeur could not be that

inspiring. And then I discovered the man's love of chrysanthe-
mums, not as a business on the side, but as a labour of true love.
That helped me put the chemical industry in perspective.

Reflecting the spirit of creativity

Whereas a love of recreation reflects one fertile source of individual
freedom, a spirit of *creativity* represents the other. Such creative
grounds contain, within them, both artistic and scientific originality
and innovation.

European civilization, as a whole, has made an enormously
creative contribution to the development of mankind. Whereas
artistic creativity has been exhibited by all nations, across the globe,
Europe's uniquely creative contribution has been in the field of
science and technology.

While grounds for such scientific and technological creativity
have stretched across Europe as a whole, a few countries – Britain,
France, Italy and Germany – have, in the last few hundred years,
played the leading part. Of these European countries, Britain's role
has been pre-eminent.

Why should this have been?

The Celtic tradition

We can trace a line of creative activity, from long before the
European Renaissance, stretching *back to the Celts* in pre-Christian
England. In fact it was the Belgic Celts, some 2500 years ago, who
first introduced gold coinage, made pottery, and had ploughs
constructed of iron.

At the same time they practised a form of art that involved
abstract patterns, free flowing curves, and fantastic reliefs. The
Celts who immigrated into Britain produced art of a much higher
quality than the Romans or any other invading group. They had
beautifully shaped pots, colourful clothes, and made exquisite
jewellery. They were also musical, possessing flutes, horns and
trumpets, and the men played a kind of hockey and exercised with
swords.

Smith was a Saxon god

Anthony Glyn points out that the British have traditionally had a
love of metals – which accounts for the most popular name being
Smith. That love dates back not only to the Celts, but also to the
Saxons, one of whose Gods, Thor, was a smith. The Saxons' great

hero, Siegfried, not only conquered and overthrew the existing establishment, but also had to be a smith forging his own sword. Legends like this are deep in the English folk memory. As a result, *the industrial revolution* that began in the North of England, hundreds of years later:

> was not so much an increased production of cotton or wool or railway engines, important though all these became in the industrial world. It *was* something deeper, *an understanding of the importance of the machine in life.*[20]

Today, this identification with the world of machines is made visible in many ways. There is the Englishman playing about with the engine of his motorbike or car, on the one hand, and the youngster tinkering with a new computer accessory, on the other. Glyn maintains that it is this combined technical and artistic heritage, stretching back to the Saxons and Celts, that explains our industrial revolution.

The well known economic historian, Walt Rostow, naturally has a more sophisticated explanation, to which we now turn.

The great scientific adventure

In his book entitled *How it all Began*,[21] Rostow sets out to explain why the industrial revolution happened, as well as when and where it did. There is no doubt in his mind that the advance of science and technology was the primary cause, rather than the commercial, demographic, and territorial expansion that was occurring in the seventeenth and eighteenth centuries. It is, as he puts it, 'the *organized creativity of the human mind*' that *made all the difference.*

Rostow traces the origins of the industrial revolution back to developments in European scientific thought, rather than to events in Britain in particular. He describes the way in which a small circle of men sought to discover the laws of heavenly and terrestrial motion.

These sixteenth- and seventeenth-century *scientists knew they were involved in a great adventure.* It was a conscious revolution engaging men from Cracow to London, from Scandinavia to France. The effort was carried forward by a combination of basic principles and practical observations. The meaning of the results was generalized beyond physics and astronomy to anatomy and chemistry.

Public authorities were very much in favour of the work that was being done, particularly in countries like Britain, where religion had less of a tight hold on people's hearts and minds, than in, say, Spain or Italy.

The question that does remain is *why Britain* should have *led the way*, at least towards the industrial, if not the scientific revolution. Here again, Rostow helps us to understand. He describes the three elements that were missing from the ancient world, and which when introduced, converted a slow-moving economic expansion into an industrial revolution.

First there was the philosophical impact of Newton's new synthesis. *Men were given a new sense of power and confidence that an order of nature was there to be found.* Few read Newton's Principia, but its triumphant message had the right impact. By changing the way man looked at the world around him, the Newtonian perception increased the supply of inventors and the willingness of entrepreneurs to introduce innovations.

The *second* element built into the scientific revolution, was the *two-way linkage between scientists and tool makers*. Scientists were willing to learn what they could from the craftsmen. The separation of the man of learning from the craftsman – to be observed from ancient Greece to medieval Europe – began to disappear.

Thirdly, the *scientists were not as yet so specialized* as to be out of contact with the language, thought and practice of ordinary men. Physicists and chemists such as Franklin and Priestley, were in intimate contact with the leading figures in British industry, like James Watt and Josiah Wedgwood. Through the 'Lunar Society', which I have already mentioned, these people met together as artists and craftsmen, scientists and industrialists, philosophers and engineers.

The names of engineers, iron masters, industrial chemists and instrument makers on the list of Fellows of the Royal Society shows how close the relations between science and practice were at the time.

The emergence of industrial design

Whereas the industrial revolution was quite evidently the outcome of creative pursuits in the sciences, it was less visibly a development of creative activity in the arts. Although Wedgwood's pottery obviously drew on each of 'the two cultures' it was science and technology that played the predominant part. So what about the creative arts? Were they relegated to the art galleries and concert halls, and segregated from the mainstream of industry? At first glance this did appear to be the case, but not if we scrutinize developments more closely.

The great nineteenth-century *Victorian engineers* were known for their technical and commercial prowess rather than for their creative artistry. Yet, as they were designing and building great structures for the railway age that owed almost nothing to past styles, and almost everything to new methods and materials that enabled them to solve hitherto unsolved problems, something else was going on.

They *were creating veritable works of 'art'* without ever realizing it, in the form of railway tunnels, engineering bridges and other engineering works. In fact Stephen Bayley, an art historian and Director of Britain's Conran Foundation, has gone so far as to say:

> The selection of machines as exemplars by artists was the first expression of a development which has not finished today. Sheet steel, pound notes and a retainer from the Board have replaced oil, canvas and a papal commission as the media and conditions of art, although the talent and processes employed have remained the same.[22]

Although this view might seem a little far fetched, it cannot be many miles from the truth. The great Victorian engineers inherited a tradition that reached back to the Saxons and Celts, as well as to Copernicus and Newton. The continuation of that tradition, in the twentieth century, ironically bypassed Britain's shores. At a time when the creative spark seemed to be setting countries other than Great Britain alight, Walter Gropius established the Bauhaus School of Design.

In 1919 industrial design was first born, as an amalgamation of art, craft and possibly even engineering. Gropius believed that the divorce between fine and not so fine art had been the cause of nineteenth-century degeneration in design. The principles of design are none other than those of unity and variety, rhythm and balance, accent and contrast, scale and proportion, colour and texture. Today we have industrial design, interior design, graphic design, fashion design, landscape design, product design, systems design and software design.

Yet, until very recently, the design function gained prominence in Italy, France, Germany, Scandinavia, America and Japan, but not in Britain – where the Victorian engineers did their great work. Interestingly enough students of the Bauhaus spread out from Germany to continental Europe and America, but not into the home of the industrial revolution.

The phenomenon of British inventiveness

Before trying to draw these various threads together connecting fine art and pop culture, basic science and heavy engineering, as well as the various forms of design, 1 must draw attention to the phenomenon of British inventiveness. The creative vigour of this nation, at least as perceived by the world at large, has been based more on its scientific inventiveness than upon any other of its achievements, at least in recent years.

Whilst its economy and technology appear to have declined during this century, *Britain is still seen to be an originator* of the very technologies which have seemingly helped to cause that decline.

It was Charles Babbage and Ada Lovelace (Lord Byron's daughter) who were the father and mother of computing. Charles created the seminal hardware and Ada was the first producer of software, in the nineteenth century. Denis Gabor – a Hungarian who emigrated to this country – created holography, which has led in its turn to laser technology. Then Crick at Cambridge (with the American Watson) discovered DNA, which has led to all kinds of developments in biotechnology and genetic engineering.

In none of these three emerging industry groups does Britain have the major companies exploiting the technologies to anywhere near the extent that the Japanese and Americans have done. So the critics say – and the British love to criticize themselves as well as others – that we know how to invent but not how to exploit. Our creative vigour takes us halfway there, but not the whole hog.

Now this is another of those half truths that has cost Britain dear, because of its negative impact on our national and economic psyche. It is a half truth for the very reasons that we are generally outstanding at producing computer software rather than hardware; that we excel, when we do produce hardware, at the small end of things; and that we are particularly good at producing games software for the leisure market.

IN CONCLUSION

Variety adds spice to life

Now let me pull the threads together. *Great Britain was created out of diverse national groupings,* and variety always adds spice to life. Of these groupings, the Celts brought with them a tradition of creativity in the arts, and in metalwork. The Saxons carried forward the engineering tradition through their worshipping of the God of iron, Thor. The popular name Smith and the British love of tinkering are both an extension of that engineering theme.

It is particularly in this country that Sinclair could flourish, at least over a period of time, by producing computers to which all sorts of bits and pieces can be added on, in order to improve their functioning. It is also a country in which the South African David Potter, founder of Psion Computers, can claim a 'quality engineering' home.

Eccentricity and tolerance

This tinkering tradition, combined with a spirit of tolerance for eccentricity and diversity, and not a little creativity, gives rise to the Newtons of this world. It is no accident that Isaac Newton was not only a scientist, but also a mystic, as well as an engineer who created his own scientific instruments. The Lunar Society in the nineteenth century in fact brought together the physicists, biologists, artists, craftsmen and industrialists of the time who between them created the industrial revolution.

As Rostow said, so perceptively in the seventies, and as Toynbee has said many times before him:

> Invention and innovation at any period of time are marginal activities in a society. They engage small numbers of human beings relative to the population as a whole. Life goes on in familiar ways, with familiar technologies, while the creative few dream their dreams and struggle with their frustrations in odd places.[23]

Only when we look backwards, after innovation has led on to large new sectors in the economy, can we understand the achievements of the inventors and innovators. By that time, however, the manufacturers and marketers may well have concealed the originally creative spirit.

But today the situation is changing. As individual businesses and whole economies evolve, the creative influence becomes more important. The balance between individual freedom and organizational order shifts in the former direction. In fact, in my view, one of the chief reasons that Great Britain slid into the economic backwaters in the period between 1870 and 1970 was the advent of large-scale production.

For such *economies of scale draw not upon the dominant British heritage*, that is individual ingenuity, and collective diversity, but upon the very reverse of these qualities. Indeed, I would go further to say that the chequered history of industrial design in this country can be expressed in similar terms.

Individuality and interdependence

It has been said that the history of design in manufacture over the last 250 years could be compressed almost into three words –

integration, disintegration and reintegration. The integrated phase reflected the days of handcraft, when designer and maker were one. In the disintegrated phase, after the industrial revolution, they became separated.

That separation between design and manufacturing fitted much better into American, Japanese and German society and industry than in Great Britain. It forms part of well oiled, formal organization. It is not surprising, then, that it is in the third phase of development that design has begun to gain new influence in this country.

For *in this phase of 'reintegration', individuality and interdependence become the norm*, now reinforced rather than opposed by technology. So Britain is back on home ground, and the designer now has his place.

Gaining freedom through order

The themes of individuality, diversity and creativity are now pervading a wide cross-section of industries in which Great Britain is gaining prominence. The 'city' has always offered the modern equivalent of Britain's early Vikings, and later merchant adventurers, scope for imagination and flair.

Unfortunately parts of it have become too much of an enclave so that the flair becomes narrowly channelled, and the countervailing traditions backward looking. A way still needs to be found of combining freedom and order, within the 'city' in the ways outlined in this chapter. At the present time, there is too little creativity (freedom) and subtlety (order).

I have already mentioned television, music, theatre and pop culture as emerging industries. Interestingly enough, computer software, which may not seem intimately connected with pop music, is often written by the same people who were playing guitars in the sixties. Computers and design come together in the creation of the new flexible manufacturing systems which will gradually replace the old assembly lines in the industrialized countries.

What we are finding now is that the values of the economist and the psychologist are coming together. Whereas the one looks for standardization and simplification, the other wants to cater for the fundamental human need for change, choice and variety. It is the very same polarity that faces the modern manager. The resolving of these polarities comes through *quality engineering and the tolerance of difference*, on the one hand, *combined with the art of recreation and scientific creativity*, on the other.

So there is some kind of amalgam between Adam Smith and Karl

Marx, on the one hand, and Isaac Newton and E.F. Schumacher on the other. Each one of them attempted to combine freedom and order in a particular way, and in a particular context. Each arose out of, or entered into, the British heritage, at one stage or another, although they had an impact worldwide. It is the wide world, as a living and national environment, that I want to enter next, starting with the 'primal' American approach to corporate culture.

REFERENCES

1 Lessem, R., *The Global Business*, Prentice-Hall, 1987.
2 Nossiter, B., *A Future that Works*, André Deutsch, 1977, p. 91.
3 Trevelyan, G.M., *The Social History of Britain*, Penguin, 1967, p. 224.
4 Nossiter, B., op. cit., p. 90.
5 Toynbee, P., *The Study of History*, Thames Hudson, 1964.
6 White, R.J., *A Concise History of England*, Cassell, 1971, p. 87.
7 Bryant, A., *The Spirit of England*, Collins, 1982, p. 112.
8 Glyn, A., *The Blood of a Britishman*, Readers Union, 1971, p. 28.
9 Glyn, A., op. cit., p. 19.
10 Glyn, A., op. cit., p. 225.
11 Nossiter, B., op. cit., pp. 88-89.
12 Masuda, Y., *The Information Society*, Basil Blackwell, 1990, p. 112.
13 Trevelyan, G.M., op. cit., p. 96.
14 Handy, C., *The Future of Work*, Blackwell, 1984.
15 Trevelyan, G.M., op. cit., p. 102.
16 Trevelyan, G.M., op. cit., p. 98.
17 Ibid.
18 Schumacher, E.F., *Small is Beautiful*, Abacus, 1973, p. 121.
19 Glyn, A., op. cit., p. 228.
20 Glyn, A., op. cit., p. 82.
21 Rostow, W., *How it All Began*, Methuen, 1975.
22 Bayley, S., *In Good Shape*, Design Council, 1979.
23 Rostow, W., op. cit., p. 172.

3 The Primal Way

BEING INTRODUCED TO THE PRIMAL WAY

Primal . . . belonging to the first stage of some continuing process; *primitive* and original; *basic* and fundamental; not dependent on or derived from something else . . .

Culture is that body of *customary beliefs*, social forms and material traits constituting a distinct complex of *tradition* of a . . . group. (*Webster's New International Dictionary*)

'Soft' and 'hard' attributes

The 'primal' way is in fact the most tangible and visible of our four approaches to corporate culture. Apparently created in America, in the early eighties, it represents the 'soft' side of the 'back to basics' movement in business and management.

The primal division between 'soft' and 'hard' was first popularized by the American Japanese watchers, Pascale and Athos. Its basic nature can be contrasted against the more rational and sophisticated 'socio' (soft)/'technical' (hard) systems identified by behavioural scientists. It has more of a business ring to it than, say, the difference between 'organic' and 'mechanistic' approaches to management.

The division of managerial interest between soft and hard was reflected, then, in 'the Japanese Mirror'. Pascale and Athos found that the *tough*ness and aggression, reinforced in America by the frontier spirit, was also present in Japan, reinforced there by the drive for national achievement. However, the Japanese generally superseded the American companies when it came to their *tender* management virtues. They had a 'soft' cultural advantage.

SOFT AND HARD

What we saw was that we (Americans) were very similar to the

Japanese on all the 'hard ball' S's – strategy, structure, and systems. Our major differences are in the 'soft ball' S's – skills, style, staff and superordinate goals (shared values).

   Their culture gives them advantages in the softer S's because of its approach to ambiguity . . . interdependence . . . We saw how the boss-subordinate relationship encourages a degree of effective collaboration that we might envy, and how consensus is used to accomplish smooth implementation, that often eludes us.[1]

Pascale and Athos go on to say that the best American companies, like IBM, 3M and Hewlett Packard, have in fact overcome the cultural disadvantage by keeping their seven S's 'in synch'. From the early eighties onwards, then, many an American and European company began to attend not only to its strategies, structures and systems but, in particular, to its 'superordinate goals'.

Shared values become significant

Whereas the 'hard' side of such American, primal management is typically reflected in autonomy and entrepreneurship, this 'soft' side is essentially represented by *shared values*. The primal approach to corporate culture and 'shared values' are often used interchangeably.

PRIMAL CULTURE

Values are the bedrock of any corporate culture. As the essence of a company's philosophy *for achieving success*, values provide a sense of common direction for all employees, and guidelines for their day-to-day behaviour.

   These values may be grand in scope ('Progress is our most important product') or narrowly focussed ('Underwriting Excellence'). They can capture the imagination ('The first Irish multinational'). They can tell people how to work together ('It takes two to Tandem').

   These formulas for success *determine* (and occasionally arise from) the types of *corporate heroes*, and the *myths and rituals* and *ceremonies* of the culture.[2]

As we can see from the above quote, the examples of shared values that Deal and Kennedy cite are basic, tangible and visible as opposed to sophisticated, intangible and invisible. The same applies to their approach to heroism, myth, ritual and ceremony, as we shall soon discover. I shall begin, though, by elaborating on 'shared values', which lie at the centre of the primal approach to corporate culture.

YOU FOCUS ON SHARED VALUES

In search of excellence

Peters and Waterman more than anyone else, in their search for excellence, brought 'shared values' into the boardroom of American, and subsequently European corporations.

MAN WAITING FOR MOTIVATION

Without exception, *the dominance and coherence of culture proved to be an essential quality* of the excellent companies. Moreover, the stronger the culture and the more it was directed towards the market-place, the less need was there for policy manuals, organization charts, or detailed procedures and rules.

In these companies people way down the line know what they are supposed to do in most situations because the handful of guiding values is crystal clear ... largely because the mythology is rich. Everyone at Hewlett Packard knows that he or she is supposed to be innovative. Everyone at Proctor and Gamble knows that product quality is the sine qua non.[3]

Tom Peters' focus on corporate culture, as well as on entrepreneurship, was symptomatic of his primal way. In attacking the rational approach to management and organization, he argued that man is not designed to fit the scientific approach to management. For it is feelings and actions that shape our thoughts:

- All of us are self-centred, suckers for a bit of praise, and generally like to think of ourselves as winners
- We want to stick out, to be independent, while simultaneously fitting into an organization that can provide us with meaning
- We reason by stories at least as often as with good data. 'Does it feel right?' counts for more than 'Does it add up?'
- We are both self-motivated and also creatures of our environments, very sensitive to external punishments and rewards
- Actions speak louder than words.

For Deal and Kennedy, shared values, if they are to be successfully adopted by management:

- stand for something, that is, they involve a *clear* and explicit *philosophy* about how management aims to conduct its business

- are known and *shared by all* who work for the company
- are *continually* shaped and *fine tuned* by management to conform to the business's economic and social environment.

Excellent companies, finally, develop cultures that reward their people for being doers and winners, and that also make them feel they belong. They reinforce the complementary and primal American virtues of enterprise (frontier spirit) and community (melting pot).

In their search for excellence, however, Peters and Waterman gave us only the flavour of 'shared values' in the context of corporate culture. For us to gain more of an appreciation of their primal way we need to turn to Peters and Austin, in their *A Passion for Excellence*.

Holding a passion for excellence

Quality

A Passion for Excellence is a treatise on quality, that is quality of the primal kind. It involves, above all, '*people, passion, consistency, eyeball contact, and gut reaction*'. The number one managerial productivity problem, as far as Peters and Austin are concerned is, quite simply, managers who are out of touch with their people and with their customers. However, the alternative, that is being in touch, does not come via computer printouts. Rather it involves '*tangible, visceral ways of being informed*'.

It means, for example, 'a remarkably successful thirty-year-old geologist/entrepreneur sinking his toes in the sand of a transgressive overlap, instead of totally relying on a computer's interpretation of sophisticated geological tools'.

Sensuality

In other words, a 'culture' that is alive is one that you can touch, feel, see, hear and even smell. For example, a company which 'smells' of innovation is one in which:

- inaction is not tolerated; everyone gets accustomed to trying, testing, that is to the *quick and dirty* approach
- *practical* team playing is revered
- *product champions* are clearly visible in the Hall of Fame
- the physical layout encourages *informal communication*
- *spur of the moment* activity is seen as the norm

- the company *'smells' of* its *products* – bragging, display and demonstration is the norm.

Management as show business

MANAGEMENT BY WALKING ABOUT

In the primal approach to culture, then, what *you can see, hear, touch and smell* is all important. 'Participating directly, seeing with your own eyes and hearing with your own ears, is simply the only thing that yields the unfiltered, richly detailed impressions' that you need to communicate with one another. Hence the importance of what is termed 'management by walkabout' (MBWA).

MBWA has become for Peters and Austin shorthand for *'bringing business* – customers, suppliers, etc. – *to life*, somehow, for all hands'. They cite a particular Texas bank as following this lead. Here are both the logic and the technique.

A bank doesn't lend money, they say; rather, it lends money so that others can productively employ it, for example build factories, restaurants. 'The bank's innovative programme involved bringing the customer to life for the operations people by shooting footage of the new construction financed by the bank, and then sharing it with all those distant from day to day contact with the customers.'

MANAGEMENT BY STORYTELLING

All business, 'primally' speaking, then, *is show business*. The primal nature of shared values, the way they are recognized, symbolized, and brought to life, is made immediately apparent by Peters and Austin when they describe the role of leadership. True leaders 'walk their talk'. They are coaches, cheerleaders, wanderers and also storytellers.

STORIES AND LEGENDS

Nothing reveals more of what a company really cares about than its stories and legends, that is its *folk wisdom*. Leaders use stories *to persuade, symbolize and guide day to day actions*. There's simply nothing better than a story to tell people what they really want to know about 'how things work around here'.

Stories engage. They help put current decisions and events into an overall framework that is readily understood, and they *embellish a company philosophy* in a new way.

The common memory created by *swapping tales imparts a sense of tradition and continuity*, and sparks interest as nothing else can. Listening to a company's stories is the surest way to determining its real priorities, and who can symbolize them.[4]

In summary, then, shared values for Peters, together with corporate culture, is reflected in material, social and ideological forms, all of which must be readily accessible to the five main senses. This is what gives them their 'primal' character.

Products (material), people (social), and business mission statements (ideological), then, need to be viscerally accessible. Values are shared, in cohesive cultures, not through abstract and lofty ideas and principles, but through management by walkabout and by engaging stories. In fact, the two Americans who have really come to champion this primal approach to corporate culture are Deal and Kennedy, to whom we now turn.

YOU BECOME A SYMBOLIC MANAGER

Symbolic versus rational management

Whereas for Peters, Waterman and Austin a coherent corporate culture is merely part of an excellent company whole, for Deal and Kennedy it is their primary concern. In fact the key values of a company's culture are central to a what they term a 'symbolic managerial orientation'.

SYMBOLIC MANAGEMENT

A day in the life of any modern manager is chock full of little things that don't matter, little things that matter some, and big things that matter a lot. We call the first *trivia*, the second *events*, the third *dramas*.

One of the chief skills of the symbolic manager is to distinguish among the three . . . To dramatize trivia is to look like a fool. To overload drama is to become a victim or a villain. *Symbolic managers never miss an opportunity to reinforce, dramatize or involve the central values of the culture.*[5]

Such symbolic managers:

- *are sensitive to culture* and its importance for long-term success. They are always speaking about their company's culture, writing about it, and crediting their success in the marketplace to the strength of their culture
- *rely on their cultural fellow travellers for success*. The ethic they hold is that 'we shall succeed because we're special'. They also take a high degree of responsibility for guarding the culture, reinforcing its beliefs, and deciding who belongs to it and who does not

- *see themselves as players* – scriptwriters, actors, directors – in the daily drama. Each meeting provides a new setting for the dramatic action. No bit player is too trivial to ignore in the great symbolic drama.

Having outlined the nature of symbolic management as a whole Deal and Kennedy go on to describe the 'cultural network' of symbolic characters that inhabit organizations.

Through the cultural network

The centre

In the centre of the cultural network lie the four characters who make up the symbolic management core. They are the *born hero*, the *compass hero*, the *priest* and the *storyteller*.

HERO

If shared values lie at the heart of the corporate culture, then the business hero provides the culture's body and soul. Heroes are pivotal figures in a strong culture. 'The hero is the great motivator, the magician, the person everyone will count on when things get tough.'

Heroes are symbolic figures whose deeds are out of the ordinary, but not too much so. They show that the ideal of success is within human capacity.

The 'born' hero is the original entrepreneur who created the company. Such a hero has established not only a business but also an institution that contributes his personal sense of values to the world. His activities and imagination will have affected the way the company does business. *His influence*, even if such a born hero is long dead, *will* still *be* – at least to some extent – *pervasive*.

The *'compass' hero* is Deal and Kennedy's second symbolic character. He or she is the exemplar, *the role model chosen to carry forward a new set of values*. For example, an entrepreneurial company that needs to consolidate its operations may choose, and promote, professional managers as such compass heroes. In doing so the company is communicating, symbolically, its intention to conduct its business more methodically.

Of course if the born hero is still in control of the company, and its core values, the compass heroes will need to complement these rather than oppose them. Between the two of them, then, they:

- make *success* attainable and human

- provide role *models*
- *symbolize* the company to the outside world
- *preserve* what makes a company special
- *set standards* of performance
- *motivate* employees.

PRIEST

Like the church, at least as far as Deal and Kennedy are concerned, companies also have priests. While the heroes create the values of the organization, the priest's role is to protect and to nurture them. He or she is the *guardian of the culture's values*, always having time to listen to a confession of guilt, or to resolve a moral dilemma.

To be a priest in a corporate culture requires a maturity beyond years. Priests seldom worry about the factual details. Instead they deal in allegories about what once happened.

STORYTELLER

Deal and Kennedy's 'storytellers' are in a powerful position because they can change reality. Storytellers interpret what goes on in the company to fit their own perceptions. As a positive force within the organization they maintain cohesion, by establishing consistency and continuity between one story and another.

Such *storytelling is the most powerful way to convey information and to shape behaviour*. 'The beauty of a story is that just by remembering the punch line you can recreate the whole occasion.' Thus a storyteller needs imagination and insight as well as a sense of detail. Stories, if they are to draw people in, must convey visual imagery rather than verbal abstraction.

The periphery

On the periphery of the cultural network, in terms of organizational impact if not physical positioning, lies a further cast of four hidden characters. These Deal and Kennedy call the *gossips*, the *spies*, the *whistle blowers*, and the *whisperers*.

GOSSIP

Gossips are the troubadours of the culture. While priests will only talk in analogues – that is, tell you the scripture – gossips will tell you the names, dates, salaries and events that are taking place in the organization now.

Gossips are not expected to be serious people, and they are not expected to get the news right. They are expected merely to entertain. Storytellers create the legends of the company and its heroes, but the *gossips help the hero making process by embellish-ing the hero's past feats* and 'spiffing up their latest accomplish-ments'.

Almost every good manager, according to Deal and Kennedy, has spies. Typically a spy is a 'well oiled buddy in the woodwork', someone loyal enough to keep you informed of what is going on. The best spies are people who are liked, and have access to many different people; *they hear all the stories and they know who is behind them.*

Most tend to be unthreatening people because they are not likely to get ahead. But they will always be taken care of, if they keep the channels of information open.

Outlaws, or mavericks, are strongly valued in a strong culture. They keep the company evolving. Knowing this, progressive corporate directors commonly place them in creative jobs, or appoint them as head of an R & D division. In such a strong culture these 'outlaws' can still share the overriding values.

However, *in a weak culture, mavericks turn against the generally shared values, and become whistle blowers*, working against the company rather than with it.

Deal and Kennedy's *'whisperers' are* often *the powers behind the throne*, movers and shakers, but without formal portfolio. 'First, they must be able to read the boss's mind quickly and accurately, with few clues. Second, to get things done, they must build a vast support system of contacts throughout the organization.'

YOU SHAPE CULTURES

How then does the symbolic manager from within or the consultant from without read, diagnose, and even change a culture.

Diagnosing a culture from inside

- Understand *career path progression*. Who gets ahead? What does an employee have to do to get promoted? Does the company reward competence in key skills? The beliefs of the corporate culture, in fact, are primarily shaped by people's perceptions of what it takes to get ahead.

- Appreciate the *content of communications*. Take your internal mail box for a week and analyse it. Keep track of what is actually discussed at meetings.
- Pay particular attention to *anecdotes and stories*. When people want to share their experience, Deal and Kennedy tells us, they relate it through anecdotes and stories. Ask yourself what was the point of a particular story? Inventory the anecdotes to determine how many relate to customers, to political infighting, or to individual initiatives.

Reading a culture from outside

- Study the *physical setting*. A company that is proud of itself and its culture will reflect this pride through its environment.
- Read what the company says about its culture. Companies with strong cultures recognize the importance of their values, and their people, and they continually *report* this *to the world*, through annual reports, employee newsletters, or press releases.
- Test *how the company greets strangers*. Is it formal or informal, relaxed or busy, elegant or nondescript?
- *Interview* company *people*, asking them to:

- tell you the *history* of the company, finding out its origins, including the mythology as well as the facts
- describe *why* they think the company is a *success*, or otherwise, and what explains its growth or decline
- describe *what* kind of *people work there*. Who really gets ahead in the long term? Who are the company heroes?
- assess *what* kind of *place* it is to work in. What is an average day like? How do things get done?

So much for diagnosing, or reading what goes on. How, finally, do you begin to change a culture?

Changing cultures

Deal and Kennedy's primal approach to reshaping a culture is relatively straightforward. This is their prescription for change:

- *Position a hero* in charge, to add weight to the change process

- *Recognize* a real *threat* from outside, to accentuate the need for change
- Make *transition rituals* the pivotal elements of change, allowing people to mourn the passing of the old ways, and to anoint the heroes of the new ones
- *Provide transition training* in the new values and behaviour patterns now required
- Build *tangible symbols* of new directions, into such things as physical settings, letterheads, and company newsletters
- *Respect people's security* during the process of transition, duly empathizing with the anxieties they are likely to go through.

Should the attempt to change a culture fail, so that a weak culture continues to prevail:

- there will be no clear beliefs or values expressed about how to succeed in business, or
- there will be many such beliefs with lack of agreement as to which are most important
- different parts of the company will have fundamentally different beliefs
- the heroes of the culture will often be more destructive than constructive
- the rituals of day-to-day life will be contradictory and disorganized.

CONCLUDING YOUR INITIATION INTO PRIMAL CULTURE

Symbolic management enters the primal culture

Shared values, without the cultural network, ceremonies and rituals to maintain and develop them, will wither away and die. The symbolic manager will not only be adept at recognizing the different members of the network, but will also recruit or promote members if there are gaps in the cultural field.

Moreover, the better that he is at his symbolic job, the more able he or she will be to play a variety of cultural roles, and to introduce a variety of ceremonies and rituals, as time and place demands.

At the same time, it is important to stress that such a symbolic manager, in a primal context, will place stress on easily accessible symbols as opposed to highly subtle or abstract ones. As a result the heroes and priests within such a culture will be more down to earth than spiritually evolved.

Ceremonies and rituals there will be, but these will be tangible occasions, celebrating well-known events and activities – like sales, recruitment and retirement – rather than esoteric ones.

Without expressive events any culture will die. In the absence of ceremony or ritual, important values have no impact. Ceremonies are to the culture what movies are to the script, the concert is to the score, or the dance is to values that are difficult to express in any other way.

Whether they are cultural extravagances or simple events when employees pass particular milestones, *ceremonies help the company celebrate heroes, myths, and sacred symbols*. Like habits, rituals are commonplace and taken for granted.

Ceremonies, meanwhile, are extraordinary; the full corporate spotlight falls on them. *Ceremonies place the culture on display and provide experiences that are remembered* by employees.[6]

Atomized structures are culture bound

Deal and Kennedy, like Peters and Waterman, foresee the demise of the centralized, hierarchical organization. In its place Peters and Waterman predict that a three-form company will emerge, as indicated in Figure 3.1.

The important point to note is that the small, and experimental units are not held together by any complex structure, but rather by 'dominating values'.

We see a revolution on the horizon that holds far-reaching implications for the American corporation. *A combination of forces* – from the rapidly changing business environment to the new work force to the astonishing advances in technology – *is forging a breakdown of the large, hierarchical, traditional organizations* that have dominated the past.

We think that the dismantling will result in highly decentralized organizations in which the work of the corporation will be done in small, autonomous units linked to the mega corporation by new telecommunications and computer technologies. This change can turn us all into entrepreneurs and in the process will transform the role of middle management. Motivation will come from the opportunity to accomplish complex tasks in an intimate, relatively simple work environment.

We see it as a no boss business. We call it the atomized organization. *For it to work, strong cultural ties and a new kind of symbolic management will be required.*[7]

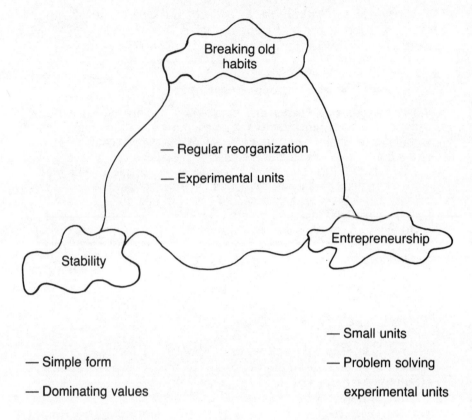

— Small units

— Simple form

— Dominating values

— Problem solving

experimental units

Figure 3.1 The three pillars of the structure of the eighties

Deal and Kennedy, as we now see, project a very similar scenario for the eighties to Peters and Waterman, under the guise of their so-called *atomized organization*, including:

- *small*, task-focused work *units*
- each with economic and managerial control over its own destiny
- interconnected with large entities through *benign computer* and telecommunication *links*
- formed into larger companies through *strong cultural bonds*.

The common, and primal theme, is the linking together of enterprise and community, small entrepreneurial units and a tightly bound culture. Not surprisingly the primal approach to corporate culture has a strong American, particularly Californian flavour to it. The rational approach is different in origin and application.

REFERENCES

1 Pascale, R., and Athos, A., *The Art of Japanese Management*, Penguin, 1982.
2 Deal, T., and Kennedy, A., *Corporate Cultures*, Addison Wesley, 1983.
3 Peters, T., and Waterman, R., *In Search of Excellence*, Harper & Row, 1982.
4 Peters, T., and Austin, N., *A Passion for Excellence*, Collins, 1986.
5 Deal and Kennedy, op. cit.
6 Ibid.
7 Ibid.

4 The Rational Way

BEING INTRODUCED TO THE RATIONAL WAY

Rational . . . Proper exercize of the *intellec*tive faculty in accordance with *right* judgment; the sum of intellectual powers; the power of comprehending, thinking and inferring in orderly and *sensible* ways, the formulation of general *principles* or laws; the formulation of *criteria* whereby ideas are tested empirically and logically.

Culture is the total pattern of human behaviour dependent on man's capacity for *learning* and transmitting *knowledge* to succeeding generations through the use of *abstract thought*. (*Webster's New International Dictionary*)

The scope of corporate culture

Corporate culture and the behavioural sciences

Corporate culture has not, in fact, been created overnight. It has been incubating, you might say, ever since a behavioural approach to management emerged in the 1930s. However, it was not until the 1970s that the behavioural scientists began to relate concepts of organizational climate,[1] ideology and values to that of 'corporate culture'.

In the course of this chapter we shall be investigating, in particular, the role played by managerial values and ideology, as well as by organizational behaviour and leadership, in the emergence of a rationally, or analytically based approach to corporate or organizational culture. But first we need to look at culture in a broader context.

The context of culture

The word 'culture' can be applied to any size of social unit that has had the opportunity to learn and stabilize its view of itself and the environment around it. At the broadest level we have *civilizations* and refer to 'Western' or 'Eastern' cultures; at the next level down we have *countries* with sufficient ethnic commonality that we talk of 'British' or 'American' cultures.

However, within a particular country it is not difficult to recognize, at a next level down, *ethnic groups,* be they Ibo or Jewish, to which we attribute different cultures. Even more specific than these is the level of *occupation, profession, or occupational community.* If such groups can be defined as *stable units with a shared history of experience,* they will have developed their own cultures.

Finally we arrive at the level of analysis that is the focus of this book – *organizations.* Within such organizations, *groups* may develop their own subcultures.

The basis of corporate culture

Corporate culture, from a rational and analytic perspective, is built upon three different conceptual foundations. The first such foundation is that of *business* or management *values and ethics,* depicted originally by the American sociologist, Philip Selznick in the 1940s and 1950s; the second area is that of *organizational ideology,* most popularly represented by the British management philosopher, Charles Handy in the 1960s and 1970s; the third, and most prolific, is that of *organizational behaviour,* represented here by the American organizational psychologist, Edgar Schein in the 1970s and 1980s.

Whereas the first and third approaches focus, primarily, on cultural uniformity, the second is oriented towards cultural diversity. Let me start, then, with the first and most traditional approach, derived from business and management values and ethics.

Ethics, values and corporate culture

In so far as 'corporate culture' represents an extension of the humanizing influence upon management, the management of organizations is viewed as efficient and effective, but also as ethical and purposeful.

Already in 1948 a leading academic authority on management had been focusing on the importance of ethics and values in leadership and organization. He was the American sociologist, Philip Selznick.

LEADERSHIP AND VALUES

The inbuilding of purpose is a challenge to creativity because it involves

transforming man and groups from neutral, technical units into participants who have a particular stamp, sensitivity and commitment.

The art of the creative leader is the art of institution building, the
reworking of human and technological materials *to fashion an organism
that embodies new and enduring values . . . the institutional leader is
primarily an expert in the promotion and protection of values.*[2]

As we shall soon see, this approach has subsequently been
extended by the American theologian, Charles McCoy,[3] to cover the
management of values in the context of business ethics. McCoy, like
Selznick, is concerned with the way leaders infuse organizations
with an overall sense of values.

Culture, ideology and diversity in management

While business ethics and the management of values represent the
most important, historically based influence on corporate culture,
'organizational ideology' is of particular relevance to management
today. By *ideology* the originator of this approach – another
American social psychologist, Roger Harrison – means the underlying *character*[4] of the organization, be it *power, role, task,* or
person based.

Charles Handy, Professor of Management at the London Business
School, has popularized Harrison's approach by likening organizational ideologies to cults or cultures. Moreover, he has placed
particular emphasis on *cultural propriety*, that is on adopting the
right culture at the right time in the right place.

In other words, as a British champion of diversity, Handy
recommends that an organization should consciously draw on a mix
of the four 'cultures' – power, role, task and person – that Roger
Harrison specified.

THEORY OF CULTURAL PROPRIETY

Each culture . . . works on quite different assumptions about the basis
of power and influence, about what motivates people, how they think
and learn, how things can be changed. These assumptions result in
quite different styles of management, structures, procedures and
reward systems.

Each will work well in certain situations, but get the wrong culture in
the wrong place and there will be trouble . . . *Different cultures are
needed for different tasks*. Cultures, too, will need to change over time,
as the tasks change, as the organization grows, or as people change.

Managers, therefore, *need to be* more aware of their own cultural
predilections, and *more aware of the cultural choices open to them*, and
to their organization . . . It was always a myth that there was one best
way to manage, but it has been a pervasive myth and a damaging one

... We need a law of requisite variety in management as well as a
theory of cultural propriety.[5]

Whereas Charles Handy was advocating diversity in cultural outlook, for management and organizations in the seventies, Edgar
Schein was seeking, once again, a coherence of approach, in the
eighties. Whereas Handy is a champion of flexible individuality
Schein's cultural focus is on organizational leadership.

Organizational culture and leadership

Edgar Schein then, a Professor of Organizational Psychology at
MIT, has divided the 'culture' of organizations into two broad
categories, one focused externally and the other internally.

Moreover, unlike Tom Peters, who is interested in the more
surface manifestations – material, social or ideological – of culture,
Schein's rational approach probes into the deeper and more abstract
realms of human thought, feeling and behaviour.

ORGANIZATIONAL CULTURE

The term *'culture'* should be reserved for the *deeper level of basic
assumptions* and beliefs that are shared by members of an organization. They operate unconsciously and define, in a basic 'taken for
granted' fashion, an organization's view of itself and its environment.

These assumptions and beliefs are learned responses to a group's
problems of *survival in its external environment* and its *problems of
internal regulation.*

They can be taken for granted because they solve these problems
repeatedly and reliably. This deeper level of assumptions is to be
distinguished from the 'artifacts' and 'values' that are manifestations or
surface levels of the culture but not *the essence of culture.*[6]

Schein differentiates surface manifestations of culture, that is,
values and artefacts, from its essence, contained within an organization's deeper level of assumptions. In addition he links cultural
considerations closely with the theory and practice of leadership,
and also with the management of values.

Having introduced you to each of the rationally based approaches
to culture – where the focus is on abstract values and beliefs rather
than concrete people and things – I want to consider each one in
greater depth. We start with Charles McCoy's approach to the
management of values.

YOU FOCUS ON THE MANAGEMENT OF VALUES

Values as a resource

In 1985, as Professor of Business Ethics, Charles McCoy produced a book on *The Management of Values*. Writing in the mid-1980s he was in a position to relate business values and ethics, that Selznick had analysed in the forties – to the emerging subject matter of corporate culture.

THE MANAGEMENT OF VALUES

Productivity, as we have known it in modern industrialized societies, has at least six well-known sources: labour; capital; technology; raw materials; markets; and managerial ideas, energy and skill.

A *seventh source*, usually ignored in the past but increasingly recognized as implicit and important all along, is emerging into view: the corporate culture, including the *climate of values* and the *organizational ethics*, that *sharpen, direct and empower* the other six.[7]

The climate of organizational values, then, just like labour or capital, is a source or resource whose deployment is to be planned, organized, directed and controlled. Moreover, like other 'factors of production' it has its particular attributes and dimensions.

Dimensions of corporate culture

The key dimensions of a corporate culture are its history, community, and character.

HISTORY, COMMUNITY, CHARACTER

The *historical* dimension refers to the *past* of that culture, providing it with its *founding* culture and the way of organizational life that has brought it to the present.

The *communal* dimension refers to the *integrated*, functional entity that is the corporation in the *present*.

Corporate *character* is the pervasive pattern of *valuing* and *future* orientation that defines the way in which the corporation is dynamic, and specifies the particular configuration and values and purposes shaping the movement into the future.[8]

We start with the company's history.

History

Corporate culture derives not only from the surrounding economic, social, technological and political environment but also *from* the *history* of a particular company.

A corporation is founded at a *particular time*, has *particular purposes* that are written into its charter, and is given its initial direction by its *particular* and original *founders*.

However, only as events and leaders are embodied in the *enduring values* of the company tradition do they enter the real history that continues to be influential.

History is not what happens but what is remembered. The past is remembered in the present by the organizational habit patterns. The past is also recalled by the stories that are told. *This history is the continuing impact of the past on the present and future.*

Community

In addition to the remembered past that continues to have power and influence, *corporate culture is a community of persons and groups* in the present.

As such a community of individuals and groups it is also *a system of customs, expectations, values and purposes*, as well as *actions and interactions*.

CUSTOMS AND VALUES

Within the organization every person and group is assigned a *role*, a *status*, and particular *functions*. Customs are those actions and interactions that have been approved over a sufficient period of time to make them social habits within the community.

Values provide criteria for evaluation which over time *shape and reshape the customs* of the community. Purposes express values in terms of goals to be attained in the future.

As customs, *values* and purposes come to be *shared* by the individuals and groups within the organization, they *form the fabric of the community* providing expectations that are mutually understood and accepted. When groups have an internal cohesion, members feel a sense of identity with one another.

ACTIONS AND INTERACTIONS

Communities are also made up of agents, that is of individuals and groups who are acting and interacting with one another.

On a *first* level the pattern of interaction in any organization has a formal, repetitive character that can be regarded as ritual. *Communal ritual serves as oil to make human interaction smoother.*

More importantly, ritual conveys tacit meanings within a community. On a *second* level social interaction embodies *relations* among individuals and groups. On a *third* level systems of action and interaction within an organizational community *convey power*.

Ritual, relations and power – shaped by ethical reflection – become intentional expressions of communal values and purposes, transformed into *policy*.

As a community with a culture, the corporation is involved continually in reflecting on values and purposes, on how these may be embodied in action, and on ways to evaluate and improve them.

Character

The third cultural dimension, after history and community, is character. '*Organizations*', according to Philip Selznick, '*become institutions as they are infused with value.*'[9] In other words, they are prized not as tools alone but as sources of direct personal gratification and as vehicles of group integrity.

This value infusion produces a distinct form and identity for the organization. Where institutionalization is well advanced, distinctive outlooks, habits, and other commitments are unified, colouring all aspects of organizational life, and lending it a *distinctly integrated character* that goes well beyond formal coordination and command.

The institutionalization of culture

Infused with value

For an organization to be infused with value means, *firstly* then, that it has a high level of integration in its total operation. Throughout various divisions and layers of management there are common understandings that provide a sense of community and relationship. *Communication is possible because there is a community of purpose.*

It means, *secondly*, that *there is a sense of corporate identity*. Not everyone has the same tasks to do or the same authority, but *everyone* possesses a firm knowledge that they are part of the same organization and are *contributing to the same goals*.

Thirdly, to be infused with values is to have *corporate integrity* based not on conformity to external directives but on an *inner cohesion emerging from common commitments*. As this integrity

becomes increasingly institutionalized, there are distinctive outlooks and habits that are reflected in coordinated action beyond that
produced by chains of command or reams of regulations.

Fourthly, there is then *a fabric of support* in which individuals
participate, both to receive support for decisions and possible
innovations and to give support to one another. It is a fabric of
community able to sustain people when they make mistakes as well
as to guide them toward success, and make it an occasion for
common rejoicing.

Fifthly and finally, there are *ceremonies and celebrations* that
both *represent the culture* and strengthen the infusion of values
throughout the corporate community.

Infused with meaning

Nothing, according to McCoy, motivates people more powerfully
than a sense of meaning in which they participate, and the meaning
that involves and motivates is that which is embodied with action.
In one sense, he says, meaning is shared values, but these values
must be acted out in specific ways. *It is through actions that embody
values and meaning*, therefore, *that corporate cultures can be
developed, strengthened and maintained.*

One form that meaning bearing action takes is story telling.
Regardless of age or location people love a compelling story that is
well told. Because a story with artistic dimensions draws people in
and involves them in its world, *stories are one of the important
ways to develop a corporate culture.* People who are impressed by
a story tell it to others. In doing so, they both pass the culture on,
and affirm themselves as part of it.

However, the *stories will help develop the culture only if they
grow out of, and are backed up by, corporate actions that demonstrate the same meaning.* There must be integrity, McCoy argues,
at the core of a corporation as the foundation of the culture. Then
it can spread and come to pervade the entire organization.

Policies which have consistency of value and purpose, finally, will
aid in building and developing a culture. *Slogans, symbols, the
repetition of goals, all these can provide the means of instilling a
culture.* So also can methods of personnel evaluation and reward.
In all these ways value commitments are projected and caught by
those involved.

THE INSTITUTIONALIZATION OF CULTURE

The institutionalization of culture seeks agreement on the basis of a
shared view of what the history, purposes and character of the

corporation are. This is demonstrated more in what the company has done, is doing, and plans to do than in the bureaucratic rules.

To the extent that there is social control in the organization and unity of perspective and action, they derive from a community of shared interpretation and *common value commitments.* When they *are* present and appropriately institutionalized, it becomes *the basis of creative interaction, meaningful participation, and continuing innovation.*

It does not require adherence to rigid codes or rules but *sharing in a significant enterprise* that *provides fulfilment* for all participants and important services for the larger community.[10]

Selznick and McCoy relate the management of values to one, overall corporate identity, community and character. Roger Harrison, initially, and Charles Handy, subsequently, have championed cultural diversity rather than uniformity. Handy, in particular, is influenced by European diversity as opposed, perhaps, to the American melting pot.

YOU RECOGNIZE CULTURAL DIVERSITY

Valuing cultural difference

The chief delight of Europe, Handy argues, is the variety it offers of climate and culture. One of the more pleasurable ways of ending a long English winter, therefore, is to drive along the highways of the continent, to watch spring and its blossoms come to meet you up the road, and to linger awhile in the sun, *adapting to another culture with different traditions, habits, ways of organizing work and of ordering daily life.*

VALUING CULTURAL DIFFERENCE

Organizations are as different and varied as the nations and societies of the world. They have differing cultures – *sets of values and norms and beliefs* – *reflected in different structures and systems.* And the cultures are affected by the events of the past and the climate of the present, by the technology of the type of work, by their aims and the kind of people that work in them.[11]

Moreover, not only is variety amongst cultures and organizations desirable, but also a successful company, as we shall see, needs to contain such variety within it. For different tasks and technologies require differing cultures and structures.

Featuring four cultures

General characteristics

In organizations there are deep set *beliefs about* the way *work* should be organized, the way *authority* should be exercised, people *rewarded*, people *controlled*. What are the degrees of *formalization* required? How much *planning* and how far ahead? What combination of *obedience* and *initiative* is looked for in subordinates?

Do *work hours* matter, or *dress*, or personal *idiosyncrasies*? What about expense accounts, and stock options and secretaries and *incentives*? Do *committees* control or *individuals*? Are there *rules* and procedures or only *results*?

These are all part of the culture of the organization, as far as Handy is concerned. This culture often takes visible form in its *building*, its offices, its shops or branches. The *kinds of people* it employs, the length and height of their *career aspirations*, their *status* in society, degree of *mobility*, level of *education*, will all be reflections of the culture.

Cultures and structures

Cultures are founded and built over the years by the dominant groups in an organization. What suits them and the organization at one stage is not necessarily appropriate for ever, strong though the initial culture may be.

For Handy there are four main corporate cultures, based respectively on *power, role, task* and *person*. He emphasizes that each can be a good and effective culture. We are all too often culturally blinkered, believing that a culture that works in one place at one time is bound to succeed in another. That is not the case.

I shall begin by outlining, in brief, the characteristics of each culture, and then elaborate on each, in turn. Finally, in this section on cultural propriety, I want to review their situational appropriateness.

The power culture

A power culture is often found in small, *entrepreneurial* organizations, as well as in larger trading and finance companies, including modern conglomerates. Its structure is best pictured as a *web*.

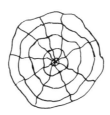

If this culture had a patron God, as far as Handy is concerned, it would be Zeus, who *ruled by whim and impulse*, by thunderbolt and shower of gold from Mount Olympus.

This culture *depends on a central power source*, with rays of power and influence spreading out from that central figure. The rays are connected by functional and specialist strings but the power rings are the centres of activity and influence. *The closer you are to the centre the greater your power and influence.*

The organization depends on trust for its effectiveness and on personal conversation for communication. Control is exercised from the centre largely through the *selection of key individuals*. It is a political organization in that *decisions are taken very much on the outcome of a balance of influence* rather than on procedural or rational grounds.

These cultures, and organizations based on them, are *proud and strong*. They have the ability to move quickly and can react well to threat and danger. Whether they move in the right direction will depend on the abilities and instincts of the people in the centre.

The role culture

The role culture is often stereotyped as a *bureaucracy*. The accompanying structure can be pictured as a Greek temple.

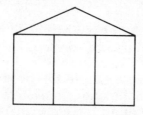

Its patron God, for Handy, is Apollo, the god of reason; for this culture works by *logic and rationality*. The role organization *rests its strength in its pillars, its functions or specialities*. They are coordinated at the top by a narrow band of senior management, the pediment.

In this culture the role, or *the job description is often more important than the individual who fills it*. Position power is the major power source in this culture, personal power is frowned upon and expert power tolerated only in its proper place.

Role cultures *offer predictability and security* to the individual. They offer a predictable rate of climb up a pillar. They offer the chance to acquire specialist expertise without risk.

The role organization will be found where the *economies of scale* are more important than flexibility or where technical expertise and depth of specialization are more important than product innovation or product cost.

The task culture

The task culture is job or *project oriented*. Its accompanying structure or picture is that of a *net*.

Some of the strands of the net are thicker and stronger than others. Much of the *power and influence lies at the* interstices of the net, at the *knots*. The so-called *'matrix organization'* is one structural form of the task culture.

The culture's God is a young woman, Athena, the warrior goddess, patroness of Odysseus, that *arch problem solver*, of craftsmen and of pioneering captains.

The culture recognizes only expertise as the base of power and influence. Age does not impress, nor length of service, nor closeness of kin to the owner.

The task culture utilizes the unifying power of the group to improve efficiency and to identify the individual with the objective of the organization. It is *a team culture* where the result of the team's work tends to be the common enemy.

This culture is *extremely adaptable*. Groups, project teams or task forces are formed for a specific purpose and can be reformed, abandoned or continued.

You will find the task culture, therefore, where the product life is short, where speed of reaction is important, and where *flexibility is at a premium*.

The person culture

The person culture is an unusual one. It will not be found pervading many organizations, Handy says, yet many individuals will cling to its values. *In this culture the individual is the central point.*

If there is a structure or an organization it exists only to serve the individuals within it. Barristers' chambers, architects' partnerships, hippy communes, some small consultancies often have this 'person' orientation.

Its structure is as minimal as possible, a *cluster* is the best word for it, or perhaps *a galaxy of individual stars.*

Dionysius is its patron deity, the god of *the self-centred individual,* the first existentialist.

The cultures at work

Each culture makes its own assumptions as to how individuals *think* and *learn*, can be *influenced*, may be *changed* or might be *motivated*. These different assumptions result in differing theories and practices of management development, attitudes to change, and systems of control and reward. Let me elaborate, for each of Handy's cultures in turn.

The power culture (Zeus)

WAYS OF THINKING AND LEARNING

Zeus individuals think *instinctively*. They move *fast* to a possible solution and test that, moving to another if the first solution does not work. They rely on a lot of *impressionistic* data and make quick decisions.

In such power cultures *like learn from like* on an apprenticeship model. 'In such Zeus cultures one will find systems of personal assistants, or a chief executive's cadre of young hopefuls. People will speak of *protégés* and *crown princes*, of heirs to the succession, who will be tested out in some organizational *proving grounds.'*[12]

WAYS OF INFLUENCING AND CHANGING

From its power base of *resources* and *charisma* the Zeus culture creates change by changing *people*. Individuals are the link pieces in this culture. If a link is failing, replace it.

You will succeed or not, therefore, and be judged, by *whom*, not what, *you know*, although whom you know will depend on *what you do*. Zeus people accept and enjoy a *world of personalities and power* based on credits and ownership.

In Zeus cultures, *money is highly valued*; but it is, usually, money as a means of achievement or *as a symbol of results personally accomplished*. However, people and information, as well as money, can be an object of the culture's acquisitive instinct. To this end, they will invest considerable time in creating *networks*, that is potential sources of people, information and money.

Zeus characters like uncertainty, because uncertainty implies *freedom to manoeuvre*. Reward these people with a *challenge*, by your *trust*, and through *resources*. Control them through *financial incentives*, or through the look in your eyes, not by pension schemes or titles.

The role culture (Apollo)

The role culture is quite different. Apollonian thinking is logical, sequential, *analytical*. The role culture would like to believe in a formally *scientific world*, where events move according to pre-determined formulae. *Intelligence* – of the convergent kind – will be a useful indicator of ability.

Learning, therefore, is to do with the *acquisition of knowledge and skills*, from those who possess both to those who do not. It is acquired additively by a transfer process called *training*. To this culture, moreover, belong both formal management techniques and depersonalized physical and *human resources* that can be planned, organized and controlled.

Power in role cultures stems not from personal charisma but from one's *role* or position. Written into that position, moreover, are a list of *rights* and *responsibilities*. The *organization chart* – generally unheard of in a Zeus culture – linking one role with another, is a diagrammatic way of representing who can give *orders* to whom.

It follows that to change Apollonian *structures* and *systems*, one must change either the sets of roles and responsibilities (structures) or the network of rules and procedures (systems).

Apollo cultures value *order* and *predictability*. Things need to fit into place, with contracts precise and honoured, and roles pre-scribed and constrained. *Duty*, obligation, responsibility and con-tribution are all important to them.

They *pursue certainty* as avidly as Zeus cultures shun it. An

Apollonian will find sense and security in budgets and job descriptions while a Zeus will view them as constraints on opportunism. Because, moreover, Apollonians value the power that is conveyed by the *formal authority* of their role, they are appropriately rewarded by an increase in such authority, and by its outwardly visible sign, *status*.

The task culture (Athena)

WAYS OF THINKING AND LEARNING

Athenians are *problem solvers*, particularly when the problems require a mix of vertical and *lateral thinking*. Fundamental, too, to the process of problem solving is the ability to *work with others*. Learning, therefore, is acquiring the ability to solve problems better, in and through teamwork.

Whereas, then, the formal acquisition of knowledge has its place, crucial learning is by *continual exploration* or discovery, accompanied by successive problem solving and *project-based learning*. Athenian cultures tend to think of people as *resourceful humans* rather than as human resources, who are ultimately responsible for their own destinies. Therefore *self-development* will be encouraged and mobility between organizations will not be discounted.

WAYS OF INFLUENCING AND CHANGING

Athenian cultures bow down to *professional expertise*. There is a lot of talk, argument and *discussion* in such cultures. Such cultures, therefore, work best when a *heterogeneous* group of *talents* finds its homogeneity through identification with a common cause or task.

The first step to influence in these cultures, as a result, is to change the definition of the *focal* problem or *task*. In such a task culture you can gain influence, in fact, by *rational argument* rather than through personal charisma or status.

WAYS OF MOTIVATING AND REWARDING

Athenians like *variety*. At the same time they are concerned with their own professional *self-advancement*. Athenian cultures concentrate on *defining tasks* rather than roles, allowing discretion in the choice of means to any given end. *Objectives* are in order, but not role descriptions.

In summary, Athenians flourish under conditions of variety, problem solving, and opportunity for self-development. They respond to *payment by results*, to group assignments and to *defined uncertainty* – the solution of identified challenges.

The existential culture (Dionysius)

WAYS OF THINKING AND LEARNING

Dionysians defy rigid classification in their thinking and habits. They will therefore resent any attempt by others to plan their futures or to develop their abilities. They want opportunities to learn, but demand the *right to choose* between them. They will therefore talk of sabbaticals, of second careers, of dropping in and dropping out and of acquiring *educational credits* on a *flexible basis*.

WAYS OF INFLUENCING AND CHANGING

It is *hard to influence* Dionysians, since they do not conceive themselves as working for the organization. It follows that any attempt to influence or change a Dionysian will have to be a *contracted procedure*. In fact, Dionysians are very difficult to manage. It is for this reason that they have to become *indispensable* if they are not to be evicted by an employer.

Dionysian organizations, Handy argues, are therefore *managed* in a *one-on-one* fashion. The 'leader' interacts with each individually.

WAYS OF MOTIVATING AND REWARDING

Like Zeus characters Dionysians want to make a difference to the world, but it does not have to be through power or people or resources. Truly Dionysian professions – like consultants or architects – are not allowed to advertise, and have to find more or less discrete ways to promote their fame.

Dionysians value *personal freedom above all*, particularly freedom of their time. They like to be consulted, but not to be obliged to participate. They are *loners* who gather within organizations only for convenience.

Balancing cultures

A particular organizational culture, then, may be predominantly power – Zeus, role – Apollo, task – Athena, or person – Dionysius based. In fact most people, at least in the developed world, are still employed by power- or role-based cultures. Whereas the task-based culture is gaining influence, particularly in the newer technology-based companies, the person-based one is still very thin on the ground.

However, and in addition, a single organization – particularly a larger one – needs to attain some degree of cultural balance within itself. In other words, a primarily role-based culture, for example, may have pockets of Athena, within its research and development division, and glimmerings of Zeus, in its sales force.

What, then, are the forces that influence the choice of mix, and the ways of changing or managing that mix, within or between organizations? The principal forces, according to Handy, are size, life-cycles, work patterns and people.

Size

The bigger the organization becomes the more like Apollo it is likely to be. 'Once you have more than ten individuals within a group, ten groups in a division, or ten divisions in a company, you have to rely on formal methods of control and co-ordination.'

Life cycles

The higher the rate of change, the larger the influence of Athena. Organizations adapt to shortening product life cycles by setting up task forces and ad hoc project groups, by accentuating development activities, by involving subcontractors and freelancers, thus *enhancing its problem-solving capacity*.

Work patterns

There are, Handy maintains, three different ways of arranging the work to be done in organizations: as *flows*, where one section's work becomes input for the next; as *copies*, where the work of each section is identical; as *units*, where the work of each section is independent.

An assembly line is the best known example of a flow pattern. Branch banking, or multiple stores exemplify the copy pattern. Finally, small enterprises and craft-based activities represent a unit pattern.

The tendency is for *flow* and *copy patterns* to *require Apollonian* methods. *Unit patterns*, on the other hand, *can be Zeus like* – most frequently – or Athenian, if collaborative work is required, or Dionysian, as with many professionals.

People

Our cultural preferences are probably thrust upon us by our *early experiences and environments*. There is also good evidence to suggest that *certain cultures are more popular in certain societies*. Dionysius, for example, has much more scope in Britain than he or she would do in Japan.

PEOPLE AND CULTURE

Youth does not value Apollo ... educated architects are often Dionysian ... the illiterate driver or entrepreneur may well be a Zeus ... The hungry obey, the contented argue ... Individualists dislike Apollo ... Conformists prefer such a role culture ...

Remember these are tendencies, not laws. As humans we have the delightful ability to be the exceptions to our own generalizations.[13]

Any one organization, then, examining itself in the light of these influencing factors, will find itself pushed towards at least two and perhaps three of the cultures. Let us look at the implications of this for organization design.

Implications for organization design

Organizations, in fact, gradually *change* their *dominant cultures.*

Most start as power cultures. The founder sees the organization as an extension of himself, only necessary because he cannot do everything on his own.

Time and success lead to growth and to specialization and to formalization of activity. Therein lies *the role culture.*

The next cultural *shift* comes about when the role culture is confronted with the need for greater flexibility. The market may start to change more quickly, or to move in different directions. More often, the sheer growth of the organization compounds its complexity. At this stage, formalization and specialization are no longer sufficient to control the diversity of problems and *the organization needs a range of different cultures.*

The leadership may seek to retain a clear set of values that was the essence of the original company, but, Handy says, the more stylistic parts of the culture must be allowed to change to fit the requirements of each part of the organization. One way to approach the problem of *finding the appropriate cultural diversity* is to look at the type of activity which primarily characterizes each part of the organization.

Steady state

Steady state implies all those *activities which can be programmed* in some way, that is activities which are routine as opposed to non-routine.

The steady state often accounts for the bulk of an organization's employees. It includes the infrastructure of the organization, the secretarial, office and accounting systems. It usually also includes the production or operations side of the business and some of the routine sales activity.

Innovation

Innovation includes all *activities directed to changing things* that the organization does, or the way that it does it. Research and development, part of marketing, the development side of production, corporate planning and parts of finance are normally included.

Crisis

All organizations have to *deal with the unexpected.* No one part of the organization will have a monopoly of crises or breakdowns, although the parts which are closest to the external environment are likely to be most exposed.

Policy

Policy making involves the *overall guidance and direction* of activities. The setting of priorities, the establishment of standards, the direction and allocation of resources, the initiation of action, these are activities which form a category of their own.

Differentiation and integration

In the final analysis, Handy suggests, if the appropriate culture prevails where that set of activities resides, then that part of the organization will be more effective (see Figure 4.1).

CULTURE, STRUCTURE AND DIVERSITY

The suggestion is that *organizations should differentiate their cultures and structures according to the dominant kind of activity* in that department, division or section.

R and D, for example, should be organized differently from the accounting department. The innovative part of marketing can be expected to be more informal, more task-oriented than the assembly line. The management of crisis should override committees, rules and procedures, regulation and formal controls.

The management of steady state activities should properly be concerned with rules, procedures, regulations and formal controls. Apply these to the innovation arms of the organization and they will suffocate.[14]

The more diverse the cultures contained within a single organization, of course, the greater the effort that has to be put into cultural

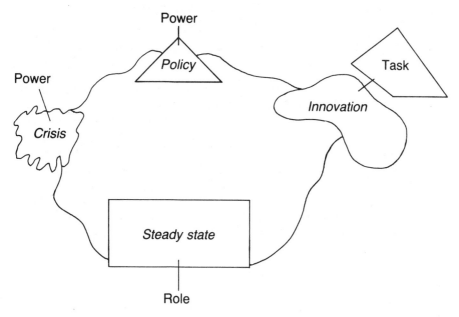

Figure 4.1   Organization culture and design

integration. Handy advocates a new form of *federalism*, as an extension of the traditional *village* concept, to achieve such integration. However, true to the European spirit of diversity, he is relatively less concerned with integration than with differentiation and adaptation.

To focus on such integration, and on a specific set of methodologies for cultural analysis and synthesis, we need to turn to the American, Edgar Schein.

YOU RETURN TO ORGANIZATIONAL CULTURE AND LEADERSHIP

Schein's approach is the most analytically rigorous of the three rationally oriented ones. He is more concerned than either McCoy or Handy with providing a methodology for analysing and adapting organizational cultures.

Discovering a culture's functions

Schein begins by describing the functions of an organizational, or corporate, culture, both in terms of external adaptation and also internal integration.

The functions of 'culture', with regard to an organization's external survival and adaptation, involve:

- securing a *shared understanding of the core mission*, primary task, manifest and latent functions of the organization
- developing *consensus on goals*, as derived from the core mission
- developing *consensus on the means* to be used *to attain goals*, such as organization structure, division of labour, and the reward and authority systems
- developing *consensus on the criteria* to be used *in measuring* how well *the group* is doing
- developing *consensus on remedial strategies* to adopt when things go wrong.

INTERNAL INTEGRATION

Similarly, Schein specifies six cultural factors that determine the state of internal integration:

1. *Common language* – if members cannot communicate with, and understand each other, the management of a group or organization becomes impossible. For instance, engineers and salesmen in a manufacturing concern may not share a common business language.
2. *Group boundaries* – there needs to be a shared consensus on who is within the organization, and who is without. For example, are subcontractors or freelancers considered part of the organization or not?
3. *Intimacy, friendship, love* – every organization must work out the basis for conducting peer relationships, including the intensity and frequency of contact both inside and outside of work.
4. *Power and status* – every organization must work out its pecking order, its criteria and rules for getting, maintaining and losing power.
5. *Rewards and punishments* – every group must know what sorts of behaviour might be considered 'heroic' and what sorts may be considered 'sinful'.
6. *Ideology and religion* – finally every organization, like every society, faces unexplainable events which must be given meaning. To avoid the anxiety of dealing with the inexplicable or uncontrollable a religious or ideological outlook may be called upon. For example, a cataclysmic event may be put down to divine intervention or to the vagaries of the free market system.

Undertaking a cursory assessment

As a professional and organizational psychologist, then, Schein makes a thorough attempt to understand an organization's culture. In the process he places particular emphasis on underlying and often invisible assumptions. He therefore leaves the visible, tangible and concrete primal world far behind him, even further behind than Charles Handy does.

At the outset of his book, though, he provides us with a rough and ready approach to cultural diagnosis. Schein tells us to:

- *observe* the *behavioural regularities* when people interact, such as the kind of language that they use
- *take note of the norms* that evolve in working groups
- *recognize the dominant values* that are espoused by the organization, like 'product quality', or 'profit before people'
- *discover the philosophy* that guides an organization's policy towards its employees or customers
- *take note of the rules of the game*, that is for getting on within the organization
- finally, and perhaps more subtly, *sense the* feeling or *climate* that is conveyed in the organization both by the *physical layout* and by the way the *members interact*.

The features of the organization upon which we therefore need to focus, for such a cursory analysis, are its:

- organization *structure*, watching out for the implications on the way that work is done, and that people relate to one another
- organizational *systems* and procedures, taking note of the implications for human and organizational behaviour and interactions
- *stories* and parables covering important events and people
- *charters* and formal statements of mission and policy, included in annual end employee reports, as well as in brochures, recruitment literature and handbooks or training manuals.

So much for the cursory approach. When it comes to a more purposeful cultural assessment, however, the undertaking immediately becomes more scientific and complex.

Building a conceptual model

EXTERNAL INTERVENTION

If an external analyst or consultant is to move beyond a cursory diagnosis of the organizational culture towards a shared appreciation of its character – including both its potential and its limitations – more thought is required. Specifically, Schein proposes:

- a *focus*, initially, *on surprises*, incorporating the unexpected
- subsequently *categorize* these *surprising observations*, duly verifying the repeated experiences and observations
- locate a *motivated insider*, within the organization, that is someone both capable of, and motivated to, decipher what is happening
- *reveal* the surprises, and *hunches to the* motivated *insider*, sticking to specific reactions
- *explore jointly*, whereby both parties *begin to probe systematically* – the outsider then assuming the role of clinical interviewer
- help the insider to search his mind, to bring out meaningful data, to *explore meaning in a relaxed setting*
- *formalize hypotheses*, subjecting the hypotheses generated to test, applying theoretical and behavioural analyses to the *building of a conceptual model*
- *engage in systematic checking* through new interviews or observations, thereby searching for fresh evidence. At this point the outsider knows where, what and when to look at and for, *through questionnaires, content analysis and interviews*
- *push* then *onto* the level of *underlying assumptions*, as elaborated upon below, before starting to
- *refine, modify* and test *the model* of the organizational culture that has now been drawn up, and then finally attempting to
- *draw up a formal description* of the culture, both as it is, and also as it might be.

In essence, then, Schein, as a good behavioural scientist, pays more attention to the intelligent interpretation of information than to an instinctive appreciation of people and things. He attaches greatest priority, in the context of culture, to the uncovering of underlying assumptions. These relate to man's fundamental being, activities and relationships.

Uncovering underlying assumptions

To reveal the essence of an organization's culture, then, Schein invites us to *appreciate the underlying assumptions around which cultural paradigms form.*

Such underlying assumptions are made by managers, in fact, on five specific dimensions, based on man's relationship to nature, to reality and truth, to human activity, to human nature and to human relationships:

1. Man's *relationship to nature* – the key members of the organiza-tion may view the relationship of the organization to its environment as one of *dominance, submission, harmonization* or *adaptation* – that is one of finding an appropriate niche.
2. The nature of *reality and truth* – this involves the linguistic and behavioural rules that define what is real and what is not, including *concepts of organizational space and time.*
3. The nature of *human activity* – this covers the 'right' things for organizational members to do, that is whether to be *active or passive*, to *work or* to *play*, to be *fatalistic* or to believe in *free choice.*
4. The attributes of *human nature* – key members of an organiza-tion will hold beliefs as to what it means to be 'human', including those attributes which might be considered intrinsic or ultimate. Is human nature, for example, fundamentally *good or evil*?
5. The nature of *human relationships* – different people have different beliefs about what may be considered the 'right' way for employees and other stakeholders to relate to one another. How should power and wealth be distributed? Is organizational life *competitive or cooperative, individualistic or communal*?

Let us consider the implications, for organizations and their managers, of each of these in turn. I shall also, through Schein,[15] be identifying specific ways and means of uncovering these implica-tions, generally through group discussions held with appropriate people.

Dimension 1 – The organization and its environment

*   Our basic *identity* and *role* – who are we, as a company, as reflected in our product or service, and customer base? What is our core mission and ultimate function in society? What is our reason for being, that is our ultimate justification for survival?

- Our relevant *environments* – what and who represent our significant economic, political, technological, ecological, social and cultural environments? What major threats and opportunities do they pose?
- Our *position* vis à vis these environments – are we dominant and in control? Or do we live symbiotically, that is in harmony with our environments? Or are we dominated by our environments, within which we therefore need to find our niche?

How, then, do we uncover the organization's basic assumptions about itself?

UNCOVERING THE ORGANIZATION'S BASIC ASSUMPTIONS ABOUT ITSELF

1. Reconstruct and analyse the organization's history by *identifying major crises*, crucial transitions, and periods of high emotion.
2. *Locate patterns* and themes across the events analysed.
3. *Cross check patterns* against strategic criteria established by the organization.
4. *Articulate the assumptions* that underlie the actions taken.
5. *Check* these assumptions against *what* actually *happened*.

So much for the organization and its environment. Now we need to consider its underlying assumptions about reality.

Dimension 2 – The nature of an organization's reality

- What is the *physical reality* surrounding the organization, which can be objectively verified? What is the *social* reality, which can only be verified by principle or consensus? What is the *subjective* reality, which is only verifiable through personal opinion, bias or taste?
- What *underlying criterion* is used by the organization for judging activities and behaviour?

Is it *tradition* – in other words, 'we've always done it this way'? Is it religious or moral *dogma*, that is to say 'this is the right way'? Is it *rational* or legal, for example 'we'll see what the marketing committee decides'? Is it based on *revelation* by wise people in authority, so that 'our president wants it this way'?

Alternatively, is it based on *conflict resolution*, that is to say 'we've thrashed it out'? Or is it based on *trial and error*, so that 'we'll try it and see'? Finally, is it based on *science* – 'research tells us . . .'?

How, then, do we uncover the organization's basic assumptions about reality?

UNCOVERING THE ORGANIZATION'S BASIC ASSUMPTIONS ABOUT REALITY?

1. *Identify* a set of strategic *high conflict decisions.*
2. *Clarify* the nature of these in terms of physically, socially and subjectively based categories of decision.
3. *Identify* the *criteria used* in the making of these strategic decisions.
4. *Look for pattern* and themes in the use of criteria.
5. *Articulate the basic assumptions* underlying the criteria.
6. *Check* the assumptions against what actually happened.

In considering the nature of organizational reality, moreover, Schein pays particular attention to concepts of space and time.

As far as organizational *space* is concerned he focuses our attention on its physical *availability* – constrained or unconstrained; on its use as a symbol of *power and status*; and on its association with formality or informality, with *social distance or intimacy* – affecting people either inside or outside the organization.

With regard to *time*, Schein alerts us to the importance of time *orientation* – on past, present or future; on time *perspective*, be it linear, cyclical or what might be called polychronic (contagious); and on time *cycles*, be they daily, monthly, annual or five-yearly in duration.

Now we move onto assumptions about human nature.

Dimension 3 – The characteristics of human nature

- What is the *underlying basis* of human nature
    - are human beings basically bad?
    - are human beings basically good?
    - are people capable of being good or bad?
- *How changeable* is human nature?
    - are human attributes fixed at birth?
    - are humans changeable/perfectible, as they grow?

How, then, do we uncover the basic assumptions about human nature within organizations?

UNCOVERING BASIC ASSUMPTIONS ABOUT HUMAN NATURE

1. *Identify* the *heroes and villains* of the organization; compare the stories regarding their respective human natures.
2. Analyse *recruitment*, selection and promotional *criteria*.

3. Analyse *performance criteria*.
4. Analyse the implicit *assumptions underlying the reward* and control *system*.
5. Look for common assumptions and *check* against what actually happens.

Fourthly, we need to consider the assumptions underlying the nature of human activity.

Dimension 4 – The nature of human activity

- Are people characteristically *active*, in control, *problem-solving oriented*, inclined to fight for their rights, and to struggle for victory against either man or nature? or
- are human beings characteristically *reactive*, subordinating themselves to nature, and *accepting* their fate? or
- are people naturally inclined towards *harmonizing* behaviour, amongst themselves and with nature, perfecting themselves, and *fulfilling* their potential?

How, therefore, do we uncover the assumptions underlying human activity within organizations?

UNCOVERING THE ASSUMPTIONS UNDERLYING HUMAN ACTIVITY

1. *Identify* a set of *problems* faced by the organization *where the* problem *source was outside*.
2. *What approaches* to dealing with them *were advocated*?
3. *Which* were *adopted*?
4. *What assumptions* were implicit?
5. *Check* the assumptions against what actually happened.

Finally, with Schein, we need to consider the impact of different assumptions about human relationships upon organizational culture.

Dimension 5 – The nature of human relationships

- What is the basis for human relationships:
  - *linear*, based on tradition, hierarchy, family?
  - or *collateral*, based on group cooperation and consensus?
  - or *individual*, based on individual aims and abilities?
- What is the basis for organizational relationships:
  - autocratic, paternalistic, consultative, participative?

So how do we uncover the assumptions underlying relationships within organizations?

UNCOVERING THE ASSUMPTIONS REGARDING RELATIONSHIPS

1. Identify a group of important recent decisions; *discover how power was exercised* in the decision-making process.
2. *Examine stories* and legends about heroes and villains, uncovering the ways in which people related.
3. *Examine critical incidents* – find out how the organization dealt with the violation of norms covering relationships.
4. *Look for themes* and patterns of response in the decisions, and illustrated through the stories.
5. *Check* the assumptions made about the desired nature of human relationships against what actually happens.

As we can see, Schein's approach is much more analytically rigorous than that adopted by Deal and Kennedy or even by Charles Handy. It focuses relatively less on visible personalities and on explicit activities and stories, and relatively more on invisible attitudes and beliefs, including implicit assumptions.

Changing cultures

Although Schein devotes himself, primarily, to an analysis of organizational cultures, he does give limited attention to methods of changing them. He cites five alternative approaches, including the 'management of cultural change' to which he devotes most attention. The 'unmanaged' approaches that he describes are evolutionary, adaptive, therapeutic and revolutionary in nature.

Unmanaged cultural change

CHANGE AS ADAPTATION AND LEARNING

The *properties of the environment* cause certain organizational responses to be rewarded or punished, and thereby *cause the organization to learn or adapt.*

CHANGE AS AN EVOLUTIONARY PROCESS

Forces for change come from within the organization and are natural and inevitable. There are *stages of evolution*, from lower to higher. We shall be paying particular attention to these later (in Chapter 4).

CHANGE AS A THERAPEUTIC PROCESS

Change comes about as a result of the *interaction of insiders and outsiders*. The aim of change is to improve the organization's adaptive ability, or level of integration. Cultural change is directly related to the action of the change agent in improving the situation.

CHANGE AS A REVOLUTIONARY PROCESS

The *working out of power struggles* between individuals or groups within or without the organization will inevitably, Schein argues, lead to some form of revolutionary process. He mentions management successions, turnarounds, or acquisitions as examples of such so-called revolutions.

However, Schein is personally most interested in a managed process of cultural change, although, as an external consultant himself, the therapeutic process is also of significant concern to him.

Managed cultural change

Schein indicates that business founders and new organizational leaders seem to know that their own visible behaviour has great value for communicating assumptions and values. Particularly in times of crisis the way in which they deal with these will determine the norms and values that are built into the organization. However, there are different requirements of leadership at different stages of an organization's development.

LEADERSHIP AND ORGANIZATIONAL CREATION

At the early stages of an organization's development the leader needs both *vision, the ability to articulate it, and the skill to enforce it.*

Inasmuch as the new members of the organization arrive with prior organizational and cultural experiences, a common set of assumptions is only forged by clear and consistent messages, as the group encounters and survives its own crises.

Thus the culture creation leader needs *persistence and patience* as well.

LEADERSHIP AT ORGANIZATIONAL MIDLIFE

Once the organization develops a substantial history of its own, *the culture becomes more of a cause than an effect*. Culture now reinforces strategy, structure, procedure and the ways in which group members relate.

Leaders at this stage need, above all, the *insight to know how to help the organization to evolve*. In some instances this may mean increasing cultural diversity. In other instances it may mean pulling people together under newly established, and shared, cultural ties.

In either case, the leader needs insight into ways in which culture can aid or hinder the fulfilment of the organization's mission, *and the intervention skills to make desired things happen.*

LEADERSHIP IN MATURE ORGANIZATIONS

If a mature organization is to change its culture from, say, an inward looking to an outward looking one, it will have to be led by someone with:

- *perception and insight* – first, the leader must be able to perceive the culturally-based problem, by having insight into the organizational culture and its dysfunctional elements
- *motivation and skill* – internal leadership requires not only insight but also the motivation and skill to intervene. To change any elements of the culture, leaders must be willing to 'unfreeze' their own organization
- *ability to change assumptions* – leaders must have the ability to articulate and to sell new visions as well as business or organizational concepts
- *deliberate role modelling* – a leader must have depth of vision and insight into the thoughts and feelings of people, in and around the organization that are normally taken for granted and therefore not expressed.

In fact, cultural change may involve a mixture of unmanaged and managed elements, incorporating adaptive, evolutionary, therapeutic, revolutionary and leadership processes.

CONCLUDING THE RATIONAL WAY

Primal and rational

Whereas the primal approach to culture is tangible, visible, concrete and immediate, the rational approach is generally intangible, invisible, abstract and enduring. Whereas the one involves a visible cast of cultural characters the other brings with it invisible and underlying assumptions.

While Deal and Kennedy refer to such tangibly shared values as 'We're the first Irish Multinational' Edgar Schein deals with the complex assumptions underlying the nature of human being.

Uniformity and diversity

Both Charles McCoy, with his managerial values and ethics, and Edgar Schein, with his organizational culture and leadership, focus on the communal and integral features of a shared culture. Though Schein acknowledges the existence of group subcultures within the organizational whole, these remain on the cultural periphery.

Charles Handy, however, like Roger Harrison from whom he originally derived his cultural theory, concentrates on the culture's parts to a greater extent than the whole. Handy is a champion of diversity, flexibility and contingency, whereas Schein and McCoy focus on community, integrity and coherence.

Cultural change and evolution

In terms of Schein's models of cultural change the primal approach is essentially 'revolutionary', drawing on heroic personalities to take over, or to turn a company around. Lee Iaccoca, at Chrysler, is probably the best known case in point.

Schein himself, like Handy, adopts more of a 'therapeutic' approach, aimed at improving an organization's adaptability and integration. The approach here is neither as ad hoc as the 'adaptive' nor as consistently and internally directed as the 'managed' one.

The next, developmental approach to corporate culture that we shall be considering is essentially evolutionary in nature. It has been popularized by Bernard Lievegoed in Holland and by myself in Great Britain. Its roots lie in biology and ecology rather than in anthropology (primal) or in the administrative or behavioural sciences (rational). The developmental way, then, is the subject of the chapter to come.

REFERENCES

1 Litwin, P., and Stringer, R., *Motivation and Organisational Climate*, Harper & Row, 1968.
2 Selznick, Philip, *Leadership and Administration*, Paterson, 1948, p. 28.
3 McCoy, Charles, *The Management of Values*, Pitman, 1985.
4 Harrison, Roger, cited in Charles Handy, *Understanding Organisations*, Penguin, 1976.
5 Handy, Charles, *The Gods of Management*, Pan, 1985, p. 11.
6 Schein, Edgar, *Organizational Culture and Leadership*, Jossey Bass, 1985, pp. 6-7.
7 McCoy, Charles, op. cit.
8 Ibid., p. 67.
9 Selznick, Philip, op. cit., pp. 38-40.

10 McCoy, Charles, op. cit., p. 190.
11 Handy, Charles, *Understanding Organisations*, Penguin, 1976, p. 185.
12 Handy, Charles, op. cit., 1985, p. 44.
13 Handy, Charles, op. cit., 1985, p. 82.
14 Handy, Charles, op. cit., 1976, p. 208.
15 Schein, Edgar, op. cit., pp. 128-135.

5 The Developmental Way

Development . . . To *unfold* gradually, to become *progressively* more *manifest;* to cause to become visible, to *reveal* hidden *potentialities;* to go through a *succession of states,* each of which is preparatory for the next one; to *undergo natural evolution* by successive changes from a less to a more perfect or highly organized state.

Culture is the *art* or practice *of cultivating;* the *act of developing* through education, discipline or social experience; the enlightenment and excellence of *taste* acquired through *aesthetic* and intellectual training. (*Webster's New International Dictionary*)

BEING INTRODUCED TO A DEVELOPMENTAL CULTURE

From primal to developmental

The primal approach to corporate culture is focused on *shared values,* dealing particularly with the cultural network – including heroes – that personify these in the *here and now.* The rational approach is oriented towards the organization's *underlying assumptions* about man and nature, relating especially to the attitudes and values of its people *past and present.* The developmental approach to culture, thirdly, is concerned with the *evolution* of the organization, including its people, its products, and its markets, from *youth to maturity.*

The primal approach, therefore, involves a heroic *personality* operating within a binding *community.* The rational orientation is towards functionally or professionally differentiated *individuals* working within a structurally integrated *organization.* The developmental focus, finally, is upon evolving *human beings* operating within an interdependent *environment.*

Whereas, then, the primal culture can be represented by Handy's web, and a rational one by either his net or Greek temple, a developmental one is best depicted by a *tree of life* (see below).

78

Such a tree, as has been outlined in my book on *The Roots of Excellence*,[1] has six major characteristics.

The 'business tree of life'

The 'business tree of life' is, firstly, *firmly planted in the ground*, preferably in fertile soil. Secondly, it *grows in stages*, four of them. Its growth and development infuses the whole business organism with life. Not to grow is to die, whether as a tree or as a business.

Thirdly, as the organism grows, it *becomes* more strongly *rooted* in the soil. Fourthly, a main stem or tree trunk develops from it, giving the tree or business a *growth centre*. Fifthly, the tree sprouts *branches*, eight of them, giving the tree *business character*.

Finally the *fruits* or foliage, in other words the products or services, *emerge*, and these in their turn produce the *seeds* of renewal. As a combined result, the business can be suitably grounded, developed, rooted, centred, characterized and renewed. I shall deal with each of these developmental features, in turn, after we have uncovered the 'laws of development'.

Developmental laws

The scope of development

Whereas the primal and rational managers view business and organizational entities as discrete phenomena, *the developmental manager views individuals, organizations, products and markets as parallel phenomena*, each subject to similar laws of structural evolution.

More specifically, for all living organisms, growth continues within a certain structure until a limit is reached. Beyond this limit the existing structure or model can no longer impose order on the larger mass. The consequence is either disintegration or a step up to a higher level of order.

This phenomenon can be observed in a single living cell or in a complex business organization. A cell does not grow indefinitely but at a certain moment divides into two new cells, which in turn grow only to their limits, and so on. The same can be observed, in the higher organisms, which pass from one phase of development to the next.

Characteristics of development

Such growth occurs both in healthy individual development and also in the evolution of whole species. Similarly, it applies to the development of individual companies, over time, as well as entire product lines, industries or economies. Development, then:

- occurs in a series of *stages*
- is principally *discontinuous*
- within each *stage* a particular *structure* tends to dominate
- the stages become *progressively more complex*
- a new structure is not added to the old; rather a shift occurs in the *whole new pattern* of relationships
- development is *not reversible* (youth cannot return!).

Let us look now at this developmental process as a whole.

A picture of development

The major authority advocating a developmental approach to management has been the Dutch organizational psychologist, Bernard Lievegoed. In his book on *The Developing Organization*[2] he suggests that development can be diagrammatically depicted as *a flight of steps*:

or it can equally well be represented as *a process of spreading,* whereby the emphasis shifts from old to new centres:

A stepwise picture of development represents total transformation from one step to the next, as is the case when a caterpillar becomes a butterfly. This in fact seldom happens in organizational life. Remnants of earlier steps tend to remain in some shape or form.

Thus the ever spreading picture is more representative of the developing organization. In other words, as an organization evolves we find remnants of earlier structures. For example a rationally managed organization will still have pockets of primal enterprise. Developmental management, therefore, is full of ambiguity and unpredictability.

Social evolution

The term 'social Darwinism' denotes the survival of the fittest. It befits the primal manager. The term 'social engineering' denotes the construction of logically determined forms of organization. It befits the rational manager.

The term *social evolution* befits the developmental manager. It *involves setting in motion organizational changes in the direction of a more advanced stage of development*, but of which only the barest outlines are known. The final form and content of the next stage can thus arise out of the actual potentialities of the culture involved.

'Culture', in a developmental context, is both nationally and organizationally based. It involves, moreover, both people and technology, art and artefact. I shall start, in the context of the 'living business', by locating fertile ground for development, thereby dealing with national culture.

YOU LOCATE FERTILE NATIONAL GROUND FOR DEVELOPMENT

A business may be based in one of the four quarters of the globe, and in a particular country within it. Both the global and the national setting will influence the corporate culture. Let us start with the West, and with the United States of America.

Western grounds

The two primal Americans, Peters and Waterman, went out in search of excellence and came back with a treasure trove of business insights. Their particular treasure was found in American soil.

Within their national soil, then, they found a series of distinctive attributes:[3]

- a hands on, *value driven* society, spurred on by the strongly held American dream of social mobility and economic achievement

- a *closeness to the customer* amongst excellent companies, reflecting the American cultural 'melting pot'
- *productivity through people* rather than through formal systems, depicting the spirit of equality in America.

These were, if you like, the 'soft' or communal attributes of America at work. Similarly there were characteristically 'hard' attributes amongst successful American companies:

- a *bias for action*, symptomatic of the inherent American restlessness and a love of experimentation
- autonomy and *entrepreneurship*, combining the American frontier spirit with its people's desire to accumulate wealth.

Eastern grounds

Peters and Waterman's search for fertile grounds was in fact stimulated by the discoveries that Pascale and Athos[4] made in Japan. The latter concluded that it was the traditional spirit and culture of the Japanese people, interspersed with modern business techniques, that was responsible for their economic miracle.

As in the American case, there are both soft and hard sources of nutriment in the Japanese cultural soil. The hard ones include:

- a *national drive* for achievement, embodied in their concept of 'risshin shusse', which symbolizes unyielding group (rather than individual) effort, for the attainment of national status (rather than wealth)
- a *restless spirit*, represented in 'Ki Ga Susumanai', that endures until such a time as a task is completed to perfection
- a belief that *rank means everything*, embodied in the concept of 'Kata Gaki'. Every person, organization and nation is ranked in order, though a subtle balance of mutuality as well as obligation is maintained between each.

The soft attributes of Japanese culture, meanwhile, include:

- *Amae*, or a sense of total dependence on trusted parties, incorporating relationships with and between suppliers and customers, workers and management, companies and ministries
- *harmony* with nature, embodied in the concept of 'shibui', whereby adaptability of people and products to their true purpose in life and nature is contained

- *humility*, reflected in the Buddhist philosophy of 'mu', whereby the individual is attached to no value or thing to the extent that his ego is at stake. He therefore remains totally open, and, in that particular sense, responsive to change.

Northern grounds

To discover fertile ground for the development of British business, I took a brief trip through Britain's social and economic history. I discovered four particularly fertile grounds (see Chapter 2).

- prolific *recreational* grounds, including widespread hobbies, outdoor pursuits and voluntary activities, represented in many a gifted amateur both past and present, and represented in such a figure as Richard Branson today
- a *tolerance* for *diversity* which is reflected in the many different nationalities that have settled in this country, and the number of businesses which have been created here by foreigners seeking refuge from persecution or prejudice. ICI is one case in point, the originators being Swedish and German.

These are the softer nutriments in British soils. The hard ones I regard as creativity and individuality:

- strong grounds for *individuality*, even to the point of eccentricity, combined with a love of personal freedom. Therein lie grounds for such enterprises as Clive Sinclair's.
- a *creative* tradition, both in the arts and in the sciences, that has served Britain well in the basic sciences, and has recently led to her re-emergence in industrial and commercial design. Many a design group, software house or advertising agency is grounded in that tradition.

Southern grounds

Southern cultural grounds, be they in Brazil or Bolivia, Zimbabwe or Zaire, are the least well charted as far as global business is concerned. Two factors stand out, however, in the South:

- the *closeness to nature*, from both a natural resource and an aesthetic perpective
- the all *pervasiveness of religion*, together with its rootedness in the land.

YOU RECOGNIZE THAT NOT TO GROW IS TO DIE

A living business

Creativity

Fertile soil stimulates growth. A seed falls to the ground, the seed of an idea. It originally emerges from and subsequently draws off fertile ground. Roots grow, forming an evolving identity. Then the trunk, branches and first leaves follow. The business, its new activities and products begin to take shape. The shape of each leaf, or product, is a manifestation of the original seed pattern.

The process of development involves the unfolding of an idea, as an individual or organization draws off the environment (soil), subsequently evolving a business identity (roots), structure (stem), character (branches), and product (fruit). This original seed is the joint creation of a person or group and their environment.

The stages in a *process of development* can be distinguished from one another. A business grows, unfolding to the point when the original structure can no longer be maintained. There is a necessary crisis as the architects of change, as it were, create chaos in the old structure. This painfully necessary process paves the way for the emergence of a more complex organization, one that is capable of undergoing further evolution. If no more development is considered possible or desirable, the organism grows rigid and gradually disintegrates.

Phases

For the healthy and growing business, there are four major development phases. In the first, *pioneering* one, the organism develops as one entrepreneurial whole, bonding together people and enterprise. With continuing growth the entrepreneur finds himself unable to cope. A crisis point is reached. The business' survival is at stake.

In the second stage of business *consolidation*, specialization of function sets in, to deal with advancing complexity. Each function or subsidiary is now in a position to make decisions independently. A hierarchy of command is established, one above the other, covering each separate part of the whole. As development continues, networks of relationships are also established, intermeshing functional order and professional freedom.

With further growth, comes another crisis. Lack of motivation, integration and innovation leads to stagnation. There is a need for regeneration, for *renewal*. The third development stage calls for interdependence and, for the first time, conscious development of people, business and organization.

As interdependence increases, however, a further crisis is reached. The organization loses coherence and identity. Ultimately, a new centre, a new vision emerges, one that is a *transformation* of the old technology and organization. A return to the roots and underlying ground is called for, but one that involves the discovery of a higher, transcendent corporate intention. 'We are no longer in the transport business; we're in communications!'

Let me now investigate, in more depth, how one culture evolves out of the other, as an organization grows and develops.

The course of business development

Stage 1 – The primal culture

In the early phase of its growth, a young organism needs vigour and enthusiasm to make its arduous way. Starting up a business, then, like each phase of an organization's development, requires both hard and soft qualities. In this case, these consist of a spirit of enterprise, and an affinity with people.

UNDERTAKING ENTERPRISE

The entrepreneurial revolution is relived every time a person starts up a new enterprise. As anyone who has done it knows only too well, it takes lots of emotional resilience – a willingness to take personal and financial risks – as well as hard work, native wit, a capacity to improvise and enough imagination to see round corners. These are the attributes of an 'enterprise culture'.

INVOLVING PEOPLE

There could be no organization without people. The ability to enthuse others, and to feel out a customer need are indispensable, within the early stages of an organization's development. Above all, communally shared values, in the context of what is generally termed a 'family feeling' is required.

The transition from enterprise to management

Ironically, it is these instinctive qualities which can prove to be the entrepreneur's downfall, as his enterprise expands. In other words, *the very success of the enterprise culture can eventually lead to its demise*. Thus Ford Motors grew too big for Henry Ford to handle effectively. In trying to hold onto the reins of power, he almost destroyed what he had created. More recently Steve Jobs, founder of Apple Computers, has been eclipsed by the professional management that he himself sought.

Stage 2 – The rational culture

During the start-up phase of the enterprise, instinct was primary, and intellect, though important was secondary. During the rationally managed phase of an organization's development the roles are reversed. The science of management replaces the art of entrepreneurship.

Intellectual aptitudes, structures of organization, and concepts of strategy, therefore surpass purely instinctive, entrepreneurial qualities. In other words, managers and management become more conscious, more explicit, more self aware, more scientific. Administrative and behavioural science overtake classical economics and anthropology. Business instinct is not able to cope with the advancing organizational and environmental complexity.

ENTREPRENEURSHIP AND BUREAUCRACY

The initiating act of business is always and inescapably *entrepreneurial* – that is, an undertaking of creativity or of innovative change by someone who pursues the belief that the inherent uncertainty of the future will turn out favourably to his undertaking.

Successive acts to sustain the originating achievement require the formalization of repetitive procedures, to economize on the scarce entrepreneurial capacity. That *requires bureaucracy.*[5]

While the pioneering enterprise is stimulated by entrepreneurship and supported by people, the consolidated organization is stimulated by corporate strategy and organizational structure, and supported by motivated staff and participative management style.

STRATEGY AND STRUCTURE

In the 1950s the American business historian, Alfred Chandler, wrote his pathbreaking book *Strategy and Structure.*[6] In it he laid the ground rules for the professional manager, illustrating how rationally designed structure follows from a rationally devised strategy. The company to which he referred most extensively was General Motors.

It was Alfred Sloane's very success in structuring a divisionalized and functionally based organization, that led to the extraordinarily successful General Motors. In its day, GM surpassed Ford because Sloane had mastered the basic principles of strategy formulation and structured organization. In a period of sustained growth and in an environment that was largely ordered and predictable, rational management won many a day.

Such an approach involves a conversion of instinctive and personalized attributes into formalized and depersonalized ones. Northern formality takes over from Western informality.

STYLE AND BEHAVIOUR

Administrative formality, however, does not rule out participative management. A balance between task and people orientation is quite plausible within the progressive and rationally managed organization. In fact, a 'human relations' orientation falls well within the second stage of a business' development. Such behavioural and stylistic interventions provide the soft edge, while administrative and strategic thrust provide the hard ones.

But times have again changed. The managerial revolution is being superseded by another one, as yet unnamed. The degree of rigidity, impersonality, and insularity created by the rationally based culture creates dysfunctional inertia. Alienation within the organization and without sets in. A new healing and growing force is required.

Stage 3 – The developmental culture

Whereas the entrepreneur concentrates on the market, thereby generating a source of profitability, the American or European manager attends to the organization, thereby increasing efficiency, and *the Japanese manager focuses on the product, thereby attaining quality*.

Profit has material 'body' to it, efficiency is a product of the rational mind, and quality is the outcome not only of thought but also of feeling. That is one of the reasons why the Japanese, with their strong aesthetic awareness, have taken so naturally to that originally American invention, 'quality circles'.

Today the industrialized nations in general are going through a design revolution. Designers are coming into their own because *as societies evolve people seek more meaning, beauty and fulfilment in their lives.*

The evolving organization, at the third stage of its development, strives towards greater synergy, on the one hand, and towards manager self-development, on the other.

CORPORATE SYNERGY

As the individual business evolves, and becomes more self-conscious, so entrepreneurial instinct and managerial intellect are replaced by intuitive individual and organizational development.

In the Japanese culture a whole tradition of aesthetic awareness has been converted into organizational sensitivity, as reflected in their concept of, and feeling for, harmony. For the Japanese, as should be the case at this third stage of business development, feeling is primary, and thinking as well as doing are secondary. That is why consensus forms such an important part of decision making.

MANAGING SELF-DEVELOPMENT

Whereas the Japanese have made a major contribution towards the design of a new corporate architecture, it is the Europeans and Americans who have contributed more towards the design of a new and individualized lifestyle. The notion of 'quality of life', as opposed to sheer quantity of material gain, has, in the last thirty years, begun to impinge upon the managerial mind.

In that context, the *development of the person as a whole* is allied with the development of the business and organization. Both search for what the American organizational psychologist, Abraham Maslow, has called self-actualization.[7] Such an actualized individual or organization, moreover, is 'in tune' with the rest of society.

As the corporate culture advances, then, from its independently managed structure to its interdependently economic and social design *so developmental replaces rational management as the guiding force*. Fluidity of process displaces rigidity of structure at this third stage. As interdependence supplants dependence or independence, joint ventures are replacing autonomous or wholly owned companies, as the norm.

Yet we still have one more stage, or revolution, to go. For the problem with the new corporate architecture is that it can become too diffuse, the alliances too loosely held, the developing individuals too remote from one another. What is now required is a new, transforming centre.

Stage 4 – The metaphysical culture

FROM MATTER TO SPIRIT

The entrepreneurial revolution in the nineteenth century followed a leap forward in man's acquisitive impulses. As the American economic historian Robert Heilbronner puts it in *The Worldly Philosophers*,[8] it is only in the last two hundred years that the desire for systematic material gain has entered mankind's immediate horizons.

The managerial revolution, in its turn, heralded an era of not only material expansion and growth, but also of the advancement of 'human capital'. The subsequent design revolution reflects a shift in orientation towards quality as opposed to mere quantity.

Now that 'culture' has entered into the corporate mainstream, we are witnessing a further evolutionary step. For it is the great myths throughout the ages – whether in the East, West, North or South – that have stirred man's inner spirit.

Ultimately it is a business' or nation's *spirit* which *controls* its *destiny*. Corporate culture, myth and ritual therefore marks the end of the journey from physical matter towards human spirit via mind and heart. Yet this form of corporate being is still the least manifest of all stages of business development.

THE TRANSFORMED CORPORATION

As businessmen or women develop their new enterprises into structured organizations, they have to undergo the sort of mental and emotional transformation that comes with difficulty to a Steve Jobs (Apple Computers) or to a Clive Sinclair (Sinclair Research). As independent entrepreneurs each of them required guts to break out of a mould, and to lead by example, through both good times and bad. But then followed the crisis of delegation.

In a certain sense entrepreneurs have to grow up from a state of youthful independence, into a state of adult dependability. In other words, they have to accept the adultlike responsibility of having others dependent on them. Formal structure is required in place of improvisation. Mind is needed to functionally differentiate and to organizationally integrate.

Once this crisis of dependence is resolved the business can move on. However, the stage will inevitably be reached, with further growth and expansion, when the hierarchy of dependence will begin to collapse.

The increasingly turbulent and interdependent world wreaks havoc upon rigidly authoritarian structures. Accountable organizations have to grow into midlife and become reciprocating organizations within a community of interdependent technologies, functions, business ventures, or institutional partners. Sensitive harmonies are required at the front line, in place of rigid forms. Heart is needed to stimulate evolution and to foster interdependence.

Yet even the evolutionary and interdependent corporation cannot last for ever. It has breadth but it lacks depth. It can evolve but it cannot continuously innovate. In order to grow up, from midlife to maturity, it has to advance from interdependence to transcendence.

The transcendent enterprise has to outgrow its personal, corporate or even transcorporate identity, and assume a universal one. So a corporation, like the Bank of Credit and Commerce (see reference 11) that has reached the fourth stage of its development, aspires towards the establishment of conditions for world peace by transforming the economic conditions around the globe.

In order to do this its visionary leaders have to embark on a heroic journey, so as to *transform* their *global vision into local action*. Such a journey cannot be made without enlisting the support of the fundamental laws of nature. There are four of these, according to the President of BCC (see reference 11): nature operates as an integrated system in its dynamic state; we live within the fold of change; infinity is the container of existence; and the moral governs all that is material.

In other words, the global corporation needs to 'interfuse' with the rest of the world's economy and environment, to recognize and flow with natural energy forces, to operate within a context of limitless possibilities, and to develop a spiritually based mission which guides its material one.

A blend of cultures

Although, finally, business transformation apparently represents the ultimate stage of development, a final point is in fact never quite reached. *Life and business involve a journey rather than a destination.* All four developmental stages, like the four quarters of the globe, will be contained in some part of a continuously developing business.

Any major corporation will have embryonic and youthful as well as middle-aged and mature sectors within it. Parts of the organization, if not the whole of it, will also be in states of transition, in-between stages. Finally, *it may well be that a business needs to regress before it can progress.*

Moreover, many, if not most businesses, stop growing in quantitative or in qualitative terms. They may never evolve beyond adulthood, that is beyond the rationally managed organization. In such a case they will be forced to regress to an earlier stage, in order to survive in the short to medium term. Ultimately, they will die, but it is impossible to predict how long they might endure.

YOU NEED TO TAP DEVELOPMENTAL ROOTS

Personal identity

A developing business, then, like a tree, grows from its roots upwards. The roots draw from, and contribute to, the fertile ground below. In the process they establish the business' identity, between itself and its environment. For the young roots *personal* and business *identity* are as one, as was the case with Clive Sinclair or Steve Jobs. Sir Clive, for example, drew on electronics and re-creation from the fertile British soil, and contributed his own fertile brand of inspiration and individuality.

Corporate indentity

As they develop, the personal roots are outgrown. In their place emerges the *corporate identity* of the company as a whole, separate from, and yet related to the founder's personal identity. The Habitat and Virgin ethos, for example, take over from Conran's and Branson's individual personalities. Habitat/Mothercare draws on the creative talent of this country and contributes its design and management skills. Virgin draws on the British propensity for freedom and individuality, and contributes flexibility of workstyle.

Transcorporate identity

As a corporation evolves, so its separate identity becomes outworn and outlived. Its own roots become intertwined with those of other corporate species, both public and private, and both indigenous and exogenous.

Genuine mergers, such as that between A T & T and Olivetti, or ongoing consortia, such as the Eurotunnel Group, are examples of such *transcorporate* entities. Furthermore, in true instances of public private partnerships, as with the enterprise agencies in Britain, an associative culture has to be developed.

Universal identity

Finally, as a company genuinely matures, it outgrows even its intertwined cultural roots. They become too confined, too limited and limiting. In fact the deeper the roots grow into the soil, the closer the attachment to their underlying foundations. Company culture with its distinct and convergent values, turns into a *universal identity* with a transfunctional, transdisciplinary, transnational approach.

Its universal values are catholic and cosmopolitan, embracing a very wide range of individuals, technologies and cultures. Unlike Peters and Waterman's closed culture, it is open, and unlike their converging myths and rituals, it is open to diversity of scientific and cultural exchange. BCC draws from the rich and widespread heritage from which it came, and contributes a diversity of knowledge and wealth to it.

YOU UNRAVEL THE MAIN BUSINESS STEM

As the roots grow, so does the trunk, the main stem of the business. For the young, pioneering business, *independent enterprise* is the central core, arising out of the founder's personal or communal identity.

For the adult company it is the *public company* which emerges, reflecting its corporate identity and public responsibility. For the business, in midlife, an *enabling company* of associated entities takes over. Finally, in maturity, a business that has continued to grow and develop becomes a *nuclear enterprise*, with its universal centre. Let me elaborate.

Independent enterprise

The *first* organizational form is that of the well-known *independent enterprise*, either *personally or cooperatively run*. It is owned by an individual or group.

This culture is either *power-* or *people*-centred, or both. *Its function is to create and maintain a profitable business.*

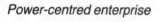

Power-centred enterprise   People-centred enterprise

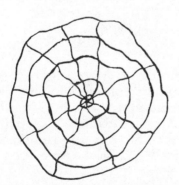

The independent enterprise is managed by its dynamic 'hero' and enthusiastic 'heroine'. Both have *finely honed instincts*.

The hero is the *entrepreneur,* with dynamism and flair. The entrepreneur spots chances, turns them into opportunities, and persistently drives his or her way through one challenge after another.

The heroine is the *animateur,* with charm and enthusiasm. The animateur involves people, shares values, and creates a family feeling within her or his enterprise.

Both are 'earthy' characters.

The public company

The *second,* also well-known form, is that of the *public company,* accountable to its stakeholders. Such an established organization has either an *hierarchical or network* form, or a combination of these two. It is owned by the public at large, strongly represented by institutional shareholders.

The established culture, then, is either *role* (function) or *task* (project) based, or both. *Its function is to deploy the public resources under its sway efficiently and effectively.*

Role-based structure   *Task-based structure*

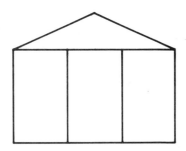
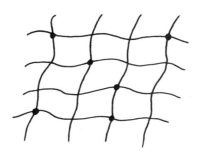

EXECUTIVE AND CHANGE AGENT

The public company is managed by an authoritative 'hero', and a perceptive heroine. Both are *intellectually capable.*

The functional or business *executive* is firm and authoritative. This executive is reliable, methodical and well-coordinated in approach. He or she formulates effective strategies and efficient structures in the organization.

The *change agent* is flexible and knowledgeable. This agent of change is adaptable, flexible and varied in his or her approach, developing changeable systems and procedures in the company.

Both are 'heady' characters.

The 'enabling' company

The *third*, institutional form, the *enabling company*, is just beginning to emerge into public awareness around the globe. It is owned by an *association*. This might either be commercially and nationally based, like a Japanese trading company,[9] or communally and spiritually based, like the Scott Bader Commonwealth.[10]

In its pure form the enabling culture is rounded in its structure and orientation, built up of overlapping circles of associated parties. *Its function is to enable its people and organizations, its products and markets, its businesses and communities, to develop.*

Characteristically, its associated organizations either consist of *public–private partnerships* or, increasingly, of *joint ventures*, which have yet to form themselves into truly enabling companies.

Public–Private partnerships　　　　　*Joint ventures*

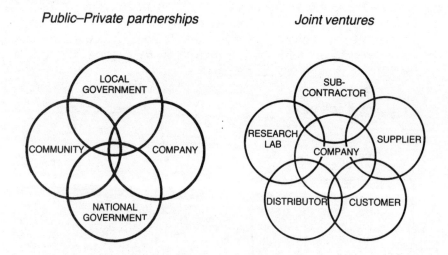

ADOPTER AND ENABLER

The enabling company is managed by its particular, faithful hero, and its farsighted heroine, both *intuitively attuned* to their environment.

The *adopter* is committed to his calling and humbled by the greater powers of the universe. Such an adopter is faithful, responsive and submissive to influences, both within the organization and without, greater than him or herself.

The *enabler* is sensitive and insightful. Such a manager is naturally cooperative and inherently developmental in his or her approach. He or she recognizes and harnesses physical, human or economic potential as it emerges.

Both are responsive characters.

The 'nuclear' company

The fourth institutional form, which I have termed a *nuclear enterprise*, has its creative nucleus at the centre, and is owned by this originative or spiritual force.

The one clear example of this is BCC, although the Bodyshop International, to the extent that its naturally based source of energy forms its centre, could be seen as another 'nuclear' case in point.

Its function, as a nuclear company, is to transform itself and the world around it, from lower forms of physical and human energy into higher ones.

INNOVATOR AND ADVENTURER

Finally, the 'nuclear' company is managed by its charismatic innovator, and effervescent adventurer, both *bounding with energy*.

The business *innovator* is imaginative, original, impassioned and creative, while the *adventurer* is active, carefree, risk prone and energetic.

How, then, do all these organizations and managers function over time?

Development in time

Businesses, if they are to grow and develop, undergo alternate structure *building* and structure *changing* phases. While the hard edge of management plays the dominant, stabilizing role, the soft edge plays the major transitional one.

THE PIONEERING–INDEPENDENT COMPANY

Having survived its birth crisis, a pioneering business becomes stabilized for a time, in a *stage of* dynamic and youthful *independence*.

Then, as complexity and variety advances, the *crisis of control* ensues.

THE ESTABLISHED–PUBLIC COMPANY

Having survived the crisis of delegation and control, a pioneering business turns into an established one, in a *stage of* adultlike *dependence* on outside stakeholders. Should it fail to recognize and negotiate its crisis of adulthood the company will return to excessively exuberant youth, or be acquired, or die.

Then, as complexity and variety advances, the *crisis of bureaucracy* ensues.

THE SELF-RENEWING–ENABLING COMPANY

Having survived the crisis of bureaucracy and alienation, an established organization turns into a self-renewing one, in a *stage of* midlife *interdependence* between itself and its associates. Should it fail to recognize and negotiate its midlife crisis the company will return to overgrown adulthood, or to excessively exuberant youth, or be taken over, or die.

Then, as complexity and variety advances, a *crisis of meaning and purpose* ensues.

THE GLOBAL CORPORATION–THE NUCLEAR COMPANY

Having survived the crisis of meaning and purpose, a self-renewing company turns into a transformed one, in a *stage of* mature *transcendence* over its material self – and environment. Should it fail to recognize and surmount its crisis of maturity the company will return to prolonged midlife, to overgrown adulthood, to excessively exuberant youth, or be acquired, or become extinct.

Thereafter, it returns to the first and youthful point in the cycle, while retaining all the other stages within it. Meanwhile individual managers, like the institutions they run, undergo similar stages of development.

IDENTIFYING THE BRANCHES IN CHARACTER

We have now looked at the underlying grounds, the roots and the central core of business. From roots we extract business identity, but not overall character. The word 'excellence', in fact, comes originally from the Greek 'arete', which means 'the sum of good values that make up character'.

I have focused on eight of them, drawn from the totality of human personality,[11] and these characteristics also develop, in four stages. At each stage of their development they shed their former existence, but retain links with it. Why, then, are there eight attributes?

The eight branches or business attributes, as I have indicated, are an extension of our own human personality. Every one of us, to varying degrees, and in differing combinations, has the following capacities:

- physical prowess
- social ability
- intellectual skill
- will power
- analytical ability
- intuitive awareness
- creative imagination
- personal faith.

These capacities are reflected in a different character, but one that retains the same underlying form, at each stage of development. It evolves from youth to maturity, forming a more highly developed set of eight branches at each stage.

The pioneering character

A new and pioneering corporate culture requires the *thrust of hard work, native wit, emotional resilience and basic imagination*. At the same time it requires the *coherence created by innate enthusiasm, improvised organization, customer feel and faith in oneself.*

Table 5.1   Enterprising functions and character

Function	Branch
Physical	Capacity to *work hard*, very hard
Social	*Enthusiasm*, and the ability to arouse it
Mental	Mental agility, or *native wit*
Emotional	Will, persistence and emotional *resilience*
Analytical	Capacity to *improvise*, rather than organize
Intuitive	*Gut feel*, and an eye for a chance
Imaginative	Imagination enough to *see around corners*
Spiritual	*Faith* in oneself

The hard and soft qualities change their precise shape and form, however, as an organization evolves.

The responsible character

As a company, and a culture, develops out of youth into adulthood, so the notion of free enterprise is, in effect, replaced by that of *accountable enterprise.*

The person who has done more than anyone else this century to spread this organizational accountability is Peter Drucker.[12] Drucker is an Austrian by birth who has been resident for many years in America. He is very much an amalgam of West and North, in that he is emotionally influenced by the spirit of enterprise and intellectually driven by the science of management. *The hard thrust* that Drucker introduces *is analytical and result-oriented; the soft coherence is integrative and integrity-oriented.*

The analytical thrust of *high productivity, management control, corporate strategy, formalized organization, analytical marketing and systematized innovation* takes over from hard work, native wit, entrepreneurial flair, improvised organization, and market instinct. The softer attribute of *effective teamwork* takes over from innate enthusiasm, and managerial *integrity* from personal faith.

Table 5.2   Executive versus enterprising characters

Enterprising branch	Executive branch
Hard work	High *productivity*
Raw enthusiasm	Effective *teamwork*
Native shrewdness	Management *control*
Sheer willpower	Competitive *strategy*
Improvisation	Formal *organization*
Market instinct	Analytical *marketing*
Imagination	Systematized *innovation*
Personal faith	Managerial *integrity*

Renewed character

To refresh our memories, then, during the entrepreneurial revolution the industrialized nations advanced from economic stagnation to rapid take off. In the same way a new enterprise emerges from nothing to all into something commercial and tangible. The result is material wealth and economic 'body'. A *primal culture, focused on heroic people and material aspirations,* prevails.

During the managerial revolution planned and coordinated expansion and consolidation took place at both macro and micro levels. This kind of development is the product of a well oiled organizational and managerial 'mind'. A *rational culture, focused on economic efficiency and social responsibility,* ensues.

Today the design revolution is bringing with it, for the first time in business and economic history, a conscious and often integrated development, of people, technology and business. This gives new 'heart' to the economy and to the firm, both of which may have been acquiring paralysis through analysis! A *developmental culture, focused on conscious individual and economic evolution,* prevails.

Table 5.3   Rational and developmental character

Executive branches	Developmental branches
High productivity	Intense *interactivity*
Effective teamwork	*Quality* circles
Management by objectives	Manager *self-development*
Competitive strategy	*Cooperative* strategy
Formal organization	Corporate *architecture*
Corporate planning	Planned *evolution*
Managed innovation	Corporate *renewal*
Managerial integrity	Social *harmony*

The adaptive *thrust of intense interactivity, manager self-development, planned evolution, and corporate renewal* takes over from high productivity, management control, corporate planning and systematic innovation. The *coherence of quality circles, cooperative strategies, corporate architecture and social harmony* takes over from effective teamwork, competitive strategies, formal organization and managerial integrity.

Transformed character

Finally, the attributes of business transformation, as compared with renewal, contain yet another blend of thrust and coherence. *Thrust is provided by the energy flow, by process and change, by the principles of natural management and by vision.* These can be contrasted against intense interactivity, manager self-development, the new corporate architecture and corporate renewal.

Coherence is provided by the corporate culture, by business interfusion, by unlimited possibility, and by a universal spirit. This can be compared against quality circles, business cooperation, planned evolution and social harmony.

Table 5.4   Transformation in character

Renewal	Transformation
Intense interactivity	*Energy* flow
Quality circles	Corporate *culture*
Manager self-development	Process and *change*
Cooperative strategy	Business *interfusion*
Corporate architecture	*Natural* management
Planned evolution	Unlimited *possibility*
Corporate renewal	Business *vision*
Social harmony	Universal *spirit*

In the final analysis, whereas commercial enterprise calls on sharply honed *instinct,* and managed organization on broadly based *intellect*, business renewal requires finely tuned *insight* and corporate transformation powerful *imagination*.

YOU DEVELOP THE FRUITS

Ripening fruits

The branches of business, whether young or old, are not the actual goods or services, which are after all what business is there to provide. The fruits attached to the branches comprise these products.

The products and services emerge from the combination of branches rather than from any one in particular. If one branch is weak then all of the fruits will suffer. As the tree matures, so the fruit grows more abundant, if occasionally over ripe.

If all the fruit is plucked, or milked like 'cash cows', no new seeds will return to the underlying ground. Seeds that are returned may or may not be absorbed. In the early stages of the business it is up to the individual entrepreneur, a Sinclair, to be receptive, and to cross-fertilize.

In the adult stage, the company as a whole needs to be receptive to new product ideas. In midlife ideas must cross the transcorporate divide. In the mature stage, finally, the whole corporate universe needs to partake in nourishing its own 'seed corn' with fertilizer from the surrounding soil. Let me now review.

Starting primal

The fruits of enterprise, in their primal state, are *basic* in form *and tangible* in nature – either from the supplier's or from the customer's perspective. At the same time, they may appeal, more or less, to both their physical or social needs.

A primary product – like tin or salt – mined in harsh conditions, or a basic commodity – like beans or sugar – sold in a basic environment, is likely to represent such primal 'fruit'. The circumstances surrounding their production and supply, however, may be *exploitative, communal,* or both, depending on the situation.

The corresponding sales outlet, therefore, will be neither a supermarket nor a boutique but, instead, a *market stall or general store*. It will be neither aesthetically pleasing nor will it offer abundant choice. However, the service may be friendly – 'Have a nice day'. Neighbourhood gossip rather than an intimate, personal interest, will be the norm.

From the customer's point of view, such products or services will *appeal to our basic physical and social instincts* and no more. A staple diet, as opposed to gourmet food; grey or khaki cloth, as opposed to colourfully designed fabric, are two cases in point. However, a *modicum of craftsmanship* may have been built into the production of an item, for example basic tourist goods in craft stores.

Should the customer be a firm rather than an individual, then items like basic nuts and bolts, for a manufacturer, and plain copier paper, for an office, will occupy primal place. Services such as office cleaning, the provision of basic canteen food, and also security services, would fall into this category. It would be a *'no frills attached'* provision, with the emphasis again on price, physical availability, and perhaps innate affability, rather than on 'service' in the broader sense of the word.

The sales outlet to companies will be a general hardware store or corner stationer rather than a Sears or Rymans. Choice will be extremely limited and haggling for price would not be unusual.

In the final analysis, the product or service is simple in nature, and is consumed without any awareness of its enduring benefits. *It is a means to an end, and a pretty basic one at that.* The situation begins to change, once the primal fruit matures somewhat, and assumes 'rational' proportions.

Bearing rational fruit

Whereas primal products and services satisfy our basic physical and social needs, 'rational' ones *appeal* more *to* our *intelligence* than to our instincts. Similarly, for the manufacturer or retailer of such products and services, intelligence is built into either the item itself or into the organization of its production and distribution.

Well engineered products might be manufactured on a sophisticated assembly line, and are *designed to provide* a degree of *standardization and reliability* that was not primally possible. That makes the customer's life more predictable, and his work or life more efficient and effective. In a selling context, innate friendliness and the instinct to haggle are both removed, which makes for a smoother, if more clinical, operation. In a working context, maternalism or paternalism is replaced by bureaucratic management.

The rationally based product will have a series of attributes that are designed to appeal to the intelligent consumer. A *product range, or composite service*, supersedes the more basic primal offering. As a result, General Motors, in the thirties, began to offer its consumers a range of colours, engine capacities, and dashboard features, while Henry Ford was saying, 'You can have any colour, as long as it is painted black'.

As progressively more intelligence is built into the product or service, however, the soft, human edge of rationality, as opposed to the hard, dehumanized one, becomes apparent. *Producer and consumer begin to communicate with one another*, albeit via the product or service rather than directly, and personally. For example, a software supplier for a hardware manufacturer engages in intensive interaction and communication.

In another such instance Bodyshop, via its naturally-based cosmetics, supplies product information that forms an integral part of the skin or hair care product itself. Supplier and customer become part of an information network, as opposed to a social community. *The product or service*, in itself, *is interesting and stimulating* as well as necessary and useful. The same might apply to a 'theme' restaurant where the customer is 'purchasing' information about, or an experience of, a country, as well as a tasty meal.

In that sense, the product or service becomes less and less tangible, and more and more intangible. *It stimulates the mind,* therefore, more than the body. Then, as the rational fruits ripen into developmental ones, we change again.

Then come the developmental fruits

Primal products and services are consumed by us, and then they may disappear into our digestive systems or into a manufactured product. Rationally-based products and services, however, especially those of the more evolved variety, interact with us, as well as with one another. I may consume a Bodyshop shampoo in the normal way, but then I am also likely to take a note of its derivation, from Rosemary oil, and perhaps read more about this oil base in *Encyclopaedia Britannica*.

In so doing I may be merely satisfying my curiosity, as a chemist or naturalist. However, there may be more to it than that. For *as a product or service evolves*, developmentally, *so it begins to tap* not only our instincts and our intellect, but also *our higher emotions*. In other words, it will satisfy me not only physically, socially and intellectually, but also aesthetically.

FORM AND BEAUTY

As a thing becomes perfectly adapted to the purpose for which it is made, and so approaches its ultimate form, it also advances in that power to please us, which we call beauty.

Use is the primary source of form. The function of a thing is its reason for existence, its justification and its end. It is a sort of life urge thrusting through a thing and determining its development. *It is only by realizing its destiny*, and revealing that destiny with candour and exactness *that a thing acquires significance and validity of form.*

This means much more than utility, or even efficiency. It means the kind of perfected order we find in natural organisms, bound together in such precise rhythms that no part can be changed without wounding the whole.[13]

As Walter Teague indicates above, there is more to such aesthetic satisfaction than immediately meets the eye. *If*, as a producer or consumer, *a product or service provides meaning and purpose in my life, then it is performing a developmental function.*

It is easy to imagine how a good play or novel might fulfil such a function, but what about a Bodyshop shampoo, a Chinese meal or a piece of computer software? On the supplier side, of course, it is relatively easy to envisage the potential fulfilment that might arise from developing a shampoo, a meal, or a computer program that is beautifully designed to fulfil a worthwhile purpose. In that context, as a Chinese restaurateur, for example, I would be offering not only good food, but a unique atmosphere.

As a consumer of cosmetics, food, or information technology, I would be looking for similar meaning and purpose via the product or service. The Chinese meal, for example, would awaken my interest in the East such that I would experience myself as being there. The software program, say a spreadsheet, would enable me to view my company in a way that I had never done before, thus providing me with a unique and fundamental insight into economic performance.

Whereas, then, the primal fruits are served up in a general store, and the rational ones in a supermarket, developmental ones are offered in a purpose-built environment, like that of an art gallery. However, instead of 'art', in the conventional sense, all kinds of products and services, designed to provide us with inner as well as outer satisfaction, would be on display. Whole food, to *nourish the whole person*, would displace the more basic, or 'value for money', variety.

Ultimately metaphysical fruit

As a Zimbabwean by birth, I am all too aware of the closeness to nature, and to God, of many Africans. In recent years such closeness has made itself apparent, as an economic as well as a religious phenomenon.

Nature, to start off with, has a primal ring to it. Animals and humans battle for survival. Basic nutriment is wrested from the land and communally-based production is based upon it. The land is in fact the primary, or primal source of economic activity.

At the same time, particularly in Britain and America, modern technology and large-scale farming methods have turned primal 'fruits' into rational ones. Mechanized modes of planting and reaping, and computerized means of storing and retrieving information on crops and livestock, have converted hands-on activities into rational processes. Similarly, supermarkets have overtaken butchers, bakers and grocers as major outlets for farm producers.

Yet, in recent years, the rising health consciousness has created an awareness of wholefoods and holistic approaches to agricultural production, that serves to introduce a developmental dimension into land-based products. At the same time, as international travel to far-flung territories increases, the aesthetic value – both materially and spiritually – of beautiful landscapes increases.

Moreover, as the spirit of the East and the South becomes more apparent to those of us in the West and North, the metaphysical dimension becomes accessible to us. As I gaze in wonder at

Americans and Europeans 'shooting the rapids' along the Zambesi river, and paying for the privilege, I wonder to what extent they are driven by the *spirit* of African adventure, and how much by *sense* of physical exhilaration.

For *as a product or service begins to bear metaphysical fruit, so it absorbs the loftiest thoughts, and draws off the deepest emotions,* of those engaged with it. Its producers imbibe such 'religious' qualities as depicted by Tracy Kidder in *The Soul of the New Machine,* as Data General's electronics engineers became 'the balladeers of computers'. Its consumers are uplifted, in the same way as the viewers of an extraordinary seascape may be, as they – like the poet Blake – 'see the world in a grain of sand'.

CONCLUSION: ENGAGING IN SELF-RENEWAL

Conscious evolution

A developmental culture, then, is engaged in a continuing process of self-renewal. That conscious process, encompassing its people and organization, as well as its technology and products, will ensure that, over time, the whole of its business evolves.

Intermittent crises divide the structure-building from the structure-changing periods, as progressive development takes place.

Progression from youth and adulthood to midlife and maturity will carry the organization forward, from an independent enterprise to a public company, and from an enabling company to a nuclear enterprise. In the process its products and markets as well as its people and organization will evolve.

Such evolution takes place when an enterprise consciously draws on fertile national soils, becoming more firmly rooted as its identity develops from personally-based origins towards its universally-based destination.

Self-development

In consciously evolving the culture of your organization, you need to start with the development of its people. Uncover the origins and maturation of key individuals:

- by charting the influence of the national and organizational culture in which he or she is rooted

- by tracing their life course from *childhood* and exploratory *youth*, to responsible *adulthood* and *midlife* renewal, projected into the fullness of *maturity*
- by identifying the *alternating* structure-building and structure-changing *periods*, interspersed with personal and vocational *crises*
- and the *significant patterns* of events that characterize each of these building and changing phases, drawing out the underlying meaning of each
- thereby, and finally, tracing the linking *thread of individuality* that is particular to each person, making up his or her evolving character.

Business development

A similar biographical assessment should be made of the company as a whole – if not each individual division or department:

- by charting the influence of the national culture, or cultures, in which it is *rooted*
- by tracing its life course from creative *birth* and exploratory *youth*, to responsible *adulthood* and *midlife* renewal, projected into the fullness of *maturity*
- by identifying the *alternating* structure-building and structure-changing *periods*, interspersed with commercial and organizational *crises*
- and the *significant patterns* of events that characterize each of these building and changing phases, drawing out the underlying meaning of each
- thereby, and finally, tracing the linking *thread of individuality* that is particular to the company, making up its evolving character.

For this company-based exercise you would need to draw on not only published literature but also interviews with the organization's founders.

Now, and finally, we turn towards the metaphysical way to cultural transformation.

REFERENCES

1 Lessem, Ronnie, *The Roots of Excellence*, Fontana, 1986.
2 Lievegoed, Bernard, *The Developing Organisation*, Tavistock, London, 1973.

3   Peters, T., and Waterman, R., *In Search of Excellence*, Harper & Row, 1982.
4   Pascale and Athos, *The Art of Japanese Management*, Penguin, 1981.
5   Horwitz, Ralph, *Entrepreneurial Management*, Westall Books, 1979.
6   Chandler, Alfred, *Strategy and Structure*, Doubleday, 1964.
7   Maslow, Abraham, *Motivation and Personality*, Harper & Row, 1968.
8   Heilbronner, Robert, *The Worldly Philosophers*, Pan, 1968.
9   Lifson, P., and Yoshino, K., *The Invisible Link*, M.I.T. Press, 1986.
10   Blum, F., *The Scott Bader Commonwealth*, Routledge & Kegan Paul.
11   Lessem, R., *Global Management Principles*, Prentice-Hall, 1989.
12   Drucker, Peter, *Management*, Pan, 1981.
13   Teague, Walter, *American Automobile Designer*, Design Council, 1946.

6 The Metaphysical Way

Metaphysics – *underlying reality* and its relations; the system of first principles, or the philosophy underlying a subject; that which is *beyond the physical* or the experiential, and is conceived as super-sensible or *transcendent*.

Culture is that complex whole that includes knowledge, *belief, superstition, morals, religion*, law, customs and art. (*Webster's New International Dictionary*)

INTRODUCTION

The metaphysical spirit

The individual who has done most to lift corporate culture out of a primal, visible immediacy into a metaphysical, invisible 'spirituality', is Harrison Owen. While for Peters and Waterman 'shared values' can be seen, touched and felt, for Harrison Owen they are intangible, invisible 'spirit'.

'The point', Owen says, 'is not that organizations become more spiritual, but rather that we might recognize that *organizations, in their essence, are spirit*, and then get on with the important business of caring intelligently and intentionally for this most crucial and essential element.'[1]

The metaphysical approach to corporate culture is concerned with the identification, generation and support of 'spirit' with a view to its transformation into material energy. Metaphysical management is equally concerned with the way physical matter and energy, whether in the form of technology, products or material aspirations, can be transformed into individual, team, or company spirit.

As Pierre Curie, who with his wife Marie created radiography, said: 'It is necessary to make life a dream, and of that dream a reality.'[2]

Organizational transformation

Innovation and transformation

The use of the term 'transformation' here, as opposed to development, is quite deliberate. For while 'development' is evolutionary, 'transformation' is 'revolutionary'.

Whereas a developmental culture recognizes and enhances potential in people or things, a *metaphysical culture creates potential*, where seemingly none existed before. Two such examples from the past were derived from the early businesses of Ludwig Mond and Alfred Nobel, the forerunners of Britain's Imperial Chemical Industries (ICI).

TRANSFORMATION AND INNOVATION

Ludwig Mond's unique *sense of predestination* enabled him to visualize the result of an experiment long before it could be established – as one sees the light at the end of a tunnel, although the tunnel itself is dark.[3]

I left in early youth
A home for distant lands beyond the sea
But strange to say, even when the ocean spread
Its grandeur round, it struck me not as new,
My mind has pictured oceans far more wide.[4]

This creative activity is well known to the great artist or inventor – as exemplified by Alfred Nobel and Ludwig Mond – though less commonly associated with the innovative manager.

Development and transformation

Harrison Owen uses the compelling analogy, in comparing and contrasting development and transformation, of the creation of a butterfly, as against a frog. Whereas a tadpole develops bit by bit into a frog, first losing its tail, then growing its legs, a caterpillar becomes a butterfly in a very different way.

The essence of transformation, as the word suggests, is a *movement across and through forms*. Transformation takes place in the 'odyssey or passage of the human spirit as it moves from one formal manifestation to another'. How this actually happens is indicated by the caterpillar transformation.

Butterflies begin as caterpillars, just as great organizations, symphonies, or technological breakthroughs start out as much simpler material forms. These forms may range from a basic commodity, in the case of the organization, to a simple melody, in the case of the symphony, to a basic compound, in the case of the innovation.

Then, when the time is right, the caterpillar spins a cocoon about itself and, after a period, emerges with beautiful colours and wings to fly. That might have been a 'development', but it is not.

For once the caterpillar is inside it literally dissolves, as a small business enterprise or simple melody might dissolve rather than evolve. The caterpillar has gone to its essence, which Owen terms 'spirit', and is then transformed into a butterfly – assuming that being a butterfly is a better way to be.

The only way to get to that butterfly state is to allow the old form to dissolve, thus freeing the spirit of the thing to achieve a new form.

This may seem, at first glance, to be like 'asset stripping'. The asset stripper, however, is dealing with material assets, at least that is the way he sees them, rather than with 'spiritual essence'. To achieve transformation in a commercial context the businessman must be able to identify, release and reform 'spirit' rather than physical, economic or human matter. How does he go about this?

The metaphysical way

There are three specific aspects to establishing a 'metaphysical culture'. They cover, in a manner of speaking, metaphysical policy making, strategy formulation and operations management.

Meta/Policy

The first *policy making* requirement is for the would-be metaphysical culture to learn a new language.

The primal culture expresses itself, for example, in terms of winning, of intrapreneuring, of sharing values, and of managing by wandering about. The rational culture uses the language of planning, organizing, directing and control. The developmental culture focuses, amongst other things, on attunement, alignment, self-enhancement and on organizational evolution.

The metaphysical culture expresses itself, both verbally and non-verbally, through *myth* and *ritual*, through *liturgy* and *covenant*, through *spirit* and *culture*.

Meta/Strategy

The second *strategic* requirement of metaphysical culture, whether in a manufacturing, marketing, financial or personnel context, is not

to have a passion for excellence, to compete efficiently and effectively, or to recognize and develop synergy, but to *transform spirit
into matter or energy,* or vice versa.

In order to do either such a culture needs to be capable of
undergoing what Owen terms 'the journey of the spirit'.

Meta/Operations

Finally, and in *operational* terms, the metaphysical culture must be
able – not to make things happen, to perform to standard, or to fulfil
potential, but – to uncover, translate, *act out* and reveal both
original and derivative stories that convey the spirit/energy of the
organization.

Should the culture not be entirely successful in this operationally
metaphysical respect it is possible to intervene, indirectly, and
facilitate effective transformation. This is achieved through a process of 'collective story telling'.

For it is these stories, in their right form in their right time in their
right place, that imaginatively and materially transform energy into
spirit and back again. I shall now deal, via Harrison Owen, with
each of these elements in their policy-making, strategic and
operational turn.

META/POLICY

In the course of describing the policy-making language that enters
into a metaphysically-based culture I shall be citing examples from
Sony Corporation. I have selected Sony not because its chairman,
Akio Morita, is a particularly 'metaphysical manager', but because
he is one of the company's founders and has chosen to reveal its
formative myths to the public at large.[5]

Mythos

Mythos is the collective term for organizational *myth* and *ritual*.
These two elements in combination make up the fundamental
building blocks of the metaphysical culture. In fact, they represent
to him what, for example, capital and labour represent to the primal
manager.

> *Myths* are the stories of a group's culture which describe its begin-
> ning, continuance, and ultimate goals. These stories are so much part
> of the institutional fabric as to define it. To know the myth is to know

the institution in a way that balance sheets and organization charts can never tell.

Ritual, then, is the dramatic re-enactment of the myth. In a ritual the group acts out its central stories in such a way that the members experience really being there and participating in the original event.[6]

The nature of mythos

A 'myth' may be defined as a likely (but not necessarily true) story, arising from the life experience of a group, through which they come to experience their past, present, and potential. The story does not reveal systematically the workings of the group or organization, but rather represents it in an immediate and gripping way.

> A myth is a good story that grips you, creates a world, and, to some significant degree, transforms it. Working with or in a given myth is like living in a good novel. The difference is that you cannot put the myth down. A myth not only reflects life. It becomes life.[7]

We can see this in Sony's early days, and in Morita's early and formative experiences in the company.

TO LIVE IS TO LEARN

Finding good magnetic material to coat our tape with after the war was almost impossible in that time of shortages. It seems incredible to me now, but Ibuka, Kihara (a brilliant young engineer) and I made those first tapes by hand. We would cut enough tape for a small reel and then we would lay out the long strip on the floor of our laboratory.

The first tapes were terrible of course, but we were proud of them. In those early days the tape was the key to the future of our business . . . and I was absolutely convinced that after all this work we were finally on the road to success . . . We were in for a rude awakening. A tape recorder was not something, in the early fifties, that people in Japan felt they wanted . . .

I was going to have to be the merchandiser of our small business.[8]

Whereas a rational culture views its systems and procedures as the natural channel for its activities, the metaphysical culture sees 'myth' and 'ritual' performing that channelling function. Where the image of efficiency for the 'organization man' is reflected in 'return on investment', for the metaphysical manager the image of transformation is reflected in dreams turned into reality.

In just a few words Morita has presented us with an image of his company, capturing its spirit of activity and learning, interspersed with creativity and humility.

The function of mythos

The true function of mythos, according to Owen, is to say the unsayable, to express the ineffable, but most importantly, to bring the participant employee, customer, or business associate into immediate, self-validating *relationship with the spirit of the organization.*

With a few lines and some colour a whole world is created. To be sure there are details, but just enough to set the stage and invite your imagination inside.

HUNGER FOR DEVELOPMENT

In 1948 Ibuka, the company's co-founder, and I, had both read about the work of William Shockley and others at Bell Labs, and we had been curious about their discoveries ever since. On Ibuka's trip to America in 1952 he first learnt that a license for this marvellous, solid state transistor might soon be available.

I must say, though, that the transistor being made at the time was not something we could license and produce off the shelf. This marvellous device was a breakthrough in electronic technology, but it could only handle audio frequencies.

In fact when I signed the license agreement with the people at Western Electric a year later they told me that the hearing aid was the only consumer product we could expect to make with it.

We wanted to make something that could be used by everybody.[9]

How Sony proceeded to create and market the world's first transistor radio might be public history, but the imagination of the employee or customer listening to Morita's brief story of creation is still free to roam.

There are so many technical, personal and social details to be filled in. It is just like looking at one of Picasso's abstract paintings. The net result of any active observation is one of co-creation. You and Morita or Picasso, subsequently, create the reality that results.

These results are more than Morita could originally have imagined, for it includes what you have contributed. This means, of course, that the function of mythos in corporate policy making is not a static one. It continues to grow, over time, as succeeding generations add their imagination – their spirit – to the original act and its recreation.

In the process of such recreation, spanning both the imagination and also reality, those involved imbibe fascination, meaning, morality and even awe into their lives.

- The first function is to awaken us to the fascinating *mystery* of life
- The second function is to interpret that mystery in order to give *meaning* to life
- The third function is that of sustaining the *moral* order by shaping the individual to the requirements of his geographically or historically conditioned social group
- The fourth function is the most vital one of fostering the unfolding of the individual, in accord with himself, his culture and the universe, as well as that *awesome* ultimate mystery which is both beyond and within himself and all things.[10]

The life cycle

UNFOLDING

Myth and ritual, just like the organization as a whole, goes through a life cycle. In the early days of a business's formation stories are being acted out, and told, in real time. They are part of *everyday reality* rather than carriers of meaning.

It is only later on, once the stories have become increasingly familiar to an ever-growing number of people, that their presence begins to offer comfort and security as well as excitement and drama. Eventually it becomes important that the stories are told in the right way, if they are to continue to be *meaningful*.

In their more flexible form, organizational stories provide an outlet for creativity and innovation. At the point where stories have become fixed in people's minds they need to be *broken* in order to give them a fresh and updated touch.

In fact, to the extent that mythos is alive and well in an organization, those who participate in it will experience the moment of breaking as one of *release*. Yet they will also experience such release as fearful.

Mythos completes its life cycle with *renewal*, whereby the individual or organization is infused with new meaning and purpose. This new spirit is generated during the time of 'breaking', and is created under conditions of what Owen terms 'open space'.

Here is an example from Akio Morita's family circumstances, in which open space was created by Akio's father.

BREAK WITH TRADITION

In Japan it was considered a serious thing to take a son, especially a first son as I was, out of his home and family environment and bring him permanently into a new atmosphere in the world of business, outside of his own family firm. Our own brewing company had been passed on from one generation to another for hundreds of years.

... Ibuka told my father about our new venture and what they hoped to accomplish, and said I was absolutely needed in the new business. When he had finished we all waited tensely for a response. With very little hestitation he said that he expected me to succeed him as head of the family and had also expected me to take over the family business.

Then he turned to Ibuka and said, 'But if my son wants to do something else to develop himself or utilize his capacities, he should do it'. He looked at me and smiled. 'You are going to do what you like best', he said ...

My younger brother volunteered to take over as the sake brewer of the Morita family when the time came for my father to retire. There were smiles all round. Everyone was relieved and happy.[11]

As the individuals participate in the story, and specifically its breaking, they discover that the *spirit* has been *freed* to explore new possibilities. In this way Akio was freed from the traditional role of first son, following in his father's footsteps. The old mythos was broken, and yet the family business could still go on.

ROLE

The role of myth and ritual, in fact, changes as it reaches different points in its life cycle. At first it serves as a mere *record of transformation*. Such a transformation may involve the initial conversion of a speculative idea into a fully established business, the handover of a business from one generation to the other, or a diversification into a new product line.

The intent of mythos at this point is not just to talk about what transpired, but rather to create the conditions under which that prior journey of the spirit (adventurous, enterprising, innovative, or whatever) may be experienced. In other words the younger generation of Morita's will have vividly experienced the transformation of the family business, through successive generations, in advance of themselves taking over.

The second role of myth and ritual is to become an *agent of transformation*. By virtue of the fact that mythos, within a dynamic regime, is being constantly broken, it exists within the corporate psyche as an uneasy bedfellow. Just as everybody has become accustomed to the tale it shifts, and exposes some new area of meaning.

For Akio, the meaning of 'brewed by Morita in Japan' became transformed into the more wide ranging 'Made in Japan'. In moving out of sake and into electronics, Akio Morita moved the spirit of innovation and enterprise into the twentieth century, his father having created the 'open space' for him to do so.

This ongoing shifting continually creates new open spaces which invite the group spirit to consider new forms of expression. For example, a previously conceived act of bold diversification may subsequently be viewed as a deliberate attempt to catch the competition offguard. This in turn leads to a new subtlety in corporate strategy and to a fresh sense of humour in its interpretation. A strategy of deliberate 'fun making' takes over from jungle-fighting tactics.

Thirdly, and finally, mythos may be itself *transformative*. Clock time (Greek 'chronos') is replaced by 'kairos', that is meaning-filled time, which in turn defines time for the group or organization. In other words, eras – for example, pre- and post-merger – replace months or years as focal points in an organization's historical progression.

Similarly, the advent of Sony signified a meaningful shift in the Morita family's role in Japanese business and society. It even heralded a transformation in Japan's role in the world. Sony's development spearheaded, and reflected back, that of Japan, from a resourceful but conservative to a resourceful and adaptive nation, technologically and commercially. Through this the country's spirit of self-sufficiency was both retained and upgraded.

REMEMBERING AND UPGRADING SELF-SUFFICIENCY

Japan

One of the most significant value concepts that we Japanese have cherished from ancient times (writes Morita) is 'mottainai'. It is an expression that suggests that everything in the world is a gift from the Creator, and that we should be grateful for it and never waste anything.

Yoishi

Yoishi Yokoi had gone into hiding when the US forces took Guam in 1944 and he had eluded capture for 28 years. Yoishi had bathed in, and had taken his drinking water from, a small stream near his cave. He had dug the cave eight feet below ground level, using a spent artillery shell as a shovel. He shored up his roof with bamboo, and he fashioned drains and a latrine for survival.

For his clothing he stripped the pliable bark from pago trees and made thread of it, which he wove into a cloth on a makeshift loom. Then he cut the cloth with the tailoring scissors he had saved – Yokoi had been a tailor before being drafted – and sewed trousers, shirts, and jackets.

He had made needles by pounding and shaping pieces of brass cartridges. He also learnt to make fire by rubbing sticks together. He trapped freshwater fish and managed to grow some vegetables. He came home, in 1982, to a hero's welcome . . .

Akio

I had to teach myself because the subjects I was really interested in were not taught in my school in those days (1930s). But I managed to build a crude electric phonograph and a radio receiver of my own.

Sony

We Japanese have always been eager to develop our own technology, absorb aspects of technology from abroad, and blend them to make suitable objects or systems. Today, at Sony, we are developing new materials for uses in machines that are not off the drawing board, but that we know will be needed along the developmental time line.[12]

Liturgy

Liturgy, of which the raw material is myth and ritual and the manufactured process is form and structure, provides the peculiar sense of time, space, and propriety indigenous to a particular people and culture.

Liturgy is formed from two Greek words: 'laos', meaning people, and 'ergos', meaning work. In literal translation it means the people's work, or what people do. In fact it is the sum of what the people do and say as an expression of their deepest being.

When myth and ritual is deeply and continuously integrated into the life of an organization, that is liturgy. 'Liturgy at its best is the conscious production and orchestration of myth and ritual such that spirit is focused and directed in a particular, intended way.'[12]

This is clearly in evidence within Sony.

Spirit and image

Traditionally, it has been the role of the priest to care for the *story* of the people, and to provide the means whereby that story can be continually remembered. In contemporary business organizations we now find the public relations function sometimes taking on the role as guardian or protector of the spirit, or of the image, of the corporation. Akio Morita had adopted this role in Sony, from early on.

TRADEMARK

I had decided during my first trip abroad in 1953 that our full name – Tokyo Tsushin Kogyo Kabushiki – was not a good name to put on a product. Ibuka and I then came across the Latin word 'sonus', meaning sound ... Sony carried the connotations of lightness and sound that we wanted ...

In June 1957 we put up our first billboard carrying the Sony name. One day we learnt that somebody was selling 'Sony' chocolate. Seeing this stuff on sale made me sick. We took these imposters to court and brought famous people in, such as entertainers and newspapermen, to confirm the damage that was being done to us.

We won the case . . . I have always believed that a *trademark* is the *life* of an enterprise and it must be protected boldly.[13]

Form and structure

While the raw material of liturgy is myth and ritual the processes for 'liturgy making' are *form* and *structure*. Form is the way we do things, as in the phrase 'good form'. Structure is the delineated field of operation within which things get done. To be effective in metaphysical terms, both form and structure should accord with, and be expressive of, the image and channel of the spirit of the organization.

FAMILY FORM

The most important mission for a Japanese manager is to develop a healthy relationship with his employees, to create a family feeling within the corporation, a feeling that managers and employees share the same fate . . .

On the 25th anniversary of Sony America, Yoshiko (my wife) and I flew to the U.S. where we had a picnic or a meal with all the employees in Alabama, San Diego, Chicago and New York. It was not just part of my job; I like these people. They are family.[14]

Covenant

At some point in the life of an organization this special sense of time and space, form and structure, will be given formal verbal expression. Initially this expression will be very sparse, limited to some general agreement of 'the way things ought to be done around here'. Over time the expression will become more detailed, eventually constituting some kind of 'rule book'. This is what Owen terms the organizational 'Covenant'.

IBUKA'S DREAM (1940S)

If it were possible to establish conditions where persons could become united with a firm spirit of teamwork, and exercise to their heart's desire their technological capacity, then such an organization could bring untold pleasure and untold benefits.

IBUKA'S MANAGEMENT PHILOSOPHY (1950S)

1. We shall eliminate any untoward profit seeking, and shall constantly emphasize the *real substance of our products*, not seeking expansion in size just for the sake of it.

2. Rather, we shall seek a *compact size of operation* through which the path of technology and business activities can advance in areas that large companies, because of their size, cannot.
3. We shall focus on highly sophisticated technical products that have great *usefulness in society*, regardless of the quantity involved.
4. Utilizing to the utmost the unique features of our firm, we shall open up through *mutual cooperation* our production and sales channels.
5. We shall guide and *foster subcontracting* factories in directions which will help them become independently operable, and shall strive to expand the pattern of mutual help with them.[15]

The extent to which the organizational covenant reflects the real behaviour of the people within the enterprise varies enormously. It will all depend on the extent to which the spirit of the organization, reflected in and through myth and ritual, has inspired the people within it. How might, or might not, this come about?

META/STRATEGY

The journey of the spirit

The journey of the spirit may be described as a series of stages which constitute, in Owen's terms, the course of organizational transformation. Each stage indicates some different quality or mode of that spirit, as it becomes progressively and strategically transformed into matter.

In illustrating the point I shall now move from Sony in the East to an embryonic mining enterprise in the South.

The Zimbabwean company involved is Karanga Mining Company (KMC), which has recently been started by a spirited indigenous technologist, Trivanu Karanga. The journey begins with diffuse spirit. However, the emerging *potential* is gradually being transformed into increasingly concrete and specific *actual* energy (see Figure 6.1).

The creation of potential

Out of the depths

At the beginning of any organization's creation there was a moment when some individual, or some small group, had what amounts to an 'Aha' experience. Something might be done, something of particular moment. We saw it with Ibuka of Sony, and now we will see it with Karanga of KMC.

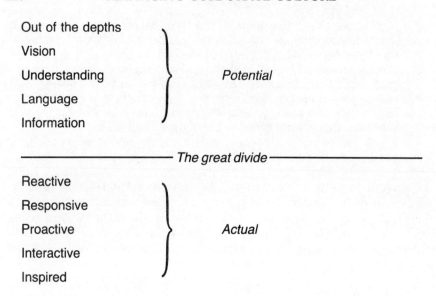

Figure 6.1   The journey of the spirit

This is the creative moment when *something emerges out of nothing*. It appears, as it were, from out of the depths. One might think of Edwin Land, when the mere possibility of an 'instant camera' popped into view or a thousand other emergent moments when the pot began to boil. At the instant, the originator may not know precisely what to do, and where it all might lead. But the thing is definitely there – hot, powerful, and moving.[16]

VOID GIVES SHAPE TO SUBSTANCE

Three years ago I (Trivanu Karanga) decided to quit – temporarily – regular employment as a mining engineer to investigate business prospects for myself in Zimbabwe. Zimbabwe, and indeed most African countries at the time, were in a chronic state of hunger, poverty and political uncertainty.

In the early eighties the country was riddled with drought. I observed that some of the worst hit areas were mining regions, but it never dawned on me that I might become a prospector for minerals. My background was far too comfortable for a risky venture like that.

So despite my concern, and love for the peasantry, my intentions to create a new enterprise brought neither them nor myself any financial reward. I couldn't get a job, let alone a bank loan that could fund any one of the thousand plus investment projects that I had identified in the rural areas.

Then, one day, I heard that my aged grandfather was dying of cancer in the communal lands. The whole of my family and clan decided to spend a weekend with him before he died, as a gesture of love. During the evening the 'spirit' (mudzimu) of my great grandfather spoke to us through the spirit medium (svikiro).

'The time has come to give wealth to our children, and they must then choose how to spread it amongst their children.' However, we had to perform certain culturally based rituals before getting such support from the spiritual world.

A month later my family conducted such rituals, and I was directed to go back into regular employment. A job was going to be secured for me in less than two weeks. A week later I was offered employment by three different organizations, none of which I had applied for. This was my first tangible experience of direct spiritual intervention in my life. My 'mudzimu' also stressed that my future fortunes lay in the mining industry.[17]

Vision

As substance is created out of the void, so a vision may begin to form, that is literally a picture or image of where the future lies.

In colour, shape and form, the idea is imbedded in some descriptive way. But the vision is not only clothed in garments of the world; the vision also reaches out to shape, form, and change that world. The nascent organization expands its power base as sympathetic individuals are brought within the expanding energy field. What the vision may lack in concreteness, it more than makes up for in raw power.[18]

TRADITION AND MODERNITY

Despite the risks associated, mining has proved itself to be the breadbasket of Rhodesia and now Zimbabwe. An interesting feature of particularly goldmining today is that the vast majority of major mines are on 'primitive' sites, on which iron ore has been mined for centuries.

The nineteenth-century settlers dispossessed the indigenous owners of their customary rights. Karanga Mining Company, on the other hand, has adopted the local Shona culture as part and parcel of its enterprise. The workers, the communal chief, and the 'mhondoro' or ancestral chief are all important members of the family. Our culture revolves around 'Ukama', that is the real support gained from the cooperation between living and deceased members of the family.

With this combination of traditional cultural forces and modern production techniques we in KMC feel we can surpass all previous production records in mining iron ore. History is set to both repeat and outreach itself, as gold mining is renewed to reach even beyond its former glory.[19]

Understanding

With 'understanding' the vision assumes clarity of form. Shape is measured, force is calibrated, products and goals are specified. Planning must be applied so that what emerged 'out of the depths' can move from vision to the real world. Trivanu Karanga has thus related the journey of the spirit to a planned development, engineered by 'architects on the board'.

ARCHITECTS ON THE BOARD

It is my belief that the liberation struggle that resulted in the transformation of Rhodesia into Zimbabwe was engineered by our ancestors, especially our past chiefs, or 'mhondoro'. They were the architects in a grand strategy to repossess the land. My own ancestors are a dynasty of successful merchants who traded in gold and ivory before the first Portuguese settlers entered East Africa in the seventeenth century.

It is in that context that I envisaged the birth and development of KMC. Since independence in 1981, egalitarian reforms introduced by the new government brought about a rapid improvement in the economy. This was so because of the vital cultural linkage between the land, the people, and the mhondoro (past chiefs of the so-called 'spirit provinces').

The government has planned for a 67% increase in minerals production over the next five years. This remarkable feat can only be accomplished by forging the same traditional and cultural linkages. Modern practices in the mining industry are inadequate to meet this requirement.

Our ancestors are the custodians of our natural resources. Land based enterprises thrive on the goodwill of these 'owners' of the land. In fact the early Portuguese settlers, in the eighteenth century, participated in the indigenous culture and rituals, and reaped their rewards in gold and ivory.

My own experience in 1985 lends support to this view. We had been prospecting for base minerals for four months without success. Despite all indications of failure we persisted in the search, basing our hope on the legends and folk stories of the wealth within the area. Eventually, though, we were on the point of packing our bags.

But a local labourer urged us to pay a visit to the area's spirit medium. He, in turn, advised us to perform certain rituals. More than 60 people danced, drank, ate and sang for three days. In the course of these rituals I was singled out by the local medium and questioned as to my motives and plans. I explained my mission and was subsequently given assurances of support. After that we had no more trouble locating mineral deposits in the area.

I attributed our success to the harmony of interest between myself, my own ancestors, and the 'mhondoro' of that particular area. I could see then that *I was fulfilling a plan* that had been designed by architects within a higher world.

KMC had therefore passed the first stage of business development, including the necessary financial and psychological investment, a stage that directly involved the world of 'spirit'. Now, as was the case in the past, our ancestors had asserted their authority over the land, and were actively keeping pace with, and leading the way for, the cultural and economic transformation of our country.[20]

Language

Something arising out of the depths, represented in a vision, and located in a context that can be readily understood, must then be named. The possibility of expression comes through 'language'. When something is named it is literally called in to existence, as a conscious element in the life of the organization. In this way TTK came to be called Sony, and KMC was named – after the dynasty into which Trivanu was born. 'It is fitting', he says, 'to name an enterprise engineered by my ancestors after them.'

Until you know the name, the products and the functions of an organization, you cannot know it in a unique sense. In that sense IBM or Sony are more familiar to us than 3M or Siemens because, in the first two cases as opposed to the second two, the company names reflect the products and functions of the enterprises.

Information and data

Harrison Owen does not separate out 'information and data', as impersonal abstractions devoid of spirit. In viewing them as means whereby progress is measured, and plans are measured and changed, he sees still a continuity of flow. In other words such data is a record of the movement of spirit, along its journey from out of the depths onwards.

'There is a continuity of flow. The same Spirit moves on through a sequence of manifestations. There is also a discontinuity of effect. Each appearance of Spirit must end before the next emerges. That is the story of the butterfly, the story of transformation.'[21]

Appropriate adaptation has led to the progressive transformation of KMC from just about a one-man band, mining in one area, into an early stage-managed organization, with a series of gold mines. However, these are still very early days: Hope and potential still far exceed actual production. In other words, potential has been recognized, and to some degree realized, but is only beginning to be actualized.

From potential to actuality

Crossing the great divide separating 'might be' from 'is' brings the organizational spirit from the level of good idea to that of being there. In this process of 'actualization' the spirit brings about reaction, response, proactivity, interaction and finally, inspiration.

Reaction

On the first days of business, Owen points out, things are more than a little confusing. Events and demands pile on top of one another. The style of management may be described as 'reactive'. You just keep things moving.

A PUNCH DRUNK BOXER

KMC, as of 1985, was myself – Trivanu Karanga – as sole proprietor. I had no capital nor prospects for getting capital. I was neither an experienced miner nor geologist. Yet somehow I had faith that my ancestors would see to the capital need as we went along.

At many a stage I could not even see my way through the next two days. Somehow I persisted despite the hardships incurred in trying to raise capital, the threats from creditors, pilfering management, dishonest workers, stringent labour regulations, and family obligations. I went through a living nightmare. The blows were getting heavier and heavier and I still came on for more, like a punch drunk boxer.

What kept me going was my instinct, faith, and the spirit of my ancestors. Eventually I gained a kind of immunity to hardship and soldiered on. Whenever I was at the bottom of the barrel something would happen that would enable me to carry on.

As one mhondoro put it to me, 'where there is honey there are fierce stinging bees'.[22]

Responsive

Once things begin to move ahead without constant disruption you will have learnt to distinguish what works from what doesn't. In other words you will have learnt to respond appropriately. As Owen says: 'It becomes clearer who you are and what your business is, so that your organization may be responsive to your own needs, and to those of the outside world'.[23]

PRODUCTIVITY AND ADAPTIVITY

When we started mining most employees were on fixed hourly rates. We found later that this practice was inadequate because most local people had an alternative job going at home or in the communal fields. Attendance and productivity therefore left a lot to be desired.

We then decided to introduce an hourly rate coupled with a productivity bonus scheme. Productivity was the key and there was no better way of emphasizing the point.[24]

Proactive and interactive

Proactive organizations are at the opposite pole from reactive ones. They not only respond appropriately but they exhibit a strong sense of purpose.

Interactive enterprises approach particular problems, albeit purposefully, as they individually arise, whereas interactive ones have a more holistic and integrated approach. They merge with their environment, seeking progressively more interactive ways of expressing themselves.

The distinction between 'in here' and 'out there' becomes increasingly more blurred, as boundaries and constraints are turned into linkages and opportunities. This has indeed been the case for KMC. 'Already opportunities are opening up for integrating vertically in processing mineral ores for manufacturing industries.'

Inspired organization

The journey of the spirit is completed when the matter it has infused becomes fully transformed. In other words, the organization through its people, as a whole, now becomes totally inspired.

Although the quality of inspiration is similar to that of the individual's original vision, it is now diffused throughout the organization. The whole enterprise has become 'spiritualized'. All forms of energy are vibrating with spirit!

SPIRIT − ENERGY − SPIRIT

The potential for the Inspired organization is given by the Out of Depths experience with which the organization began. The experience was powerful in the sense that something dramatic and new appeared from nowhere. What it was and what it would become were all unknowns.

Over the course of the succeeding stages of the Odyssey, that primordial Spirit, having emerged from Out of the Depths, became more focussed and particular. The Spirit appeared in successive modes of being, each one of which allowed for a fuller expression of its potential. Yet even at the Interactive level, form and structure were important and constraining considerations. The Inspired level brings the possibility of going beyond these constraints.[25]

KMC, as a youthful enterprise, has a long way to go before it might become an inspired organization. Yet much potential has already been created. Trivanu Karanga has certainly emerged *out of the depths*. The *vision* he now holds powerfully motivates him to link Zimbabwe's spiritual and cultural heritage with its material resources.

Through his enriched *understanding* of indigenous business and society, moreover, he has fused together ancient Zimbabwean culture and modern European technology. He has even created a new business *language* through mhondoro (spirit) and ukama (cooperation) into his mining operation. That operation will be monitored, via this special language, and through 'purpose built' *information*.

Furthermore, Karanga has crossed the 'great divide' between potential and actual. In doing so he at first *reacted* instinctively to adversity, carrying on relentlessly and fuelled by the support of his family and ancestry. He is now beginning to tackle *responsively* technical, social and economic problems as they arise, and has been *proactive* enough to draw on traditional practices to reinforce current productivity.

He has not yet reached a stage in which his *interactive* activity is as commercially evident and viable as it is, communally. For at this point he has not yet won over a sceptical business establishment, for reasons that will soon become apparent. So KMC is still being called upon to react to adverse financial circumstances.

Finally, when and if Dube creates a wholly *inspired* organization, and so actualizes his vision, he is likely to be ten or twenty years down the road. 'We must not fail and cannot fail because the stakes are too high for not only KMC but also for Zimbabwe and Mozambique to whom we are spiritually bonded.'[26]

FACILITATING THE JOURNEY

Policy and strategy

The journey of the spirit is an odyssey that a metaphysical manager, like Trivanu Karanga, undergoes over a long period of time. At one stage he will have emerged from out of the depths gradually to formulate his vision. He will have established his *metaphysical policy*.

Over time the vision will have been placed in context, and converted into a business language that those around him could understand. In his own mind he will also have planned a series of steps for its accomplishment.

In fact this process, whereby potential is created, will often recur during the metaphysical manager's lifetime. If KMC is to continue to develop Trivanu Karanga will have to descend into the depths on many more occasions. In subsequently turning actualizing potential he will continually and successively react, respond, become proactive and then interactive, and then infuse his whole organization with inspiration. That is, if you like, his ongoing *metaphysical strategy*.

This strategy or journey takes place, however, in the wider context of an organization, as revealed in the first part of this chapter. As Figure 6.2 indicates, spirit is inevitably and necessarily moulded by corporate culture. The 'family culture' pervading Sony and the 'Ukama' culture pervading KMC are ever present.

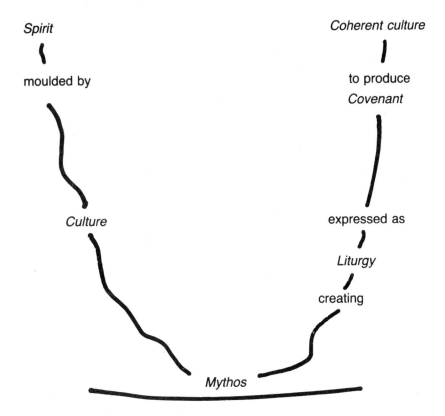

Figure 6.2 Spirit and culture

This culture is in its turn represented through myth and ritual (mythos), with which both Akio Morita and Trivanu Karanga have imbued their organizations. Japanese and Zimbabwean mythology, whether pertaining to self-sufficiency or honey and stinging bees, have become part of the organizations' fabric. The heroic exploits of their current and ancestral originators live on through stories acted out, ritualized and represented.

Mythos creates liturgy, the everyday activities of people in the organization, which is more or less infused with myth and ritual. Every time Sony makes a technological breakthrough the spirit of 'mottainai' is relived. Every time a new mine is discovered the chiefs of the 'spirit provinces' are remembered.

Liturgy is codified, at a later stage of the organization's development, as the organizational covenant (see Ibuka's management philosophy, p. 118) which serves, in its turn, to produce a coherent spirit. In the business' early stages, as for KMC, the covenant and the vision are as one.

Operations

Whereas the metaphysical manager undergoes the journey of the spirit, the developmental manager can, at least to some extent, facilitate it within the organization as a whole. This is a useful developmental role because organizational members seldom perceive their institution as spirit, represented by mythos. Moreover, even for those who are so inclined, really seeing your own culture, your own stories, and your own spirit, is difficult because they are so much part of your life.

Harrison Owen's approach to facilitating the journey of spirit involves four distinct steps. In step 1 a general understanding of the organization is developed through a consideration of its *history*. In step 2 the facilitator focuses on the *leader*, and on his personal vision and understanding. Finally, in steps 3 and 4, the organizational *culture* is studied, described, and reflected back to its members, through a variety of methods.

Particular and novel use is made of what Owen calls a *mythograph*.

HISTORICAL SCAN

The process begins with a historian's approach to the organization, unravelling at the outset objective facts and figures. When did the organization all start, where, and under what conditions? Who are, or were, the major figures, founders, associates and adversaries, and what have been their major characteristics and contributions? What is the structure and shape of the organization, including its external affiliations? What are the major locations and product lines?

Having found out all this the facilitator must uncover what significant events have occupied the organization's past. He is therefore interested in the development of brand new products and services, market breakthroughs, mergers and takeovers, reorganizations, struggles for succession, and so on. His aim is to uncover, at this initial stage, not only facts and figures but also the key words and names, particular to the organization, which recur.

Owen calls these *heavy words*, because of their depth of historically based meaning and significance. Sony itself, from the original Latin 'sonus', meaning sound, is a good case in point. After completing this historical scan, and having identified several 'heavy words', the facilitator interviews the leader of the organization.

UNCOVERING THE LEADER'S VISION

During this interview – step 2 – the essential question that the facilitator asks is 'Where does the organization think that it is going, or would like to go?' The question is asked of the current leader, and is aimed at uncovering his vision and understanding of the organization.

The discussion starts with facts and figures – production targets, plans for relocation, and recitation of major problems and opportunities – but should proceed to the uncovering of the leader's personal and qualitative vision of the long-term future. The question 'What would it look and feel like if success were achieved?' addresses the quality of spirit desired.

CULTURAL ANALYSIS

Exploration

Step 3 begins at the conclusion of the interview with the leader, at which time he or she is asked to identify a dozen important people in the organization. 'Importance' may be defined in any way the leader chooses, though he would inevitably include several members of his or her senior staff.

In interviewing these important people one cannot begin by asking 'What are the key myths and rituals around here?' Rather one centres upon three questions: 'Who are you and how did you get here? What is this place? What should it be?'.

Who are you?

The first question is designed to set the stage and allow the person to talk about himself. It serves to place him or her in the context of the organization, and its historical evolution.

What is this place/What should it be?

The second two questions go to the heart of the matter, but they get there indirectly. Inevitably the person interviewed will initially respond with facts and figures, but will be likely to turn to stories and incidents that emerge out of, or exemplify, these. Their words might go something like: 'You really don't understand this place . . . it's like . . . well last week', and out comes the tale.

In listening to the interview responses, it is important to remember what, in particular, you are investigating. The factual information is of interest, but only from the point of view that it establishes the context. The real concern is for the 'little stories' that are told. Sometimes the telling of a tale will be an extended performance; other times it may involve just a few key words, for example 'John is a mysterious character'.

Although only a select few stories will be told by those twelve people, in Owen's experience the seminal ones will recur. The actual number of major myths (stories 'pregnant' with meaning), in his opinion, is unlikely to succeed half a dozen, even within a major corporation.

Preliminary assessment

The role of the focus group

Once the initial interviews are complete, they must be analysed in terms of the stories present. Of particular importance is the way in which these stories function togther to represent the spirit of the organization. Areas of similarity and difference between the leader's vision and that of his 'followers' should be identified.

Step 3 of the process comes to an end when the findings are presented to a pre-selected focus group of the organization's leader and his key associates. The function of this group is twofold: firstly, to validate the stories, and secondly, to assess the proposed interpretation and corrective actions.

The role of the full group

In step 4, stories are sought from all levels and sectors of the organization. Specifically this means interviewing a representative sample from the executive, middle management, and working levels of all major departments and divisions. This may involve a total of, say, 100 people in an organization of 10,000. The facilitator simply proceeds until stories begin to repeat themselves, continually, at any one level or in any one sector.

Observing ritual

In addition to uncovering these stories through interviews, it is important to observe closely the rituals that characterize different parts of the organization. These may range from board and departmental meetings, to sales drives, to 'rites of passage' for new recruits, to company prize givings, to golden handshakes. One needs to identify their precise range and character.

Constructing the mythograph

Classification

Once the tales and ritual acts have been gathered, the problem is to make sense out of this collection by arranging the material in such a way that the quality and direction of the spirit emerges. Furthermore, one needs to identify how strongly focused or weakly diffused the spirit may be, and apply any corrective actions that may be appropriate.

The means whereby this analysis is accomplished is Owen's so-called *mythograph*. The mythograph is a formalized representation of the organization onto which may be plotted the elements of myth and ritual. By way of an example, and applying more than a little of my own imagination (in absence of the complete facts) I have used KMC to illustrate the mythographic points (see Table 6.1).

Table 6.1 The mythograph of KMC

Levels	Sectors		
	Operations	Banking	Community
Executive	11 Dynasty of merchants	12 The guy's crackers	13 Nehanda at the gallows
Supervisory	21 The Wedza 'bira'	22 The Zimbabwe ruins	23 The dying grandfather
Workers	31 Where there's honey there are stinging bees	32 His father went under	33 Ukama

Assessment

In assessing the mythograph, the key thing to remember is that each element (myth) represents, and in a sense contains, the spirit of the place. Furthermore, it provides indications of the quality, force and direction of the spirit (see Table 6.2).

Under ideal circumstances, when the metaphysical management of the organization is functioning effectively, all cells would show the same seminal story, with minor and due variations, according to level and sector. That sort of coherent picture would represent a

Table 6.2 A mythographic analysis of KMC

11	'Dynasty of merchants'	Trivanu's ancestors, stretching back hundreds of years, were all gold and ivory traders.
21	'The Buhera Bira'	In the Wedza area, after Karanga had unsuccessfully prospected for 4 months, he held a 'bira', that is a traditionally communal festival – and iron ore was subsequently found.
31	'Honey/ Stinging'	There is a traditional story, within the local Shona culture, that tells of the bees that sting (hardships incurred) by those gallant folk seeking honey for all.
12	'The guy's crackers'	The European bankers in Zimbabwe are sceptical of 'spiritual' forces, especially in business. Most regard Trivanu, the self-styled visionary, as not only a poor investment, but also 'crackers'.
22	'Zimbabwe ruins'	The indigenous banking supervisors, more receptive to Karanga, tell the story of the ancient Zimbabwe ruins, in which gold was mined 500 years ago – Karanga is seen to be following in those footsteps.
32	'His father went under'	The low-level staff within the banks, easily influenced by the big bosses, tell jokes about the family of bankrupt Karanga's, Trivanu's father having himself gone in.
13	'Nehanda at the gallows'	The spiritual leader Nehanda vowed, as she was taken to the gallows in 1890, that her bones would rise to liberate her country.
23	'The dying uncle'	As Karanga was beginning to despair over his self-determined future, the spirit of his dying grandfather intervened, and pointed towards Trivanu's future in mining.
33	'Ukama'	Many a story has been told within the traditional culture of how, through a spirit of cooperation, great things have been achieved.

'one-pointed' spirit, creating the potential for an unimpeded, powerful flow of physical and human energy.

In this situation not only is the culture coherent, but the spirit remains free and flexible – free to develop and transform.

As we can see from Table 6.2 the company and the indigenous community are in harmony. One story, whether current or historic, KMC- or Zimbabwe-related, reinforces the other. The company-community spirit is coherent at all levels.

In contrast the banking establishment is out of step. Its spirit lies somewhere else. 'The guy's crackers.'

The futility of direct intervention

Corrective metaphysical action will smooth out the flow – avoid side eddies and bottlenecks – toward the achievement of the business's vision. Such action must recognize the present situation in which the spirit flow is disconnected in one particular respect, and mutually reinforcing in all others.

Simply telling someone, the banking establishment in this case, to adopt a different mythos can never work. Such statements as, for example, 'don't shut yourself off from the spirit of Karanga's ancestors', literally fall outside of the frame of reference of the listener. Consequently it is 'nonsense' to him.

In fact a direct challenge to the European's own mythos that 'mining empires are created by heroic personalities with material resources at their command', will merely strengthen his original position. As Owen says: 'Since mythos represents the field of meaning, denial of mythos will subject the holder to meaninglessness, which is obviously not a condition that anyone will willingly enter into.'[27]

The futility of indirect intervention

The alternative route that Owen proposes is 'leadership by indirection'. The object is to create a new and composite story out of the existing elements contained within the mythograph. By using the existing mythos the basic, conservative nature of culture is acknowledged. However, the very power of the newly shaped story, overrides the existing negativity. Let me illustrate.

In constructing the new tale a place must be found for the heroes and rebels of the past, as a basis and connecting point for the future. In KMC's case, a linkage needs to be established between such characters as Rhodes and Jameson, the heroes of the European establishment, and Nehanda, the heroine of the indigenous Zimbabweans.

Furthermore, in the process of reconstruction the spirit of Zimbabwe's ancestors needs to be interlinked with that of Rhodes himself, who indeed lives on through the European's historical connection with 'Rhodesia'.

Collective story telling

The new mythos cannot be created impersonally, but has to be installed through a process of collective story telling.

COLLECTIVE STORY TELLING

Weaving the new tale is the essence of leadership and lies at the heart of the process of transformation. In constructing it, it is necessary to *consciously link back* to the organizational potential, created through its depths, vision, and language, and also to the ways in which the potential may have become actualized in everyday business life.

Whatever this new tale may be it *cannot simply jettison all that went before* . . .

The leader may start with a 'story line', but that is just the framework around which need to be orchestrated all of the other elements. In fact it should be possible to *touch, smell*, and *move* with a story that is well told. Each part should be able to contribute in its own way, and none should be allowed to dominate.

But most of all, the story should be constructed with sufficient *open space to allow members of the organization to partake in its creation*, through their own imagination. The story must become their story, 'our story' . . . Telling a four dimensional story is a real art. Indeed it may be the highest form of art.[28]

CONCLUSION: THE CREATION OF LITURGY

A story once told will be quickly eroded unless it is retold and embedded within the organization. It must become real, and an ongoing part of organizational life. In other words it must become liturgy – or what the people do.

No longer is it the leader's prime function to direct the organization. Rather it is his responsibility to *orchestrate the new story* in all its forms. The structure of the institution, its physical fabric, the cycle of organizational activities – all need to reinforce it.

Suitable 'rites of passage' for new recruits to the enterprise need to be developed. Celebrations, at regular intervals, must reflect the ethos, the mythos, and the appropriate heroes.

In the KMC case Trivanu, as leader of his enterprise, would

assume a position central to not only his workforce and the indigenous community but also to the commercial and political establishment in Zimbabwe. Akio Morita has already assumed such a position in Japan.

The rounded structure of his organization would reflect the spirit of Ukama (cooperation) indigenous to the country, and pictures of Cecil Rhodes (colonizer) and Mbuya Nehanda (liberator) would be located alongside one another. Sony has achieved this harmonization of opposing forces by Westernizing its Japanese operation, in one sense, and Easternizing its American one, in another.

New recruits to KMC would be able to share the story of its birth and growth, alongside stories of the founding of both Rhodesia and Zimbabwe. The 'bira' festival, which had such a formative influence on the KMC's development, would be regularly celebrated. In Sony Akio Morita makes a point of addressing all new recruits in Japan, once a year, and revealing to them the journey of Sony's spirit.

In time, and over time, the spirit of the organization, moulded by the Sony or by the KMC culture – through the prevailing myths and rituals – needs to create an enduring liturgy, expressed in the form of a written covenant, serving to produce a coherent spirit. Should this process not happen naturally it is possible to intervene, albeit indirectly, and help the transformation of energy and spirit along.

It is that spirit, for Harrison Owen and for all metaphysically inclined cultures, which is the most precious and powerful of all organizational resources. In Chapter 10 we shall take a practical look at the metaphysical process of transformation – of energy into spirit and back again.

At this point, however, having reviewed the four different approaches to cultural immersion, assessment, evolution and transformation, it is time to apply theory to practice.

REFERENCES

1 Owen, Harrison, *Spirit Transformation and Development in Organizations*, Abbot Publishing, 1987.
2 Owen, Harrison, op. cit. p. 72.
3 Goodman, Jane, *The Mond Legacy*, Heinemann, 1984.
4 Nobel, Alfred, *Nobel*, Crowell, 1980.
5 Morita, Akio, *Made in Japan*, Fontana, 1987.
6 Ibid., p. 52.
7 Ibid., p. 64.
8 Ibid., p. 48.
9 Ibid., p. 87.
10 Campbell, Joseph, *The Hero with a Thousand Faces*, Princeton University Press, 1949.
11 Morita, A., op. cit., p. 18.

12 Ibid.
13 Ibid.
14 Ibid.
15 Lyons, Mick, *The Sony Vision*, Crowell, 1976.
16 Owen, H., op. cit., p. 74.
17 Karanga, Trivanu, *KMC*, MBA Project, 1986.
18 Ibid., p. 14.
19 Ibid., p. 7.
20 Ibid., p. 12.
21 Owen, Harrison, op. cit., p. 117.
22 Karanga, Trivanu, op. cit., p. 3.
23 Owen, Harrison, op. cit., p. 91.
24 Karanga, Trivanu, op. cit., p. 2.
25 Owen, Harrison, op. cit., p. 11.
26 Karanga, Trivanu, op. cit., p. 11.
27 Owen, Harrison, op. cit., p. 224.
28 Ibid., p. 11.

7 The Primal Approach to Corporate Culture*

The conventional wisdom, on the subject of corporate culture, is what I have termed 'primal' in nature, and American in origin. A good case in point is that of the JMS Seed Company.

John M. Schultz created more than a business. He created a culture that could support the business through good times and bad, one consistent enough to provide stability and stable enough to allow it to sustain the changes of time and circumstances.

The essential culture at JMS Seed Co. has not changed since its creation, as the same shared values are evident and the company is basically in the same business. Both simply expanded to encompass advantageous opportunities and survive the changes of time.

It is because of the culture's expansion and continuity that it has become the driving force of the company; still strongly joined to the founder's ideals and his memory, yet able to survive successfully without him physically present.

This indeed was J.M. Schultz's intent. He actively and openly conveyed the values that now bind the culture in an attempt to make them important, and shared, from the very beginning. For he knew that if they became significantly dominating and protected, they could become self-perpetuating. Also, by involving his immediate family he added an additional assurance that his values and spirit would continue through both a conscious reverence for an ancestor as well as through the inherited characteristics and ingrained spirituality, that, if physically part of the organizational network, would be ever present in the company.

What follows is a primal analysis of the culture that is JMS Seed Co. This is the obvious choice of approach (as opposed to, say, a rational analysis) because it ties in so well with the founder's

* This case study has been compiled, in its essence, by Audra Schniederjon, Michael McNiel, Jeremy Monk and Chad Tan, students at the City University Business School, London, with the very kind help and cooperation of Mrs Frances Adams Schultz.

original vision, and because the firm as it is today lends itself so naturally to a primal assessment.

SHARED VALUES

A strong sense of shared values at JMS Seed Co. has become the bedrock of its corporate culture. As general guidelines of day-to-day behaviour, they provide a sense of common direction. But, more importantly, they serve to communicate the company's clear and explicit philosophy for achieving success.

The shared values today that are the most powerful were established with the birth of the company and have prospered ever since. These values are basic and strong because they have proven successful over several decades. And yet they are continually being shaped and fine-tuned by management to conform to the business's economic and social environment.

The *first* and most important value is that JMS Seed Co. will *provide the highest quality product to its customers*, with the underlying assumption that although cheaper products are available, the extra quality received through the purchase of a JMS product will more than pay for itself in the end. Management is continually looking beyond the present market to determine how it can bring in more customers, more business, and higher profits, and yet it will never compromise quality.

The *second* shared value, extremely apparent at JMS, is a *commitment to their employees*. Because the corporate headquarters continues to remain in Dietrich, Illinois, the small (pop. 1200) farming community where JMS has developed and grown for years, the company is currently employing the second and third generations of some local families. At the same time, there is a conscious effort to treat all employees as individuals based on their own personal capabilities.

THE JMS FAMILY

An employee who had been with the company for thirty years had become mentally impaired and although it was not cost effective for the company to keep this particular individual employed, they just kept him on the payroll and gave him adjusted duties in order to help him to maintain his family and self-worth.

A similar example involved another employee who drove himself into debt by living beyond his means. When JMS Seed Co. was informed by this man's bank that his wages were to be tied up to service the debt, the president of the company met with the employee to see what could and should be done. The company agreed to pay off all the employee's debts and refinance the debt with the agreement that the employee would follow a personal budget. Within three years the debt was paid, his house was renovated, and he had a good car and savings in the bank.

A third shared value at JMS is that of *flexibility*, especially in *job roles*. Everyone knows he/she is supposed to be aggressive and efficient in his own job as well as maintaining flexibility and recognizing the opportunity to help out another employee or department in times of need. Because agriculture is a highly cyclical industry, the workload in the various company departments varies considerably from season to season. It is for this reason, as well as the fact that the firm desires to maintain a permanent (rather than cyclical) staff and thus job stability, that employees are expected to go where they are needed. An accountant may be doing payroll one week and billing the next, or on rare occasions be expected to go out back (in the very busy harvest season). In fact, the company accepts the premise that it will never be so grand that management cannot go out back to help in the busy season.

Loyalty is the *fourth* shared value. There is loyalty to maintaining a superior product, whether in the form of expanded R & D to produce a product capable of competing with new technically advanced varieties of soybean, grass, or wheat, or whether in the form of special employee motivation programmes to keep workers excited about what they are doing, no matter how routine.

There is also loyalty of top management to other business entities that stand by JMS in shaky times.

During the bad farming season and economic pressures of 1929, JMS had difficulty in obtaining loans. But one bank over a hundred miles away offered to cover the firm's needs. J.M. Schultz never forgot this and every year since, all banking has been done with this bank (nearly 60 years).

SYMBOLIC MANAGEMENT

Ritual events and activities

Symbolic management has played a major role in keeping the culture's shared values alive and thriving. The symbolic managers throughout the organization have a special skill in being able to recruit and promote members of the cultural network to maintain and develop the company's ceremonies and rituals. These tend to involve tangible events celebrating well known occasions and activities.

A very popular annual JMS ritual is the company Christmas party
where all the employees, from the back warehouse to the front
office, gather together as they do for the annual summer picnic. The
purpose and importance of these rituals is to reinforce the 'family
atmosphere' and to give the employees an opportunity to mix and
see each other as individuals making up one organization; as
members of the family rather than simply as position holders.

Daily ceremonies include the morning coffee break where the
department manager sits in with his employees to discuss the day's
activity over coffee, ending with a period of social informal conversation. This 'family atmosphere' is extended through the daily
operations. There is no 'time clock' in the offices. Most employees
arrive early and stay late. Employees become ingrained with the
idea (shared value) that they are giving and working for the
improved quality of the firm and its product rather than getting in
their closely monitored eight hours.

The cultural network

In a primal context, the JMS symbolic managers place stress on
easily accessible symbols. Therefore it is evident that the culture's
heroes and priests are more down to earth than spiritually evolved
(as in Transcriba).

JMS nevertheless uses symbolic management in that managers
never miss an opportunity to reinforce, dramatize, or involve the
central values of the culture.

The primary means of communication within a corporate culture
is the network, that hidden hierarchy unrelated to official positions
or titles. The network of a strong culture is powerful in that it can
reinforce the basic beliefs of an organization, enhance the symbolic
value of heroes by passing stories of their activities and accomplish-
ments, set a new climate for change, and provide a tight structure
of influence for the CEO. The network is not only important because
it transmits information, but more importantly, it interprets the
significance of the information for employees.

CHARACTERS IN THE CULTURAL NETWORK

Heroes personify the values (which are the soul of the culture) . . . they
create the Role Models for employees to follow . . . the great motivator,
the magician, the person everyone will count on when things get tough.
They have unshakable characters and style. Heroes are symbolic
figures whose deeds are out of the ordinary, but not too far out.

Priests are guardians of the corporate culture. They preach the 'gospel'
that has been handed down from the founding fathers . . . Priests

interpret the founding fathers' acts and formulates codes of behaviour from them.

Storytellers interpret what is going on in the company, to suit their own perceptions. A memorable punchline can recreate an entire occasion. A storyteller is someone capable of creating an atmosphere. Stories may serve to downplay rather than support existing culture.

Spies are people loyal enough to keep the good manager informed of what is going on. People who are well-liked, and have access to many different people. They hear all stories and know who is behind them. Spies are likely to be unthreatening and unambitious.

Gossips embellish the hero's past feats and latest accomplishments giving precise names, dates and events.

Whisperers are able to (1) read the boss' mind quickly and accurately (2) build a support system of contacts throughout the organisation so they can make things happen.[1]

Born heroes

Heroes represent the ideal of success. 'Born heroes' are those visionaries who have not only built an organization but have also established an institution that survived them and added their personal sense of values to the world. Several characteristics guarantee a born hero's survival.

First of all, he is right, and right in a big way, about a product, a way of doing business, an organization. Thus, 'nothing succeeds like success'. In addition, these heroes are persistent in seeing their vision become reality. And lastly, the visionary hero has a sense of personal responsibility for the continuing success of the business.

John M. Schultz is very clearly the 'born' hero, as the original entrepreneur and creator of the corporate culture that enabled the company to rise to its current position, allowed it to survive and prosper in the present agricultural situation, and will help JMS Seed Co. to continue in the future. He is the visionary hero whose influence will last for generations. As such a hero he established not only a business but also an institution that demonstrates his personal sense of values to the world.

As previously mentioned, John M. Schultz valued quality above all. Each bag of soybeans, wheat, or grass seed that left his plant bore his initials JMS. This is still the case today. Thus, with each bag, quality is guaranteed to be the highest because it represents the name on the outside, a name revered because it is the founder's as well as because it still represents the family which is so much a part of the present culture.

Another personal value very evident still in the company is an appreciation for employee suggestions. There were never new ideas that he dispensed with before examining them. When workers complained to JMS about using hand trolleys, he instituted forklifts almost immediately.

JMS had a keen ability to look beyond the basic or obvious. In this case employees simply complained about work, but he discovered a way to create a benefit. He gave employees a feeling that he took their complaints seriously as well as ultimately improving the efficiency of the department.

The born hero also affects the way the company does business through his activities and imagination, especially those activities kept alive in stories.

KEEPING GOING

John M. Schultz as a 6' 4" teenager helped out on the family farm. But while most farmers would go back to their houses for lunch, JMS was known to stop his horse and plough, pull out his sandwich and finish lunch quickly to get back to ploughing immediately.

This story of a relatively basic activity has long motivated employees to put in extra time when it is needed such as in the busy harvest season.

John M. Schultz's imagination and pride is apparent in another activity.

SHOWMANSHIP

When grass seed made up a big portion of company business, especially a type known as 'red top', JMS would appear at every seed convention with a large red hat on to live up to the name of the 'Red Top King', as he was often referred to in the 1930s and 1940s.

This 'showmanship' still persists as does J.M. Schultz's pervasive influence, even though he is no longer a physical part of the organization.

Compass heroes

An employee who started working in the company at the age of fourteen was handed the keys to JMS at the age of twenty-five by the founder. He issued the instructions: 'I give you the keys and the responsibility of being manager of my company.' This new role model chosen to carry forward a new set of values was John H. Schultz, son of the founder. He is the 'compass' hero.

It was upon his retirement as president, some forty years later, that he handed the same keys to his son in turn, John M. Schultz

II, thus reinforcing the example of the loyalty and trust that succeeds from generation to generation.

The 'compass' hero, John H. Schultz, is presently chairman of the board, and although removed from day-to-day operations, maintains contact with all employees through frequent visits to the plant. He in fact knows most on a first-name basis as well as their families. He symbolizes to most employees J.M. Schultz Seed Co., the basic values and culture instituted by his father.

HEROIC FUNCTIONS

John H. Schultz started as a worker in the back warehouse, performing most of the very menial jobs even though he was the owner's son and heir apparent. He thus showed his ability to perform those tasks that he would someday ask others to do.

And not only did he simply perform. Upon asking employees who worked with JHS in his younger years what he was like, the unanimous reply is that he could outperform any other worker out back. This characteristic and perpetuating opinion has given credibility to each position JHS was appointed to throughout his career. The other employees felt he deserved promotion and looked up to him from the beginning because he made success appear attainable and human for those who worked for it.

He stood above the crowd, and yet was part of it. He became a role model in his business and in person. Employees as well as citizens have been the recipients of his generosity in instances where, through JMS, he has made improvements in Dietrich including donations for a park and tennis courts, with the designated purpose of family leisure. In this way, he is sharing his personal values of family and recreation, with the local community as his father did.

Examples like this serve to motivate other employees when they are asked to put in the extra that makes a difference in the end. It also represents the fact, mentioned earlier, that John M. only expected of employees what he himself was willing to do. And yet, this loyalty to employees goes even further.

In the profitable years, as a shareholder, the hero was handsomely rewarded for a successful year and he demanded that the employees also share in the profits, as they were behind the success. However, in the lean years, when the board determined that the usual wage increases could not be given to employees, JHS insisted that his and all managers' salaries be lowered by up to one-third to demonstrate that the cost-cutting tactics would extend from top to bottom. This may seem a little dramatic, but it only reinforces the fact that heroes personify the corporate shared values and epitomize the strength of the organization.

Storytellers

Stories must convey visual imagery rather than verbal abstraction if they are to be effective in conveying information and shaping behaviour. They have the power to change reality or maintain cohesion within set guidelines.

Storytellers are important because they preserve the institution and its values by imparting the company legends to new employees, and revealing what it takes to get ahead in the organization. A storyteller needs imagination, insight, a sense of detail, but most importantly, access to a great deal of information.

A lifelong backwarehouse manager at JMS, who has dealt with all three generations of Schultz presidents, is the most evident story-teller in the culture. He is able to reflect back on the early years of the founder, the growth years of the son, and the restructuring years of the grandson, as well as being able to turn to the future. He offers freely and dutifully a perspective to all employees, especially those employees who did not have the opportunity to meet any of the three.

Priests

While the heroes create the cultural shared values, priests protect and nurture them, as guardians. This position requires maturity and seriousness beyond years, as it requires the most responsibility of any in the cultural network.

Priests are familiar with all matters of the company's history and relate it to current situations through allegories. Thus, they are not as concerned with details as the storyteller. Priests also aid people through defeat, frustration and disappointment.

At JMS the true and powerful priest is J.H. Schultz's wife, Frances. She is the 'guardian' of the corporate culture: preaching the founding father's 'gospel', interpreting his acts, and formulating codes of behaviour from them. Frances can serve as priest because she can easily reach the members of the culture and be easily reached by them. Moreover, she is considered separate and distinct from J.H. Schultz and his 'hero role'.

Not only has Frances published a book about the founder and his company which she has dutifully circulated, but she writes quarterly newsletters to be distributed throughout the company, and to any requesting outsider. Frances does not hold an official title at the company but rather sits on several boards in the community, further associating the Schultz name with donation and charity.

Her most explicit and active role as priest has been to act as a sounding board for disgruntled employees unable to approach the corporate hero. As one of the hero's closest confidantes, at the same time, she constantly serves as a guide in helping him to make morally correct and culturally consistent decisions.

Gossips

A gossip's role is to reinforce the culture through embellishing both the hero's past feats and latest accomplishments. He will know all the trivial, day-to-day happenings of the organization that entertain, if not always entirely accurately. And once he gets hold of a good story, it is repeated throughout the company.

A backwarehouse worker at JMS who has been with the company for over forty years serves as the gossip. He has no proximity to power, yet has proven very useful in raising the status of other, particular employees. He is able to recount from childhood memories, the stories and views of the founder.

He actively searches for new information that he can embellish and pass on. In the same way that he regards the hero as 'larger than life', so are the stories he retells about anything, from an event eighty years old to the latest breakthrough in the research department.

Spies

Almost every good manager has a 'well-oiled buddy in the woodwork – someone loyal to keep you informed on what is going on'. He is an unthreatening, unambitious and well liked person who hears all the stories and knows who is behind them.

A trusted employee and citizen of Dietrich has been able to offer a perspective to the president that otherwise would have been unobtainable. He never has a truly bad word to say about anyone, which makes him as much loved as needed. However, he does effectively keep close tabs on what is going on, both physically and emotionally within the organization, and conveys these to the manager on a 'friendship' rather than 'duty' basis. Added insight, into employee work efforts, needed changes in duties, or even attractive opportunities within the local or business community (such as profitable farmland purchase) is gained through the spy.

Whistle blowers

In a strong culture, 'mavericks' are valuable, but in a weak culture 'mavericks' turn against the generally shared values, and become whistle blowers. At JMS, there is one particular employee who has been a 'thorn', constantly trying to break the consistency of the culture. He has been unsuccessful thus far because of the company's unique way of handling him.

In one particular instance, he decided that the company policy of clearing a dumping area weekly was inappropriate and that monthly clearing would suffice. Following his own opinion rather than fulfilling his weekly duty turned out to be a major error when his disobedience caused his department two weeks' loss of production. It would have been expected that this individual be instantly fired, yet because of his current economic and family situation he was permitted to stay. This employee's status and potential following was diminished and, in fact by keeping him on, the company was seen as charitable and 'good' while he was regarded as 'evil'.

Whisperers

Anyone who wants something done heads for the whisperer. He is the 'power behind the throne'. Essential to this position is strong loyalty. In addition, though, the whisperer must be able to read the boss's mind quickly and accurately and have a vast organizational support system through which to stay current on important issues.

An in-law of the Schultz family has dealt with the company as a customer for several years in his farming operations and so has access to 'external' information. As a shareholder and part-time employee in the busy season he also has access to 'internal' information. His personal perception and criticisms, as well as those of other customers conveyed through him, are directly transposed to the president or hero. Thus they offer a 'real' view of strengths and problems with the company's service to its customers.

When the decision was made to go to Brazil, and local farmers criticized the move because they thought that it would cause increased competition in the world market, the whisperer was able to point out that through this move, the company would be buying land outside of the local area rather than competing for land in the locality. This he showed to be an extreme benefit to these farmers, because if the company were to buy acreage in the local area, it would cause land prices to increase thus making it even more difficult for local farmers to expand.

Within the JMS organization itself, the whisperer has a somewhat more frightening image, as someone whom no one wants to cross. Yet because of his 'easy-to-talk-to' personality and knowledgeable understanding of the boss, people are drawn to him to air their suggestions as well as to attempt to acquire more information about the hero, the company, the possible future changes, and how each individual in the culture will (or should) be a part.

CONCLUSION

Folk wisdom

The folk wisdom at JMS Seed Co., the stories and legends revealing what the company really cares about, is rich and important, particularly because it reveals the guiding principles not only of the founder but of the company that grew from him.

The culture today still uses these stories to persuade, symbolize and guide day-to-day actions and to reinforce how things work at JMS.

These stories embellish the company philosophy by helping to put current decisions and events into a readily understood framework. They impart a sense of tradition, priority, and continuity. They thus reinforce the principle that the company will be as successful as the founder if the characteristics in the stories continue to be the features that presently guide JMS.

JMS BOUNTY

In the late 1940s, an order was placed for 100 shares of stock at $100 per share, which translates into a $10,000 investment. When the confirmation order came back it was for 1,000 shares of stock (a $100,000 investment). The company was unable to make the payment with their current reserves and finally had to get a loan to meet the $100,000 payment. The fault was not that of the Seed Co. or of J.M. Schultz, but that of the stockbroker who took the order.

In the end, in fact, the purchase proved to be a good one. The financial officer was instructed to determine whether the 1,000 shares should be maintained and with this further research, it was discovered that the purchase was even more profitable than originally anticipated. JMS held on to this stock over the years and the profits have been bountiful.

If the founder had simply made a quick decision and demanded correction of the mistake immediately, ruling out any possible positive outcomes, sizable profits could have been lost. This ability to look beyond the generally accepted state of affairs and pick out an opportunity for enhancement not only aided JMS in becoming successful, but has become a striven-for quality throughout the current corporate culture. Employees realize, through stories, what qualities have been important to success and work hard to perpetuate them.

Shared values, symbolic management – including rites and rituals and a strong cultural network – have maintained and developed

JMS's primal approach to management. Through enterprise and community – the American way – the company has prospered.

Now we turn from primal to rational, from America to Britain, from enterprise and community to freedom and order.

REFERENCE

1 Deal and Kennedy, *Corporate Cultures*, Addison & Wesley, 1982.

8 A Rational Diagnosis of Corporate Culture*

INTRODUCTION

The most thoroughgoing of the methodologies for analysing corporate culture is that of Edgar Schein (see pp. 65-76). In this book his approach has been applied to a large software house in the UK, which has a strong design and development orientation.

ARK Computer Services (ACS) was started 25 years ago by a charismatic innovator, Jim Hines, who has had a strong influence, subsequently, on the overall development of the industry, in Britain and in Europe. Over the last five years Jim Hines has been the orchestrator of two friendly mergers with manufacturing companies who make extensive use of ARK's software design expertise.

Hines became chairman of the enlarged ARK group in 1983. So whereas the ACS division, which we are investigating, employed some 200 people in 1988, the entire ARK group was responsible for some 2000 employees. Within the group, finally, were four semi-autonomous companies, each of which drew heavily on ACS' software expertise.

This particular cultural analysis is focused on the design and development side of the business, as distinct from the four operating divisions.

APPLYING A RATIONAL MODEL

The sequential approach involved in applying Schein's methodology, involves the series of steps outlined below. We shall be dealing with each in turn:

* This chapter is based on the research work into ACS undertaken by Angela Clark, Andrew Gilbert, Andrew Lemonofides, Sally Rowland and Patricial Todd – final year undergraduates on City University's business studies programme. The cultural analysis, though based on business reality, has been fictionalized to preserve confidentiality.

1. undertaking a *cursory assessment*
2. initially *focusing on surprises* and on the unexpected
3. subsequently *categorizing* such surprises
4. *locating a motivated insider* with whom to deal
5. *revealing the surprises* and hunches to him or her
6. *exploring jointly*, and probing systematically, the surprises together with the motivated insider
7. exploring *meanings* in a relaxed setting
8. *formalizing hypotheses* about the company's culture
9. systematic *checking* for fresh evidence
10. *uncovering underlying assumptions* behind the organizational culture
11. *refining*, modifying and testing the *model* of culture
12. *describing* the organizational culture *as it might be*.

Undertaking a cursory assessment

A cursory assessment was made after our first two-hour visit to ACS' headquarters:

Physical impressions

- We were received in a *warm* and friendly manner
- the interior decor and dress was casual and *relaxed*
- people were working in *small groups*
- the working atmosphere seemed to be *informal*
- technical *language* was predominant, with formulae stuck up on boards above each workstation
- people seemed *mobile*, not desk bound
- it was only *partially open* plan.

Group norms

- Individuals were huddled together in *project teams*
- there was a great emphasis on *display* of client systems
- prototype *models* were visible for all to see.

Dominant values

- *Innovation* orientation, e.g. software packages developed over the past five years, were prominently displayed
- *quality* design and development
- an overall *action* bias

- *Hines*-led, e.g. his insistence on creative thought processes being made visible on display boards above workstations
- *close to the customer* in so far as their systems featured.

If these were our instant impressions what, in the course of time, proved to be the cultural surprises?

Focusing on surprises

The first visit to the company, including a background meeting with the development director and a tour around the head office premises, revealed several surprises, that is to say:

- the extremely *informal* atmosphere
- the *haphazard* layout of the building
- the *clutter* lying on desks and on the floors in the studios
- the *trendy*, market clothes worn by everyone
- the *young* age of the majority of employees
- the *friendly* attention we received
- the degree of *conflict* within the design and development unit
- the high rate of employee *turnover*
- the comparatively *low salaries* and poor benefits package
- the *lack* of formal *training*.

Categorizing the surprises

The surprises could easily be grouped into three main areas:

- *informality* – dress, clutter, friendliness, haphazard layout
- *conflict* within the unit, not only between business managers and technically based professionals, but also between the different professional groups
- *personnel policies* – low salaries, poor benefits, minimal training.

Locating a motivated insider

The client, initially, was the development director, who was worried about the lack of cohesion between management and software engineers. However, it soon became apparent that he lacked the inside knowledge of attitudes and behaviours that were the bricks and mortar of our investigation.

Fortunately, in the early stages of our research we came across June Merton, the unit's personnel coordinator. In fact she had only recently been promoted from personnel assistant to the divisional director into her new post and was therefore very keen to help us in our investigation.

Revealing surprises and hunches to the motivated insider

We used our early informal contacts with June Merton to begin to reveal some of our surprises to her. June had been working for ACS for two years, as a temporary secretary, and had no previous background or experience in computing or computer services. This enabled her to appreciate our views as outsiders, and to share, empathetically, in the surprises we underwent.

Exploring jointly and probing systematically the surprises

We conducted, at an early stage, an individual in-depth interview with June, during which she was able to relate specific events to us, arising out of her experience within ACS.

The description of these events served to *enrich our understanding* of the relationships within ACS, and between it and the rest of the ARK group.

These descriptions were not comprehensive, given her relatively junior position within the company, but they were good enough to *provide us with themes* which could be explored at a subsequent stage.

Exploring meanings in a relaxed setting

Before and after the twenty-eight interviews that we subsequently conducted we had an informal conversation with June, during which she briefed us on the individual concerned, given her in-depth knowledge of each person.

As a result of the interviews, and June's subsequent embellishments, we gained a rich impression of the ACS culture, with our particular focus on both attitudes and atmosphere.

Formalizing hypotheses about the company's culture

Prior to conducting detailed interviews, however, we formed our initial hypotheses, arising out of discussions with our client and motivated insider, and our own physical observations:

- the working atmosphere is *inherently informal*, arising out of both the *young and trendy* people involved in the business, and the *freewheeling* influence of Jim Hines himself
- the software engineers, and designers, gain a great deal of *pride* out of their company's high profile position in the industry
- there is *poor communication* in the group as a whole, and in ACS in particular, not only because of the *two cultures*, that is orderly managers and freedom-loving professionals, but also because ACS is still finding its way out of a pioneering stage into a consolidated stage of its development
- there is *conflict* with the clients arising out of not only the *different ACS and client cultures*, but also because of the *incomplete state of the intercorporate mergers*
- there is *insufficient structure and discipline* to hold the degree of complexity that has now been reached within ACS and the overall ARK business.

Checking systematically for fresh evidence

Having formed our hypotheses we set about checking for fresh evidence through a series of in-depth interviews conducted at three different levels of the company, covering senior, middle and junior levels of management or professionals.

To ensure uniformity in our interview questions we prepared a series of interview guides covering:

- the *background* of the interviewee
- the nature of their *job* and working methods
- a description of *key projects* in which they had been involved
- their general *impressions* of ACS and its management
- their own *plans* for the future.

These guidelines, in a sense, provided the vertical axis, or sequential base for the interview. Our initial hypotheses, at the same time, provided the horizontal base, in that we ensured that such areas as working *atmosphere*, corporate *image*, interpersonal and interdivisional *communications*, as well as organization *structure* and *processes* were covered, whenever it was conversationally opportune.

In other words, our interviews were a combination of structured and free form. The overall conclusion we reached was that *The ACS culture was not sufficiently strong and elaborated to accommodate the diversity of its client cultures.*

Uncovering underlying assumptions

Edgar Schein (see Chapter 4) uncovers the underlying assumptions behind a corporate culture, on five specific dimensions, based on a person's (or an organization's) relationship to the environment, to physical and social reality, to human activity, to human nature and to human relationships. Subsequent to our data gathering we were in a position to address each of these, in turn.

Dimension 1 – The organization's relationship to its environment

RECONSTRUCT AND ANALYSE THE ORGANIZATION'S HISTORY BY
IDENTIFYING ALL MAJOR CRISES, CRUCIAL TRANSITIONS, AND OTHER
TIMES OF HIGH EMOTION

The first major *crisis* that Hines faced was in 1964 when he almost became insolvent, in the face of a chronic lack of orders. Having barely overcome this crisis he was faced, two years later, with a traumatic demerger. Twenty years later, in 1986, the company was faced with a hostile takeover bid.

In 1963, when Hines 'opened shop' for the first time, with his brand new, customized software concept, the fifty-five staff involved with him experienced elation and euphoria.

Crucial *transitions* took place, first, when Hines, in 1962, decided to go into business as an embryonic computer services company; second, in 1965, when he merged and then demerged with a fellow software house; third, in 1981, 1983 and 1985 when he underwent a succession of friendly mergers with high-tech engineering companies.

Periods of *high emotion* have been many, including both pain and ecstasy. Successive moves in the nineteen sixties, seventies and eighties into new premises have provided such highs and lows. Moreover, new designs and developments have always been accompanied by high emotion.

FOR EACH EVENT IDENTIFIED, RECONSTRUCT HOW MANAGEMENT AT
THAT TIME DEFINED THEIR IDENTITY AND ROLE, RELEVANT
ENVIRONMENTS AND POSITION

When Hines initially set up in business he saw himself as an innovator, a man slightly ahead of his time in the UK. However, existing trends and applications in America and Scandinavia indicated that the time for such software developments was ripe.

Although Hines was anticipating demand in Britain, he was sufficiently in tune with the international market to know that he would ultimately evoke a positive market response for his customized software.

Subsequently, when ACS merged with two successive engineering companies, the transactions were a friendly response to a mutual recognition of interest. ACS was looking for suitable market outlets for its innovative systems and the two companies were in need of revitalization.

LOCATE PATTERNS AND THEMES ACROSS THE EVENTS ANALYSED

Four patterns emerge from these events. First, Hines has remained, over the twenty-five years, the *dominant person* within the company. Second, a *spirit of technical innovation* has never waned, spearheaded by Hines himself. Third, ACS and then the ARK group has *vacillated* between being in and out of *control* of its business and economic environment. Fourth, *business and social innovation has been out of step* with its technical counterpart.

CROSS CHECK PATTERNS AGAINST CURRENT STRATEGIC CRITERIA

The chief executive of ACS is an analytical manager who is out of step with Hines' more innovative and intuitive approach. Whereas Cummings, of ACS, sees his rational approach to be an effective antidote to the environmental fluctuations, Hines is largely averse to such rationality.

Whereas, then, the professionally-based culture is aligned behind the Hines perspective, the emergent band of business managers are prone to come out on Cummings' side. To add to the complexity, Hines still sees the ACS division, because of its design and development orientation, as very much his baby.

At the present time *a meta culture has not yet arisen that can transcend the division* between impulse and intuition, on the one hand, and planning and analysis, on the other.

Dimension 2 – The organization and the nature of reality

Spatial reality

IDENTIFY A SET OF DECISIONS THAT INVOLVED STRATEGIC ISSUES
AND HIGH CONFLICT PRIOR TO RESOLUTION

'Spatially' related decisions can be divided between those involved with physical reality (fact); social reality (agreement) and subjective reality (personal feeling).

The removal of Jean Wilson Jean Wilson had originally been brought in, from one of the group's engineering companies, to introduce administrative systems into ACS. The way she had gone about it, for all her good intentions, proved to be insensitive and highhanded. As her unpopularity amongst the software engineers grew the MD decided to get rid of her.

As a subjective reality Bert decided that she was a disruptive influence on his division. As a physical reality, he had received at least a dozen serious complaints in the previous six weeks. As a social reality he sought out the opinions of his senior management, before making the decision.

The opening of the Japanese office The decision that Jim Hines made to open up a new design and development office in Tokyo was a totally subjective one. He did not consult with anybody, and his announcement of intent came as a total surprise to the management at ACS. The physical reality underlying Hines' decision was thus hidden from management and, as a social reality, no agreed strategy had been put on the table.

IDENTIFY THE KINDS OF CRITERIA THAT MAKE PEOPLE FEEL THAT A DECISION CAN BE REACHED

Whereas Bert Cummings seeks consensus, in his approach to decision making, Jim Hines adopts a more arbitrary stance. Whereas Cummings' decision to remove Wilson was a response to group feelings, Hines' decision to move into Japan was a response to his own market feel.

LOOK FOR PATTERNS AND THEMES

Cummings is constantly looking for implementable solutions, that is ones that carry majority agreement. Hines, on the other hand, is guided by his own personal inspiration and market intuition, often irrespective of his people's judgement.

ARTICULATE THE ASSUMPTIONS UNDERLYING THE CRITERIA

Cummings, and his fellow business managers, need to invoke co-operation from the software people, not being one of them! Hines, on the other hand, is not only the respected founder of the company, but as a software engineer himself, can command a great deal of respect among his fellow professionals, automatically.

Temporal reality

WHAT ARE THE ORGANIZATION'S BASIC ASSUMPTIONS ABOUT THE NATURE OF TIME, AND ABOUT THE WAY TIME IS STRUCTURED?

Orientation to the past There is a strong corporate orientation towards the past in that Hines almost singlehandedly transformed Britain's software industry, in the 1970s, bringing in a *spark and* a *flair* to it that had previously been lacking. Although he is now more of a businessman than a designer, employees still look back and up to him, as an innovative software engineer.

Orientation to the present Much of the unit's work is *project based*, and subject to tight deadlines. Moreover, there is a need to keep constantly on one's toes, ready to respond to a client's immediate needs. Although some design projects are of a one- or two-year duration, the majority have to be completed within six months.

Orientation to the future Hines' vision of the future, through which *Britain will lead the world* as an innovative software force, is never too far removed from his business and engineering surface. However, in the past three years, as the whole group has struggled to come to terms with itself as a merged entity, the futuristic vision has become somewhat blurred. If anything, within ACS, Cummings' five-year structure plan has become a more visible future prospect.

Time perspectives ACS is dominated by *polychronic* time, although both linear and cyclical time have their place. A multiplicity of projects occur at any one time, and an individual engineer will be involved with several of these at once.

At the same time, there are a few large projects, in which an individual will be totally *and linearly* involved for a period of, say, two years. Finally, due to clients' annual budgeting procedures there is a *cyclical* aspect to both marketing and project activity.

Dimension 3 – The nature of human nature

IDENTIFY ORGANIZATIONAL HEROES AND VILLAINS, SUCCESSFUL PEOPLE
AND FAILURES, AND COMPARE THE STORIES TOLD ABOUT THEM FROM THE
POINT OF VIEW OF WHAT IS SAID ABOUT THEIR HUMAN NATURE

Identify heroes *Jim Hines* is seen by the members of the design and development unit as *the ultimate hero*. He is uniformly respected as an innovator in his own right. As a *charismatic* personality, his mere presence inspires his engineers and designers to work harder and reach new heights. As the ultimate hero, his singlemindedness and uncompromising views are usually accepted without question.

Some of the hero worship directed at Hines is also extended to *Christine Welbeck*, the group design and marketing director, who has been with Hines from the beginning. Unlike Hines, Welbeck is an extremely approachable person, having more of a *magnetic* rather than charismatic personality, while also being an experienced software engineer.

Bert Cummings is the newly arrived hero of ACS itself. He is generally perceived as *authoritative*, well organized and business-like, rather than being a person with flair. At the same time, as a trained accountant he is willing to remain in the wings when specialized knowledge of software is required.

Identify villains Jean Wilson represents administration and *bureaucracy*, without carrying the authority and humility that Bert Cummings possesses. The many stories told of her interfering, unsympathetic and domineering personality have shown us that it is her personal characteristics as much as her role in the company which served to label her as a villain.

Mark Beck, recently appointed marketing manager within ACS, has been described as unpredictable, moody, an empire builder, sarcastic and abrasive. As a *temperamental* software engineer he has some of Jim Hines' negative qualities, but few of his positive ones. He is not respected as a designer, even if he has the 'artistic' temperament. Colleagues and staff are seldom sure of where they stand with him.

As we can see, heroes and villains are judged more according to their personal attributes than through their role in the company or their particular, professional background.

ANALYSE RECRUITMENT, SELECTION AND PROMOTION CRITERIA

Recruitment Christine Welbeck recruited the majority of the present ACS management, thus providing a channel for indirect influence through Jim Hines. Day-to-day recruitment of engineers and designers is undertaken by departmental directors. Bert Cummings gets involved with recruitment of senior staff, and there is, at present, no personnel manager to assist with recruitment.

Selection Software engineers and designers are selected partly on the basis of their design skills, but also on their degree of commercial awareness. The ARK group provides a pool of skilled managers from which ACS can benefit. The new systems implemented by Cummings are a product of his training in one of the recently acquired engineering companies.

Promotion There is a policy of promotion from within. All vacancies must be advertised internally. Bert Cummings is involved with promotions to assistant director and director level, where it is more likely that external candidates will be considered. Promotion is based on job performance and on the availability of suitable vacancies.

ANALYSE PERFORMANCE APPRAISAL CRITERIA: WHAT ARE PEOPLE
LOOKING FOR, WHAT KINDS OF COMMENTS ARE WRITTEN DOWN,
WHAT SEEMS TO BE VALUED AND WHAT IS NOT VALUED?

Divisional performance   A uniform bonus scheme operates in all ARK companies, and has been applied to ACS with little success. For if business is slack within a constituent engineering company ACS, through no fault of its own, will be penalized. The basis for the bonus award is divisional performance, that is actual versus budget.

Individual performance   Eighteen months ago a job plan review scheme was installed for the first time. Every six months employees are assessed on the basis of both their performance on the job, and on personal attributes.

Every person is assessed on five key areas by his or her immediate manager:

- acquired experience
- creative flair
- commercial awareness
- knowledge of software design
- personal flexibility.

Performance under each point is rated as excellent, good or fair.

ANALYSE REWARD AND CONTROL SYSTEMS FOR THE IMPLICIT
ASSUMPTIONS THAT UNDERLIE HOW THINGS ARE PROCESSED

Job appraisal, in practice, is kept to a minimum, and results are seldom followed up, implying great trust in the engineers and designers' abilities to do their jobs well. There is a great deal of faith placed in the judgement of design and development directors on personnel matters, such as promotion and recruitment.

LOOK FOR COMMON ASSUMPTIONS

The underlying assumption stems from Hines, that design and development personnel work more for *creativity and self-expression* than for security and self-advancement.

Heavy prominence is given to subjectively based personal attributes, as opposed to purely objective, professional criteria, drawing on the assumption that personal flair overrides depersonalized competence.

The bonus scheme promotes more competition than cooperation, arising out of the assumption that a competitive spur has to be imposed on top of an innate desire to cooperate amongst fellow professionals.

Dimension 4 – The nature of human activity

IDENTIFY A SET OF PROBLEMS FACED BY THE ORGANIZATION, IN ITS
HISTORY, WHERE THE PRIMARY SOURCE OF THE PROBLEM WAS OUTSIDE
FORCES THAT ACTED AS BARRIERS OR CONSTRAINTS

The problem identified here arose through a project undertaken with a major external client. The client, in fact, is a large multi-national in the mining business, Mintek.

WHAT WERE THE APPROACHES ADVOCATED FOR DEALING WITH THE
PROBLEM? DID THEY REFLECT ON THE COMPANY CULTURE?

ACS approached its client as a sensitive enabler, rather than as a hands-on problem solver, thereby trying to get the Mintek people to identify their thoughts and feelings towards their own corporate requirements. That caused immediate problems. Because Mintek is a company of accountants and mining engineers, rather than computer buffs, it lacked the overall intellect and insight to come up with any answers.

In other words, Mintek was looking for cut and dried solutions, whereas ACS was trying to involve the client in coming up with a customized package.

WHAT APPROACHES WERE ACTUALLY ADOPTED? DID THEY REFLECT ON
THE COMPANY CULTURE?

The design team continued to resist offering straightforward expertise, which left Mintek with the impression that ACS didn't really understand its problems. So Mintek felt it was not getting proper professional support.

WHAT ASSUMPTIONS WERE IMPLICIT IN THE APPROACHES ADOPTED?

Whereas ACS saw itself as an innovative and enabling company Mintek was demanding hand holding. While ACS saw itself as a group of talented designers, seeking client participation in decision making, Mintek was looking for technical support.

Dimension 5 – The nature of human relationships

IDENTIFY IMPORTANT RECENT DECISIONS AND EXAMINE WHETHER
THEY WERE MADE BY INDIVIDUALS, GROUPS OR BOTH, AND HOW
POWER WAS EXERCISED IN THE DECISION-MAKING PROCESS

The most recent important decision faced by ACS was whether or not to create a major new department specializing in retailing. Initially Bert Cummings consulted with two of his directors, Tim

Brock, head of manufacturing applications, and Mark Beck, head of divisional marketing.

Both of these directors were in fact potential leaders of the new department. Mark came back with immediate approval, having been issued a feasibility report, and Tim came up with a series of reservations. In the event Bert himself decided to go ahead with the new department, but to recruit someone from outside to run it.

EXAMINE ORGANIZATIONAL STORIES AND LEGENDS ABOUT HEROES
AND VILLAINS, TO DISCOVER HOW SUCH PEOPLE RELATED TO OTHERS
IN THE ORGANIZATION

There has been both resentment of, and admiration for, Bert Cummings. As a non-designer he is on a different wavelength to Jim Hines, and designers find him difficult to identify with. As a result his decision to bring in a retailing director from outside was not well received. On the other hand, all staff admired the way he got rid of Jean Wilson when it became obvious that her brand of bureaucracy was ineffective.

In essence the designers value his sense of fairness, and obvious administrative prowess, but they devalue his impersonality and cool objectivity.

Conversely, Mark Beck has another kind of double edge to him. He recently had a vehement argument with June Merton about a personnel issue. She, uncharacteristically, shouted back at him which made Mark all the angrier. In fact he stormed out of her office in a rage. June then burst into tears and received a lot of emotional support from colleagues.

A day later, though, the other side of Mark made itself apparent. He came into the office all remorseful and presented June with a bunch of roses, behaving as charmingly as he had behaved abrasively the day before.

As we can see, such displays of emotion, both negative and positive, are part and parcel of everyday human relationships at ACS.

EXAMINE CRITICAL INCIDENTS, SUCH AS INSTANCES OF
INSUBORDINATION, TO DETERMINE HOW THE ORGANIZATION DEALS
WITH VIOLATIONS OF AUTHORITY NORMS

The entire organization at ACS is characterized by informality, notwithstanding recent attempts to introduce more system and procedure. Bert Cummings has a conciliatory approach to violations of group norms. When, for example, Jean Wilson was removed from her post she was transferred to a more formally run part of the ARK group, rather than actually dismissed.

By and large people who do not like the system leave of their own accord, rather than being fired, and there is no shortage of jobs in the industry.

Bert Cummings usually starts by trying to reach decisions by consensus, but because of personality clashes often ends up behaving autocratically. Ultimately power lies in his hands and he is not afraid to use it.

The *conflict between design and flair*, on the one hand, *and system and management*, on the other, remains largely unresolved. Traditionally, and through the example set by Jim Hines, the former has been more important than the latter. More recently the balance has begun to swing the other way, but not yet markedly.

Staff turnover amongst professional engineering and managerial personnel at ACS is running at 15 per cent per annum. Although this is not above the industry norm, it is surprisingly high, given the high respect held for Jim Hines himself.

For all the attempts being made by Cummings to manage by consensus, the combination of relatively poor terms of employment and recurrent personality clashes makes for continuing dissatisfaction.

At the same time, it is important to stress that the software engineers and designers gain enormous satisfaction from the work itself, and from the innovative example that Hines has set them.

Refining, modifying and testing the model of culture

At this point we need to refine our original hypotheses, in the light of our findings to date. These hypotheses pertained to:

- the *informality* in working atmosphere
- the *pride* that the engineers and designers feel, because of their high profile within the industry
- the *poor communication* within the ARK group as a whole, and between professionals and management within ACS
- the *conflict* between ACS and group clients
- the comparative *lack of structure* and internal discipline.

The informal working atmosphere

This informal atmosphere was initially established by Hines himself at the pioneering stage of his company's development. It suited not only the stage of the business' development but also the creative nature of the task and people involved.

However, as ACS has grown and developed, together with the group as a whole, the family feeling has declined and personality clashes have accelerated. Cummings' desire to invoke consensus is thus often overtaken by the need to make autocratic decisions in the wake of such clashes.

It would seem that the culture has not grown up with the size and scope of the business to the extent that *informality*, supplemented by appropriate systems and procedures, could be mediated by consensus. While the ultimate hero, Jim Hines, projects more in the way of creative cut and thrust than familial coherence, the villains of the piece certainly exercise social *disruption*.

This disruptiveness is accentuated by the differences between Hines himself, the innovative designer, and his love of *creative chaos*, and Cummings, the authoritative executive, and his desire for stability and order. Whereas, if resolved at a higher level, this combination of freedom and order can be ideal for technical and commercial innovation, if left to run their own separate and unresolved courses, these opposites can tear one another apart.

Group pride

We observed considerable *pride* in the attitudes of the staff towards the group. The prestigious Hines name continues to attract high quality engineers and designers, despite the comparatively low salaries and fringe benefit.

This pride is reflected not only in the visible respect for Hines, and for the kind of design and development work that he advocates, but also in the attention paid to quality.

At the same time this very pride edges into *complacency*, to the extent that loss of business is seen to be debilitating not so much to ACS but to the client. The hunger for business, that was part and parcel of the pioneering company, seems to have gone.

Finally, the combination of pride and complacency can also lead to a degree of *insularity* in that the innovative stance that Hines had adopted has also led to a degree of dogmatism and defensiveness, which sometimes cuts ACS off from wider developments in the software field.

Poor communication

Communication within task and project groups is very strong. On the other hand, *communication across departments and projects is very weak*. The professional engineers and designers at ACS often feel they are kept in the dark, especially over important management decisions. While Bert Cummings has a policy of keeping his senior managers informed, this policy has not yet filtered down to the lower echelons.

As a consequence the professional workers have developed a resilient and widespread grapevine, conveying gossip and rumour at speed, often greatly distorting the truth. At the same time the troops feel that criticism flows freely while praise is all too scarce. The job plan review scheme, installed in part to remedy this situation, has proved to be ill-fitting within the informal culture.

Seemingly, also, the fact that Jim Hines is now relatively remote from ACS itself, what with his wider concerns as group chairman, means that the unit is cut off from many of the creation and resurrection stories that characterized their past.

Internal conflict

We found the engineers and designers to be of the opinion that the line and staff managers within the group, responsible for buying in their services, treated them in an impersonal, offhand manner. They were certainly not treated as one of the family.

This situation seems to be exacerbated by the so-called block fee system, whereby each ARK company pays a predetermined amount to cover design and development costs for a fixed period, thus *turning* such *development work into a commodity* rather than a creative and customized activity.

The fact that ACS is an integral part of the ARK group has in fact often proved less of a help and more of a hindrance. The constituent companies have resented having to keep their business 'within the family'. Moreover, the close links that supplier and customer necessarily have stops them from maintaining a professional distance.

Lack of structure and discipline

Until the appointment of Bert Cummings there was little attempt to impose formal control systems on ACS, other than those required to control specific projects of a fixed time duration. Traditionally that form of more pervasive control has been exercised by Hines himself.

Cummings was appointed, one year ago, with the objective of imposing more formal structure on ACS. At the same time Jean Wilson was brought in, as operations director, to inflict more structure at the operational level.

Because Cummings respected the software engineers for their technical and design competence, they respected him for his managerial ability. On the other hand, with Jean Wilson, no such mutual respect ever existed.

Meanwhile there continues to be a backlog of structural problems that had been swept under the carpet for many years, and formal planning processes, for the long term, are only beginning to be introduced.

Finally, despite attempts through the job review scheme to address the issue, software designers have remained commercially undisciplined. These *unbusinesslike attitudes* often spill over into relationships with clients, resulting in a poor impression of the company as a whole.

Our modified hypotheses therefore are as follows:

- the *informal* working atmosphere *is functional in* that it stimulates creativity and good working relationships within a project team, or *small group*; in its pioneering form it is *disfunctional in* that it is incapable of accommodating tasks and relationships in a *larger group* setting
- the engineers and designers, retaining their *pride* in their high profile group and founder, are at the same time somewhat *insular* and *complacent* when it comes to a wider commercial awareness and client empathy
- the relative *failure to upgrade the pioneering family feeling* into a more formalized and participative consensus, has resulted in poor communications within ACS as a whole, and between ACS and its internal and external clients
- a *comparative lack of structure* and discipline arises out of the failure of professionals and managers to differentiate and integrate their functions in a mutually satisfactory way.

Describing the organizational culture – as it is and might be

AN INFORMAL ATMOSPHERE

Informality becomes interspersed with formality, as part of a natural 'growing up' process. Formal job review and evaluation processes are intermeshed with informal *peer group pressures*.

The 'family feeling' that was associated with ACS' early days is resurrected, in a new more articulated form, through not only conventional newsletters and periodic get-togethers, but also through *deliberate enhancement of the natural* 'animateurs' and storytellers within the unit.

GROUP PRIDE

Pride in the company is deliberately fostered, as an *innovative entity technically, organizationally and commercially.* Role models of each are set in place. Hines' own development is reassessed in that triple light.

Interdivisional pride is fostered by not only a sharing of each other's history, but also by the *orchestration of joint projects.* Insularity is counteracted by the deliberate introduction of ideas and people from outside.

COMMUNICATION

The development of a *personnel and organization development function* that is woven into the design and development of systems, minimizes the chances of rejection. Integral to such a function is the maintenance and enhancement of communication, both formal and informal.

Personality clashes, dramatized through role plays in a developmental context, are used as a means of learning and *conflict resolution.*

Job review procedures, like a new profit bonus scheme, are subject to the same design and development disciplines as their technical equivalents. A software package is thus developed for these motivational and control purposes. *Design engineering and business management become irrevocably intertwined.*

STIMULATING COMMERCIAL AWARENESS

A strong element of the job review process is an assessment of commercial acumen, based not on a rational imperative but on an *aesthetic demand for wholeness.* In other words, the isolation of the technical and the commercial leaves an ugly gap in the business.

Conflicts between client and ACS are maximized in training exercises, and minimized in reality. Elements of conflict in reality are used as a basis for on-the-job learning. *Development becomes an integrated concern, not a technological feat in isolation.*

CONCLUSION

The rational approach developed by Edgar Schein is comprehensive, but only within its own sphere of reference. Being analytically based it inevitably highlights problems more than opportunities, and serves to inform rather than inspire, to reform rather than to transform.

Moreover, because of its scientific overtones, Schein's approach is strong on hypotheses, and the formulation of underlying assumptions, but weak on primal impact, developmental insight, or metaphysically-based inspiration. Having already worked with the primal approach to managing cultural change, I now turn to the other two.

The developmental approach to cultural evolution is manifest in the story of Psion, a high-tech company based in Britain.

9 The Story of Psion

Adam my son, listen. What is light? It's a kind of heat – an emission of energy. The rate of energy is power. Miss Ropley is wrong. I'll prove it to you.

MY CHILDHOOD*

'We became strong, tough and self-reliant'

A psychiatrist friend of mine recently asked me about my childhood. *It seemed as if my early life had been a normal one all round, except for one thing.* I didn't have a father. At least he died when I was very young.

In retrospect I can see that it had a big effect on me. I don't know what it is like to have a father. All I can remember is his voice.

My mother, therefore, had to bring up my sister Maryann and me on her own. She worked for long hours as a nurse to support us. I hardly saw her in the week – and in some ways she played the role of a father. I can remember her bringing back chocolates at eight o'clock at night, as we were going to sleep.

It was my *grandmother*, really, who played the role of mother. She was a wonderful person. She had a very full life and *was avant garde for her time*. Grandma went to university in 1908. I can remember her reading Winnie the Pooh to me in Latin! In fact she was not only an intellectual in her own right but also married to a professor.

The result of all this was that my mother and grandparents led very busy lives. They didn't have time to offer us the attention that other kids my age were used to receiving. Maryann and I couldn't help but notice our friends' parents coming along to their swimming galas. We were never in that position.

* This story is told in the first person by Psion's founder, David Potter, directly to the author.

So we reacted very strongly. *We built up our own little world. Maryann and I developed a remarkable sense of independence.* In fact, we dismissed other kids, who depended on their parents, as utter wimps. *We became tough, strong and self-reliant.* We made a fetish out of being that way.

That sort of childhood gave me certain strengths and weaknesses that I recognize to this day. I am less fearful and more confident in myself than other people I know. That's my strength. However I tend to rely on myself at times when I should be sharing my stresses and strains with others. That's my weakness.

'I was fascinated by machines and mechanical things'

I was *fascinated* as a young kid *by machines* and mechanical things. I used to take them to pieces to see how they worked. In those days, forty odd years ago, watches were made with a spring. Once you got the spring undone, no matter how hard you tried, it was impossible to get it back in working order. So, at the ages of six and seven, I must have undone a lot of watches and clocks!

At an older age I remember an old RAF aeroplane sitting in a garden nearby us. This was in Salisbury, in Rhodesia, where I spent much of my childhood and youth. The crashed aircraft was coated in aluminium. It had lots of *levers and instruments.* I was *absolutely intrigued* by them.

By the age of nine I had started to build things, like go-carts. *I went through a series of models, one more sophisticated than the other.*

I started by putting wheels on a piece of wood, sticking on a bolt up front, and using a piece of string to steer. That was the simplest version. It wasn't satisfactory. In fact it crashed. That was pre-historic engineering. By the age of ten I'd devised a super one to replace it.

I put together a series of metal levers, made up my own steering wheel, and fitted on the two sets of wheels underneath separately. I then went along to the local garage and *persuaded two hefty characters in charge* to braze or weld the whole thing together.

There was still one model to come, though, *the Lincoln Continental* of my motorized world. For this I took an old steering column out of a car, which had been lying out in some wasteland. I cut out the aluminium sheeting from the crashed aircraft, and moulded it to the frame, before spray painting the outside. *I loved producing it.* Occasionally friends would come along and help, but I did it, essentially, on my own.

IN THE COURSE OF MY YOUTH

'I was a very persistent problem solver'

In my early teens I gravitated towards more normal things, like making model aircraft, and *by the age of 13 or 14 I was becoming more intellectually aware.* Calculus, for example, really began to interest me. I was good at maths and mental arithmetic, slower than some of my friends, but *a very persistent problem solver.*

At the same time, I became interested in motor bikes. I can remember, at 15, getting hold of a 50cc model, and reconstructing it. *I can vividly recall testing the magneto by holding hands with my friend while we grasped onto each end of the wire.* We pushed the bike and the shock passed through us. Incredibly we got it to work.

To this day I love little machines of all kinds. My three young boys and I, at this very moment, are putting together a radio-controlled airplane at home. We ran in the engine last weekend. I don't know who enjoyed it more, me or them. *They're such beautiful things, those little engines.*

'I was a romantic at heart'

Science and engineering weren't my only passions, though, as a youth. In fact I can remember this dreadful character in Salisbury giving me a psychological test at the age of 16. I scored very high in two discrepant areas. One was mathematics, that was an interest rather than an aptitude. The other was *the outdoor life.*

I've always had this kind of *physical and visual sense.* I have always enjoyed nature. When, at the age of 20, I came from Africa to Europe, I can still remember how it hurt, physically. In fact it left a big *hole in my life.* There is, and always has been, this sense of belonging to Africa which is the unfulfilled part of me.

So I have this fond image that in my sixties I'll lead a different kind of life from the one I am leading now, in Africa or in the East. The image is one of myself as a teacher. Teachers should be older people, drawing on their lifetime experience, on the wealth of ideas and experiences that they have accumulated.

In fact when I was living in Rhodesia many businesses around me were at a pioneering stage of their development. In my teens I became interested in *business* as an idea. Business and trade carried a romantic image – *one of the roots of the world.* Money was merely a means to an end, a means of developing things, of rendering ideas practicable and achievable.

I have always been a romantic at heart. I was shocked the other day to hear the daughter of a wealthy friend of ours say, at the age of 20, that money was the most important thing in her life. At that age I would probably have said ideas and sex, with sex representing the broader physical and sensual aspects of my life.

My love of ideas, and my interest in learning, drew me then, as it does now, to befriend many of the Jews in Salisbury. Because my stepfather was Jewish I had some blood connection with Judaism, but more as a way of being than as a religion. I have always respected both the feeling of warmth and the love of learning of Jewish people.

In my late teens I had also become politically conscious. My maternal grandparents were Victorian Christians who had a profound belief in God. My mother and I were irreligious. In fact I hated going to church and to Sunday school. But the sense of morality pervaded throughout. Most of my mother's friends were politically liberal in their views, and this percolated through to me.

After leaving school I applied for a scholarship to Cambridge. In between finishing in Rhodesia – because of the difference in academic timing between the two hemispheres – and going onto England, I went to the University of Cape Town. Intellectually it was dull, but it certainly was an experience.

ENTERING YOUNG ADULTHOOD

'I wasn't one of them, or them'

Staying in residence, I found the initiation ceremonies that we underwent quite bizarre, even appalling. *They certainly taught me about human nature, at its most raw.* I saw people literally destroyed by the initiation rituals. It was *nineteenth century* when the rest of the world had moved to the twentieth.

I came to England in October 1963, at the age of 20. It was a complete *culture shock*, in more ways than one.

At Cape Town *I had been top of the academic tree.* I graduated in my year with four firsts. But suddenly I found myself, at Cambridge, no longer the top dog. People of my age were much more cultured and sophisticated. I found myself feeling intellectually deprived.

I had also *entered into the British class system*, with a vengeance. There were 200 at Trinity, the majority of whom were from public schools. A good proportion of these students were there through class privilege, but the best of them were terrific. I can remember one young fellow who was an expert on Egyptian archeology at the age of 19. He had an international reputation in his field already. I had some catching up to do.

That got my back up. *I had to prove myself.* I wanted to show everyone that those lost souls from the empire could compete. I wanted to test my mettle.

All in all these were dangerous as well as exciting times, or so it seemed to me then. It was like entering Lord of the Rings, or Dungeons and Dragons. One wasn't sure of oneself. I had come from sunlit Salisbury to the blackened fog of London. *England was black and Victorian in its feel.*

Satanic and dark. Huge cities with large buildings. All black and grimy. *I was all by myself.*

I dragged myself through this quagmire, and got a first for part one of my physics degree. I learnt a huge amount. I had been culturally very narrow. I lacked any idea of Marxism or Socialism. I learnt rapidly. After all, there was a revolution going on in the sixties.

The public school boys still walked around in ties and grey flannels. They were the 'Eli', as H.G. Wells would have said. The 'Morlocks', in his terms, were the grammar school boys from the North, dressed in donkey jackets and jeans. The Beatles were just emerging. Macmillan was on his last legs. Harold Wilson was about to project 'the white heat of technology' onto the general populace.

I had friends from both sides of the class divide. *I wasn't one of 'them' or 'them'* and so could be accepted by both. Both groupings saw me as 'that peculiar colonial with a funny accent'. I also had to support myself through my studies, on and off, and took odd jobs like driving lorries and working in warehouses.

'Physics taught me how to gauge quality'

Intellectually Cambridge was enormously stimulating. *I enjoyed mathematical physics hugely.* I remember the night when I learnt to understand relativistic electrodynamics completely. I got a huge kick out of it. Maxwell, Lorenz, Einstein . . . *it was an incredibly beautiful theory* – the most beautiful constructs made by man.

These contemporary concepts drew on a huge amount of historical and scientific background. As a result you were able to express, in a few lines, statements which covered a great diversity of physical experience. The existence of such *theory illustrates that there is an unbelievable harmony* in nature and in the universe.

The process of problem solving and the nature of such harmony is the same thing for me. One sets oneself a proposition and the problem comes and shows that the potential solution is consistent with the tenets of the framework in which you operate.

Mathematical physics is the most beautiful subject, and the most banal, because it deals with things that are simple. You can only apply the rigours of mathematics to natural, physical phenomena. It's a terrible discipline to impose on oneself. It *teaches one how to gauge the true quality of an idea.*

'I am stretched two ways – between engineer and physicist'

Loving electrodynamics, then, I wanted to pursue my theoretical work in that area. I was tempted by solid state physics but, after graduating from Cambridge, decided to pursue my doctoral work in plasma physics. I enjoyed the intellectual aspects of astrophysics, on the one hand, and the potential applications of fusion physics, on the other.

I was being stretched apart by *the problem that has always enveloped me – intellectual involvement* on the one hand, *versus practical application* on the other. If you'd have asked me, in childhood, what I wanted to be, I'd have said 'an engineer'. If you'd have asked me in my youth, I'd have said, 'a physicist'.

The group I joined for my doctoral work, at Imperial College in London, was working on thermonuclear fusion. This research involved taking a piece of the sun and containing it within a magnetic box. It was a wonderful idea, holding in prospect an endless source of power and energy.

The subject was a young one when I started my research. It needed more study. The specific research in which I became involved, though, was slightly different. The mathematics underlying nuclear fusion is complex and non-linear. *It lent itself to computer-based analysis.*

THE RESPONSIBILITIES OF ADULTHOOD

The creation of Psion

'I became an acknowledged expert'

So I began, in my late twenties, to become involved in studying these mathematical systems by computer. *I investigated the computer as an applied tool.* We studied such problems as why galaxies form themselves into bars and spirals.

We began by working with basic, physical principles, branched out into complexity, and then simplified down. I suppose that is what I was doing instinctively as a kid, when I was building ever more sophisticated go-carts.

With the computer, though, you can simulate complex models. This fascinated me. I became one of *the first* researchers, in fact, *to apply the computer to the analysis of multidimensional phenomena in plasma physics*. It was very stimulating, intellectually. I was invited to America and became an acknowledged expert in the field. So I became involved in an academic career.

I had originally intended to enter into a business or engineering environment after my doctorate. But an academic career has its own momentum like a canoe disappearing down rapids. It was enjoyable. I was now married. It was a difficult path to turn off.

'I turned £5000 into £50,000'

In 1974, at the age of 31, I went to UCLA in California, to pursue my academic career. That was the year in which the stock market came crashing down. In November I wrote to my bank manager in England. *I had been following the fortunes of a few companies pretty closely*. So I told him to divide up the £3000 I had on deposit and invest equal amounts in six different companies.

I had this belief, you see, that *the market was ruled by fear, fashion and instinct*. I knew, therefore, that the fashion would change. *I knew I had to make money*. My salary was about to take a nosedive, once I returned to Britain, and I had a new family to support. My wife Elaine and I had established roots in the UK, and we wanted to return.

I learnt a lot, then, about the world of public companies. I realized by this time that because I was good at research I could devote myself to studying sectors of the market with great care. I was very successful as a result.

I turned £5000 into £50,000 in two to three years. After Elaine and I had used up £45,000 on a deposit for a new house, I turned the £5000 left over into another £50,000.

'I wanted to contribute to the Silicon Age'

The nineteen sixties was the era of mainframes. While I was at UCLA two important things happened. Firstly, *I saw a couple of guys* in Santa Barbara *build a specialized computer in their garage*. To be able to build such a sophisticated machine in a back yard amazed me.

Secondly, the concept of a processor on a chip had arrived. *The computer was beginning to become an 'everyman' thing*. Instead of talking to 20 or 30 people, *I suddenly saw the chance of talking to 30 million*.

It had become clear to me by the late seventies, that something as profoundly important as the invention of the lathe was going on. In the 1800s the lathe had generated steam engines, motor cars, and petrol engine aeroplanes for a century to follow. Now the silicon chip was about to move us radically on. After the stone age, the bronze age and the iron age *we were now moving onto the age of silicon.*

There are chances in one's life to participate in great movements. I wanted to be part of this one. We can't all be Einsteins. That does not matter. One can still make a contribution. The prospect of remaining a mere expert in a narrowly-based academic discipline appalled me.

Moreover, *I still had this sense of independence* that enabled me to venture out where others feared to tread. I wanted to bring together the intellectual, the practical and the commercial sides of me. I was also a romantic at heart.

'I believe in starting small'

I founded my company with £50,000 start-up capital. Elaine and I had two children at the time, both of whom were very young. *I had responsibilities*, therefore, *and was not prepared to gamble my money away.* There were, in fact, two ways to go – the organic approach or the big bang. I profoundly believe in the first. Start small. *Get the essence of the thing working before you move on.*

Take the example of a contemporary company, IPS. An American team of technologists and managers were recently encouraged to set up a silicon-based company in one of our development areas. The government supported the operation to the hilt.

The idea was to produce silicon chips that were not only logic devices but could also accommodate a great deal of power. Take a computer printer, for example. You have to control it logically, and also drive its motor. It makes sense, therefore, to put the logic and the power together on one chip.

That was the concept. These guys had the expertise in design. The market potential was there. They should have used the design and marketing expertise they uniquely possessed, and subcontracted the manufacturing to an existing company, like Motorola, who had excess chip-making capacity. In other words, they should have begun with 5 million poundsworth of capital instead of the fifty million they raised to start an entire foundry.

'I was in touch with the technology and the marketplace'

Now IPS has gone into receivership. That was the big bang approach. I stood at the opposite extreme. I started by myself in a small room. I had no clear business plan. *I was open to a wide range of opportunities. I knew the technology and was in touch with the way the market was evolving.*

People were still playing with the newly emerging electronic devices. Apple II and the Commodore PET had both just come out. People were wondering what to do with them. The technology was still terribly primitive.

In 1980 Sinclair came out with his ZX80. It was a classic marketing coup. A personal computer for £99! It seemed a ludicrous idea at the time. Computers were things only used by billion pound bureaucracies like the Gas Board!

I didn't have the capital to become involved with hardware, but I had the knowledge and experience to know what I was doing in software terms. *I could identify the wheat from the chaff.* By 1981 I had also got to know both Sinclair and Acorn, the major British players in the personal computing fields.

'I bulldozed my way into Sinclair'

In fact I bulldozed my way into Sinclair. I was a nothing in the industry but *I had 'chuzpah'*, or what you may call cheek! Once I saw the ZX80 in operation, and was suitably impressed, I wrote to Clive Sinclair and said I wanted to meet him. I told Clive that I could organize a distribution deal for him in South Africa, because of my contacts there. He said he wasn't interested, personally, but passed me onto his export people.

I approached them in London. They said 'Nice to meet you, but we already have a distributor in South Africa'. So I decided to check them out. I flew out to Johannesburg, armed with a ZX80, and first ensured that I would be able to pick up some customers. Having secured potential orders I then made it my business to find out how good Sinclair's local agent was. It turned out that the South African company was very limited.

So I told the export people when I returned to London and, sure enough, they gave me the business.

'The name we came up with was Psion'

In the meantime Elaine and I had talked a great deal about a company name. I had, in fact, bought a company off the shelf for £100. It was called Redcheer! The name we came up with for the business was 'Psion'. PSI not only stood for Potter Scientific Instruments but also was a Greek letter. I added 'on' for the sake of uniqueness. We needed a name, moreover, which would be acceptable anywhere in the world.

'I packaged the product in an upmarket way'

While I was negotiating a sales agreement with Sinclair, in 1980, I was developing a new business on the software side. I probed my personal contacts and combed the magazines for computer games software. I sorted out the good from the bad. A classic example of what I considered 'good' software was a chess game produced by an eccentric engineer from British Airways.

Andy Laurie worked on mainframes, in the company, and played chess at home. He was also what you might call a computer freak! He produced a chess program for the ZX80 in his spare time, and sold a few by advertising in the trade magazine. I came to Laurie with a proposition. I told him I could sell many more of his product, by a more professional marketing approach, if he was willing to operate on a licence basis.

Once he agreed I got him to tidy up a few things on the programme. *I packaged the product in an upmarket way and found a manufacturer to duplicate in volume.* I did it all, moreover, *cost-effectively*, sending samples to distributors all over Europe. With this particular product, and subsequently with selected others, I began to ship serious quantities.

Cassettes began to pile up in my room, bulging out into the corridor. With the income generated I brought in Charles Davies, who had done his doctorate with me at Imperial. *He was very bright and able.*

'Now there were two of us, and more'

So there were now two of us sitting in a little office in London's Edgware Road. We began to develop our own games software, working first with the Acorn machine. We started selling products on an even bigger scale. The stocks were now all over the place. We just had to find bigger premises.

I searched for ages. We had been paying a mere £40 a month, which was cheap. Eventually I found Huntsworth Mews near Baker Street. There were 3500 square feet of studio space going for only £2 per square foot. We jumped at it. This was at the end of 1981.

We rapidly recruited four new software people, including a New Zealander, Chris Jacobs, who seemed to appear from nowhere. He was an electrical engineer with software experience who had an outstanding degree to his name. Another of our new recruits, David Mugglestone, was a refugee from South Africa.

By this stage *we had become far more sophisticated than our competitors* in the leisure software field. We also had recruited people with flair and originality who were willing to accept a pretty unconventional job. Whereas Acorn was a child of Cambridge, we fed off Imperial College, but were generally more catholic in our recruitment than they were.

The transition from pioneering to management

'Psion was beginning to stand out'

By 1982 we had been approached by both Sinclair and Acorn to produce software under licence. At this stage the big retailers were just beginning to become interested. We were moving out of the embryonic stage. *Psion* moreover, with its high-level software team and good facilities, *was beginning to stand out*.

In February 1982 the buyer of W.H. Smith came to see us. He wanted to order big quantities. At the same time Sinclair approached us. They proposed an even bigger deal, but under the Sinclair label. The name Psion would be written in small letters at the lower end of the cassette cover. I decided to do the deal with Sinclair, because of the potential wider market. So I had to turn down W.H. Smith orders. That hurt terribly.

The volume of sales, through Sinclair, was so big that it surprised us. We sought suppliers all over the country. *We knew that the quality of supplies would be crucial.*

It was remarkable what we had achieved by the end of 1982. Our turnover in 1981 had been £120,000 – with a net profit of £12,000. A year later it had gone up to £1.5 million, with a net profit of £620,000. Our return on sales was 40 per cent and on capital astronomic. It was usurious.

'We grabbed the opportunity'

Meanwhile, in the Spring of 1982 Sinclair had come to us with a new machine. It seemed to be a great product, but he had no software for it. *We grabbed the opportunity.*

Sinclair gave us the prototypes to work on early in the day. The trouble was that they were still at an embryonic stage of their development. That presented us with a problem. So Charles Davies and I came up with this inventive idea.

We realized that Sinclair's architecture was similar to that of the more expensive TRS80, which was already on the market. So we bought ten of these Tandies, developed the software on them, and then switched the memory from the TRS machines to the Sinclair.

The problem we still had, though, was our lack of any hardware expertise. So we recruited Andy Clegg. He'd been working for

British Aerospace. Andy was academically outstanding, but he had a bit of a chip on his shoulder from his experience of bureaucratic middle-management. He was a difficult character to manage at first, but he has since turned out to be *the salt of the earth*.

In 1982 we developed a huge range of software. I myself wrote some of it, working around the clock. My half-brother in South Africa, Colly Myers, was also writing material for us. I can remember how he produced this spreadsheet package, Vu-Calc, in just a week. It was dramatic. *He went seven days without any sleep*.

People were amazed with the way Sinclair's 'Spectrum' eventually turned out. It took off like a train. By the autumn of 1982 we had 16 people, but we all got involved in the shipment of boxes.

The consolidation of Psion

'We began to have time to think'

By this time we also began to have a bit of time to think about our future. That made a big difference. We were making huge profits and were building up considerable cash reserves. So we started to ask one another, should we continue to plough our energy, skills and resources into games software?

It was a low entry business. We'd done it ourselves on a shoestring. I began to question the longevity and utility of the games market. Perhaps it was my Victorian attitude coming through. *We couldn't really see the useful applications.*

We had produced some superb games products, like Psion Chess and Flight Simulator. We also produced a 3D Graphics pack for £9.95. It was in fact based on very sophisticated mathematics. *We wanted to open people's minds*, to interest and to intrigue. Flight Simulator, in fact, had a real aerodynamic model.

So *our corporate culture was earnest, academic and intellectual*. We were not interested in producing video games. I was approaching 40. We didn't wear ear rings. We knew about very sophisticated things on computers.

We pondered upon all of this and eventually decided on two things. Firstly, *we were going to diversify into products of longer-term benefit*. Secondly, *we had to invest in the best possible facilities*.

'It was now time to build our foundry!'

We had a team of outstanding quality. Charles Davies, Colly Myers or Chris Jacobs could stand up to or, indeed, outstrip their peers anywhere in the world. We could afford to invest in the long term, so as to be able to apply our abilities to the full. *It was now time to build our foundry!*

So we bought in an entire VAX super minicomputer system from DEC for cash. We wanted to use the system for development purposes. Only Marconi in Britain and a few other large companies in America were using such equipment for similar purposes.

We decided to diversify into two areas. On one hand we wanted to develop *integrated application software* for business use. We thought of this at the end of 1982, before Lotus 1, 2, 3 and Symphony had appeared on the scene. It was a massive task to undertake. In addition, we wanted to develop a *handheld data base machine.*

At this stage we were a development company, adding value through software. We did not have any marketing people as such. Our products were sold through original equipment manufacturers particularly through Sinclair. *I ran the whole business side*, though Amanda, who is still with us today, had joined as an administrative assistant.

In the early part of 1983 Peter Norman was brought in as our first business executive, to look after sales. We also brought in a second executive, at the time, to look after our suppliers.

Although I had sewn our first marketing seeds in the earliest stages of Psion's business operation, our added value since had been provided by design and development. That produced both strengths and weaknesses. The main strength was our lack of marketing costs. Our main weakness was our dependence on Sinclair. We realized all that and decided to broaden and expand.

It was Charles' idea to bring in the VAX machines. That decision proved to be as important for us as the invention of the wheel or the lever was for society at large. *Instead of dealing with a particular microprocessor we brought in a tool that could deal with all of them,* in the production of software.

'Eureka'

The background to the development of our hand-held machine was important. Towards the end of 1982 IBM and Victor (Sirius) came out with their first 16-bit machines. I was very impressed. These machines had real quality. The graphics were superb and they had the capability of large amounts of memory. Moreover, they were purpose-built for the office environment.

The trouble was, though, that *people were using the machine for arcane purposes,* like storing suppliers' lists. It was madness. I can vividly remember Charles and I having lunch together and saying to one another, 'If we could produce such a machine for simple databases more cheaply and simply there had to be a huge market'.

The idea tied in with our proposal for integrated applications software, which we subsequently called 'Xchange'. One system, in both cases, would deal with lots of applications. It's like the natural law that covers a diversity of physical experience.

We knew that with our limited resources we could only compete if we were totally radical in our approach. So during the course of 1983 we recruited talent on both the development and executive sides. During that year our turnover increased to £3 million, with a net profit of £1.5 million.

The aim was to launch both of our new products in 1984. On the applications software side, in fact, we had been approached by Sinclair in the spring of 1983. He had come up with this new business-oriented machine, the QL. We had submitted our proposal for the software, and we won the contract. We looked forward to a sure-fire royalty stream.

Soon afterwards ICL came along to us, via Sinclair. The main board of ICL's 'One Per Desk' was the same as the QL's. A deal had been struck between Wilmot and Sinclair, though ICL was operating along a longer timeframe.

So we had the two biggest computer companies in Britain come to little Psion. It should have been a cornucopia. But by the end of 1983 Sinclair was getting behind schedule. I started negotiating with some development capital people to cover a prospective shortfall in 1984.

'Laying deep foundations'

At the same time, with the development of our handheld database machine, which had since evolved into a small computer, we had to create a sales force. We had to gear up for the production, marketing and launch not only of our applications software but also of our handheld 'Organizer'.

1984 was a seminal year for us. We were becoming concerned about Sinclair. He was responsible, at this time, for 97 per cent of our sales. This was not a position of integrity for the long run.

The QL was launched at the beginning of 1984. In fact we couldn't believe it. It was so far from being finished. Also the microdrive that Sinclair had developed to replace the more expensive floppy disk seemed to us highly suspect. The launch was a great extravaganza. But product shipments turned out to be way behind schedule. We were going to be in a difficult position.

We launched our 'Organizer' in June 1984. Sales were disappointing. We were covered financially by a deal I had made with a merchant bank. Then when another prominent merchant bank heard of the deal they put their oar in. They wanted a part in the action. The two banks got together and began to put the screws on us.

Ten days before signing with them I was contacted by an old friend, Theo Loeb, who had access to finance. 'Why haven't you approached me?', he said. I was delighted to hear from him. I didn't like the way the two banks had clubbed together at our expense. So I told Theo I'd give him ten days to come up with a better deal.

In fact Theo and his financial partner came up with similar terms, and within the time I had allotted. Since then my relationship with Theo Lamb and Danny Fiszman has evolved excellently.

In 1984 Psion made a substantial loss. In financial terms it was a very bad year. *In real terms 1984 was a turning point for us.* It was the year when our long-term future was laid.

'We created a marketing function'

Our future was laid in two particular ways. Firstly we succeeded in starting up a crucial second side to our business, that is the marketing side – the image and communications facet. In fact *we laid down the skeleton of our self image.* For the first time some of the values of the company were articulated. Secondly we *brought* both of *our* new *developments*, the applications software and the handheld computer, *into volume production.*

While that was going on our relationship with Sinclair was deteriorating. The OEM side, in fact, underperformed seriously. If it hadn't been for our successes in developing our own sales the situation would have been terminal (see Figure 9.1).

Of course during 1984 and 1985, on top of Sinclair's impending demise, there was the great hiatus in the whole microcomputer market. There had been an absurd bullishness in the market in the two preceding years. Then, in a matter of weeks, for example, INTEL's book to bill ratio – that is prospective sales compared with actual – changed from 1.8 to 0.5. Disastrous. The company suffered massive losses in 1985. Sinclair went to the wall. Acorn had to be rescued twice.

The speed of it all surprised us, but *we knew the downturn was imminent because of the weak companies and the weak markets.* The microcomputing and PC markets had mushroomed extraordinarily in the early eighties. Everybody jumped on the bandwagon. They expected that everyone – including people, chickens and pigs – would be using the products!

The whole industry was very young, all the way from the components to the machines. Because of that immaturity it had a rough and tumble character to it. It's a bit like the motor car industry must have been in 1910. There's an atmosphere of the wild west frontier.

So during 1984 we still had some revenues from our OEM sales, but not as much as we would have wanted. At the same time Organizer 1, our handheld computer, sold 30,000. It was only modestly successful financially.

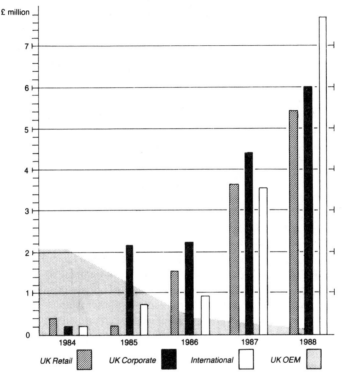

Figure 9.1   Sales history (in millions of £s)

The fundamental engineering design of the machine was very good, but *we were a small company trying to educate a large market*. The question of brand image, we discovered, is a major one. Rolls Royce or Hewlett Packard have developed theirs over many many years. Yet our modest sales did fund our historic and prospective research and development. In addition *we learnt an awful lot about our marketplace*.

What we didn't succeed in doing, first time around, was establishing a wider distribution market. In fact, unexpectedly, we found ourselves selling mainly to large corporations for specialized applications. The most prolific case in point was Marks and Spencer.

ENTERING MIDLIFE

Transition between managed organization and enabling company

'We enabled one another to develop'

Over the last 30 to 40 years large companies like Marks and Spencer have become more and more reliant on their systems. These systems have been combined together to become like their *nervous system, capturing and recording information for use by the body of the corporation.*

Today, however, 40 per cent of the workforce is mobile. That causes problems. *Imagine a human being with his fingers and toes detached from his nervous system.* People are on the move and they require the portable communications systems to connect them with the central nervous systems of their organizations. *That's where we come in.*

Marks and Spencer approached us in 1984, but with a slightly different problem. They were going to introduce their charge card in April of the following year. A year or so before they had put the problem to their computer services department of how they would control and validate their card.

They expected to be handling several million accounts by 1987, making the company one of the biggest credit card operations in the country. How were they going to validate their use? As we knew, Marks and Spencer believe in controlling and systematically managing absolutely everything.

The team responsible for their card validation approached us, having heard about Organizer 1 through our general marketing. *We listened to what they had to say. We said we could do it in the required timescale.* Our charges were, to their eyes, tremendously low.

So they invited us to illustrate how our system would work. We did that in a week. *They were very excited.* They said they'd order a few hundred from us. They wanted to see the concept, including the software, working. We pulled together a software team and accomplished the task in the required timescale.

On the basis of what we had achieved, in that January of 1985, they said they would proceed, subject to a trial in Scotland by February. That trial represented a substantial software task. But we succeeded, and in March received substantial orders from Marks.

We supplied all that they required and by the end of March our systems were installed in all their stores. *They worked beautifully.* They were ready to introduce their charge card system right on time in April.

Marks and Spencer, as we have since been told, *have never lost any information on a Psion system*. The company was impressed. The board got to know all about it.

They could see, as we did, all manner of other applications for our handheld machine. In fact they asked us to implement a trial for a price look-up system. This was a much bigger project than the charge card. The trial, in May-June 1985, was very successful. So it was implemented nationwide by the autumn.

Meanwhile, during the month of May, we were intrigued to find a pile of cash registers dumped in our Huntsworth Mews premises. These were followed by a succession of executives from Marks and Spencer. 'Now that you have produced a charge card and a price look-up system for us', they said, 'how about coming up with a complete point-of-sale system?'

They wanted to be able to log central data at the till point without any cumbersome wires. In other words they were looking for a computer till with information on it running off batteries. They wanted us to rip out the innards of the machines they had supplied and implant our own system.

'We'll take the money we had originally allocated to NCR', they said, 'and give it to you to develop a system for a trial in our Islington store in September. At the same time, we're undertaking trials with IBM and with ICL in other locations.'

We implemented the till system to their specification, and within the time schedule specified, including both the hardware and software. On the basis of that trial the board decided to go for a SPOS (stand-alone point-of-sale) system, that we had developed in conjunction with them, in the majority of their stores.

Then came the next step. 'You've got superb expertise in software and microelectronics', they said. 'Now *get into bed with a partner* on the cash register side. The people we'd like you to go with are Sweda. They have the expertise in cash register maintenance and manufacturing.'

They then sent our original SPOS specification to all the major vendors, including IBM, ICL and Thorn EMI. They were all asked to pitch for the contract, and three were shortlisted, including ourselves. However, after we had formed a very good relationship with Sweda, they were suddenly taken over by Hugin. Neither Marks nor ourselves were pleased with this change, but there was nothing we could do about it.

Finally, when it came to the implementation of the big trial, we delivered our side of the contract on time and Hugin failed to deliver on theirs. So Thorn EMI got the contract. SPOS, developed by Psion, was supplied and implemented by Thorn. A sad cameo.

But while Hugin no longer supplies anything to M & S, this year we did record business with them. *Psion's handheld computer is used more and more pervasively within Marks*, not least of all as back-up to SPOS. It's also used for stocktaking, for the cashing up of tills, and for a whole plethora of retailing applications. Yet, having learnt from our Sinclair experience, this time we have made sure that Marks and Spencer represents no more than 10 per cent of our overall sales.

In fact, our two companies meet every week. It so happens we are physically located close to one another. *They're a very demanding customer but a fulfilling one at that*. We've learnt a lot from them. They've been tremendously supportive. We're much closer to them than a conventional supplier. *They can use us as a* kind of *stalking horse*. We've acted as pioneers, on their behalf, for all sorts of things.

We're young and nimble. They're old and wise. *It's like big brother, little brother*.

'We're becoming the largest supplier in the world'

It's an interesting facet of Psion that, as a smaller company, we've been able to work extremely well with large ones. I suppose we have that element of seriousness, of quality, and of organization that attracts them to us. We could have taken over the whole of the M & S contract from Hugin, but that would have meant sacrificing our development on other fronts. I made the strategic decision not to do that.

As a result of the technical and market experience we had gained, coupled with the onward march of the silicon industry, our handheld machine underwent a major development from September 1985 to the end of April 1986. It *evolved radically in terms of capability and adaptability*. Above all, through the development of our software systems, we were ready, in the spring of 1986, to launch Organizer II.

Organizer II is like Apple II. Both are hugely successful products. I never heard of Apple I! Organizer II is like Apple II in more ways than one – applications, distribution channels, degree of innovation. From what I know in *1988 we'll be the largest supplier of handheld computers in the world*. By that time we're likely to be shipping nearly 200,000 units plus per annum.

Indeed the potential markets run into millions of units. We're *innovating and creating a whole new market area*. In May 1986 we were producing 200 units a month; by the summer of 1988 we had gone up to 20,000.

'Enabling a customer to solve his problems'

In essence we had developed a whole new market. One of the things we had learnt, moreover, was how unique the computer was as a product. The computer is unique to sell because, unlike a pen or a car, it is not an end in itself. The computer itself does not do anything. It needs software for that. Therefore *a good computer product is one that can accommodate thousands of potential applications,* each one of which can enable a particular customer to solve his problems.

That's the most interesting thing about a computer, which also makes its design extremely difficult. How do you build such generality of application into its architecture? That quality applies just as much to handheld computers as to mainframes.

We managed to build a plethora of prospective applications into our machine.

In other words, we made Organizer II tremendously 'soft', so that the customer could mould it to his own requirements. We built in a general operating system and a powerful language that enabled users to program the machine for a multitude of applications. Finally, we also generalized the peripherals.

'We've developed in stages'

Like our product, our organization has developed in stages. *If a company is learning, it inevitably evolves and grows.* The way we were structured, as 5 people, is totally different from the way we became organized, as 35. Again, as 120 people we are now totally different. In fact we are getting to the size where we might be in danger of losing our family spirit.

We're going to have to solve that. A new recruit can find himself, now, removed from the heart of the company. Yet our strength has always been the tremendous sense of involvement that we have been able to generate. So I have begun to think of ways of restructuring in order to make us spiritually more effective.

It's all about learning. If there is growth there is flux. Organizations fail when they begin to stop questioning. Through 1982 and 1983 Psion was led from the top. It was *leadership by example.* The less able looked up to the more able. Individuals sought to gain respect, and exercised respect. There was also tremendous peer group pressure.

In 1983 and 1984 the first attempt was made to introduce some form of management structure. Up to that time the structure was informal and implicit. Now we brought in executives with titles.

Formal structures were introduced in the face of increasing complexity. I no longer made all the business decisions. We introduced groups and departments into the organization.

In 1985 and 1986, as the company grew larger, we began to develop a wide range of formal controls, both computer-based and manual. We were also influenced, at that stage, by the difficult year we had undergone in 1984. If you like, we began to articulate our nervous system. We introduced sophisticated budgeting systems, though we built in ample scope for discussion around them.

We don't believe in hierarchy for hierarchy's sake. Everyone here calls me David. But we do believe firmly in planning and control, and in clarity of communication.

'We've achieved a fusion between development and marketing'

When you think about it, *you communicate in everything your company does*. You communicate within the company, to your staff, and around the company, to your agencies – writers, designers, artists.

The first thing I did with the onset of Organizer II was to produce a booklet on its features and benefits. I produced it three months prior to launch, covering the what, where and why of the product.

When the product was launched we focused on a restricted set of people. *We concentrated on the computer* cognescenti, that is the opinion leaders in the data processing world. We produced large, and very detailed brochures. We pumped out hundreds of thousands of them, directed at the computer literati. We knew that they were our prospective ambassadors. They, in turn, would communicate with a wider group.

It is only now, more than a year after the launch, that we have begun to advertise in the lay press. 'Organizer II, like Rover – woof, woof – is a man's best friend.' We can advertise like that now because we have laid all the groundwork. We've repeated the same process in France, *creating progressively wider ripples*.

In the same way as we are broadening our market, so we are broadening our product line. We have been engaging in intensive research and development for the last three years, working on what we call our SIBO technology – a range of products from laphelds to voice. We're holding back our launch of new products until 1989, because we're in advance of the times. These products will really come into their own in the 1990s.

The new developments in which we are engaged represent *a partnership between ourselves and our component suppliers*. Andy Clegg has spent a great deal of time in America and Japan with INTEL, on the one hand, and Toshiba and Hitachi on the other. The sorts of products we're designing are lapheld word processors, solid state dictaphone machines, and secretaryless typewriters, all with a *common underlying architecture.*

Personality and organization

Another aspect to this communication process has been the introduction of administrative and financial systems to ensure that there is proper control. We're now a rather bureaucratic company, in a sense. We believe in planning.

I remember, by way of contrast, the MD of Sinclair saying that he didn't believe in planning and control. There's a nice aspiration behind this. It's *the Cambridge concept.* Assemble a bunch of bright young people, put them together in a pot, and let the sparks fly. This is the way you are supposed to conquer the world. You, the management, therefore must not let control interfere with creativity. *What a load of nonsense!*

To this day I still feel that Sinclair's psychology was highly aberrant. When the chips were down he apparently seemed more concerned with his own personal position than with that of his company as a whole. In the process he effectively destroyed a world brand with substantial potential.

As a major creditor of the company, in 1985, I had access to his balance sheet. He could have turned the company around. 'Why didn't he?', I have often asked myself. It could only have been this crazed belief that personality and personal control was more important than the organization that got in the way.

It's interesting that Sinclair had such a high profile. It's a bit like Rupert Murdoch or Captain Bob. Their egocentricity is reflected back to them by the media which, in turn, makes them even more egocentric. *The man, rather than the product or company, gets promoted.* It's sad for them and sad for the country.

The result, in Sinclair's case, is that he failed to nurture a growing plant, even with all its flaws, into a substantial Sony-type organization, that is one which has provided products of quality and substantial employment.

Balancing freedom and order

Psion is different. We believe profoundly in creativity, and in play. But it's a tough world out there. *Unless you think that, you will perish. Development people need to create, but not in a vacuum.* In fact they're much happier working within a framework. Planning is not inconsistent with creativity.

Organizer II is a development concept that was launched in the exact week we planned it to occur. That's how good our planning is. There was good organization and leadership throughout.

In our early pioneering years the stress was on development and creativity; as the company grew, there was initially a period when we lacked control. Then, as we consolidated, we began to install management systems and procedures. At this later stage we believed in balancing creativity with planning, creative freedom with structured order.

In some ways, of course, all creativity is based on structure. What is particularly interesting about a creative period is the underlying structure upon which the creativity is based. I think it's a special feature of postwar Britain that there has been a rebellion against Victorian values and the underlying structures upon which they were based.

In fact Clive Sinclair is part of the same phenomenon, the lone inventor and free ranger striving against all the establishment odds. He happens also to be a very creative marketeer; his main failing is in engineering.

Good engineering results in quality and value, which has been creatively developed and meticulously implemented. It involves *producing things of use to people which work*, which are cost effective, which don't break down, which have quality about them.

It's not the lack of marketing skills which plagues Britain. We have communication skills par excellence. We're controlling the marketing world at this particular moment, what with Saatchi and Saatchi and J. Walter Thompson. Our failure stems from those attitudes we have, arising out of our reactions against our grandfathers in the Victorian era.

I remember when I was working as a lorry driver to earn my keep, I passed by Snapes Printing Works in Oldham, Lancashire. That company was owned by my great grandfather. Perhaps my own peculiar cultural history gives me both a perspective and an involvement in this country that is unusual.

You see, in my era at Cambridge the last thing you did was to go into industry. You went into the Civil Service, the BBC, or into a merchant bank. *Business was dark and satanic and destructive of creativity*. There was this natural reaction against Victorian capitalism. Now companies like ours are turning the whole argument on its head.

So much for the story of Psion, and its cultural evolution. We can see how founder and company, product and market, individual and organization, have evolved in tandem. We now turn finally to Transcriba, and to the metaphysical.

10 The Metaphysical Approach to Cultural Transformation*

INTRODUCTION

In this chapter we shall be applying the metaphysical approach to corporate culture, through which the creation, destabilization (chaos) and prospective resurrection of a particular business, through its culture, will be documented.

The company concerned, which we shall call 'Transcriba', is in the publishing and communication business. The founders, having started by publishing company magazines in French and English, gradually diversified into technically based books and magazines, translated into dozens of languages. By 1980 they had become a significant force in the field of scientifically based publications around the globe.

Though its corporate origins reach back to Britain in the 1950s, its co-founder came from Eastern Europe, and was born in 1912. Her name was Bella.

We shall begin with 'Creation', and with an assessment of the original spirit which subsequently materialized as the company.

CREATION

The originative spirit

As spirit is an abstract entity its journey is completely void of time and space. Hence the journey of the spirit is not a function of time.

* This chapter is based extensively on the research and consultancy work undertaken by Mike Hollands, Michal Ron and Ben Stoddart as students of The City University Business School, London. Whereas the companies concerned are real, names and some of the content have been changed to preserve anonymity.

The creation of each spirit is unique and distinctive. It may be a gradual process over time or it may be an instant moment's inspiration.

Harrison Owen states that 'the genesis of every organization is a moment when some individual, or some very small group of individuals, has what amounts to the Ah-Ha experience. . .'. He identifies this as the creative moment when something emerges out of nothing.

Prior to the Ah-Ha experience there is a significant gestation period. It was during this period that the essence of the Transcriba spirit reappeared over time in different manifestations.

It is crucially important to differentiate between these primal manifestations and the eventual corporate spirit. Bella was the carrier of these primal manifestations which were to become part of the corporate spirit (the Transcriba spirit).

In its most originative form the spirit reveals itself through Bella at the age of four:

> I am indebted to those prisoners of war from Russia and Italy, who stayed on with us after the First World War, for teaching me their respective languages. Amongst these prisoners was a Russian called Jozko. I loved sitting on his lap and listening to the endless stories which he told me in his own Russian dialect. After a while I began to understand these stories; they were full of werewolves and witches, all of whom lived in great, dark forests full of howling wolves and a lot of snow. They were most wonderful descriptive stories. It was through these stories that I managed to learn and speak four languages by the time I was four years old: Czech, German, Italian and Russian dialect. This became the basis of my lifelong hobby and eventually my career – languages.

The spirit reappeared in a different form later when Bella was a teenager, as exemplified by her humanitarian and communicative qualities.

As a teenager Bella and her student friend Stella went on an adventure which led them to Finland. Later on they walked all the way through Lapland until they arrived penniless, hungry and exhausted in Norway. They came across a luxurious liner. They knew that unless they travelled upon it they would be left to suffer the arctic cold of the Norwegian winter, or have to walk 500km south. Having no inhibitions, Bella approached the captain, and convinced him to take them aboard.

> The captain was a good psychologist. He realized that a couple of sunburnt girls with a strange tale to tell would amuse his guests who were getting a bit bored with all those fjords. He arranged to have us seated at a table with the richest of his passengers. His gamble paid

off. I entertained them endlessly with our adventures in English and broken Norwegian, and Stella played the piano for the benefit of the guests.

Another manifestation of this originative spirit appeared in the Second World War, when Bella was on a British Naval boat. Determination and the will to help others became apparent.

> We had neither paper, nor pencils, nor a blackboard and particularly – no classroom. My friend had said 'count me out, these idiots are not fit to learn a language'. This was, of course quite untrue, as we had many very brainy and educated men on board. We all had a lot of fun, and much later several men told me that my lessons had actually helped them. This made me rather pleased with myself.

These are early manifestations of the Transcriba spirit, but as the company had not yet been created they were incomplete. It was not until Transcriba became a reality that the spirit was released in its fuller, wider form.

In fact you might think of the original outlines of the corporate spirit as an architectural plan of a building prior to the three-dimensional construction.

Business foundations

Prior to the company's foundation, and out of necessity, Bella and her husband Anton seized every opportunity to make money: a children's holiday home, hedge clippings sold in Covent Garden, the rearing of geese, ducks and chickens. They were both involved in publishing, Anton as a scientific illustrator, Bella as a publisher of a bilingual technical magazine.

> I had my little publishing office going, employing people part time. We bought our first secondhand IBM, and were forced to eat potatoes for a week as we bought our first dictionaries.

It is at this point, when the foundations of the company were first established, that the direction of the company's spirit becomes channelled and focused . . .

> One of our publishers in St Albans was manufacturing flight simulators. Concorde was on the drawing board, but the English and the French didn't understand each other. So we started to translate letters, drawings, meetings – in a small way. Then we became the official producers of the French and English company magazine. We

couldn't work for Concorde as Bella and Anton Haupner, so we drank tea and dreamed up the name 'Transcriba'.

We anxiously waited for Anton to come back from Concorde. He crawled out of the old Ford, and just stood there on the drive, giving the thumbs up sign and grinning all over his chops as you have never seen him grin before! All the publishers and typists were hanging out of the windows – and they cheered in quite unseemly fashion – as if they had watched a most important goal being shot in a football match. I just waited for Anton to get out of the public eye to give him a big kiss and cuddle (what a way for one Managing Director to welcome the other!).

The naming of Transcriba is the significant staging post where the spirit crosses the 'great divide' from potential to actual.

The name captures Anton's vision of communication and understanding between people and across international barriers. It also encapsulates Bella's animateurial and caring qualities.

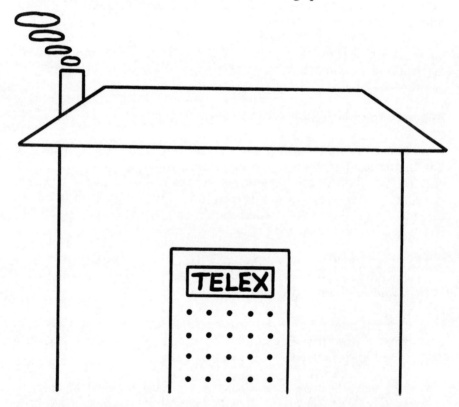

It wa⌐ Anton's idea to install a new telex machine so translations could be received and returned at high speed. This was reported around the world.

In his vision, Anton saw that global communications would lead to a better understanding of other cultures. 'Mutual understanding is an important factor in continuation of our life as a race, as a species.'

The Spirit of Transcriba fed initially off Anton's 'brainwave' (the telex machine). In fact, it became so powerful that 'it led to Anton giving up reading his thrillers. They became boring compared to our every day lives.'

So why was it that the spirit eventually manifested itself through Transcriba when there were so many opportunities beforehand in other forms of enterprise? Looking back in hindsight at Bella's childhood it could almost seem predestined.

The Transcriba spirit

When researching through material written by the founders, Bella and Anton, as well as stories and myths still told today by the elder members of Transcriba, we felt the presence of a very distinctive, unique spirit – the spirit of Transcriba.

> The photographer went mad. He is used to taking pictures in offices, factories, workshops. When he was let loose on our sunny lawn, pretty girls sunbathing while translating for good money, millions of daffodils and free lunch in the garden – he just went mad. When it was time for him to go, at long last, he asked 'Why are you still working? You have everything. Why are you carrying on?'
>
> It made us think.

Once identified it was impossible to mistake or confuse the spirit with external and internal influences operating on the corporation. This was the unique essence of Transcriba. Although the spirit cannot be defined by means of formal substance, we felt that the distinctiveness of the Transcriba spirit could be characterized by certain modes, movements and even features.

The recognition of the spirit was similar in experience to submission to a strong, unique source of energy.

This energy, once recognized, is spellbinding and the receptive individual interacting with the spirit becomes entwined with it and inseparable from it.

Once this source of energy is identified mentally by the individual it acts in a very similar way to a faith, a religion.

Hence, we see the Transcriba spirit in its early manifestations as a unique religion or source of faith. The features of this spirit could be seen as a positive generation of belief in people's ability to love, achieve and create collectively.

In-house translators from the old Transcriba were very casual, working on the lawn in the summer.

The spirit of an individual and the spirit of an organization are strongly entwined. On the individual level the spirit develops and appears through visions, special understanding, and conceptualization unique to that individual.

The more developed an individual's personality, the more aware he or she is of their own journey of transformation. An individual's recognition of his own spirit could be very powerful and act as a catalyst, enabling the spirit constantly and rapidly to transform and eventually to achieve self-actualization.

Bella's understanding of her ability to communicate with people across national borders and language barriers transformed idea into reality whenever the opportunity to translate and publish arose.

Her sensitivity towards people and enterprise enabled her to make the progress from organizing and caring for her own direct family to the administration of people in a new organization.

We were also not surprised to read about Bella's relationship with her own god, especially on two occasions which indicated new heights and depths of spirit not recognized previously by herself.

. . . I was not brought up to be a practising Jew, but I always knew and considered myself to be Jewish and I always had the greatest respect for God and a very good relation with him in my own private sort of way. We do understand each other. It happened twice in my life that I prayed sincerely and deeply for God's help. In both instances what I prayed for was wrong, but the help I received was much greater than the one I had asked for . . .

Anton's vision was to increase global communication, with translations sent electronically across the world. For Bella, it was much more personal; she treated everyone as a friend and breathed life into the most downhearted person.

The energy generated by two compatible individuals (Bella and Anton) within an organization where the company spirit is powerfully manifested, will inevitably break the one plus one equals two rule. The combination of these spirits will lead to a greater energy than the two component levels.

> Anton and Bella often played with all the children of the employees. Anton in particular used to entertain the children by playing them songs on his guitar. He always played and repeated the same song so that the children would recognise the tune and join in the singing. (Irene Haupner)

Once the organization spirit is revealed and recognized by the fellow members, then a greater passage from potential to actual has been facilitated.

The company spirit draws not only from individual spirits, but also from its interaction with its physical, cultural, and intellectual environment.

For instance, the perception of the company spirit by other companies or opinion-forming individuals will also contribute to the new shape or manifestation of the corporate spirit.

Hence we believe that although inseparable from each other, as the individual spirits erupt into the corporate spirit alongside other elements, the corporate spirit is potentially greater; this will obviously occur only if there is sufficient compatibility within the organization on a mutual spiritual level.

It is during the pioneering stage of the company that the separation between the two spirit levels is difficult. As the Transcriba example demonstrates, these two levels of spirits tie in firmly and interact in a give and take relationship.

Though they play different parts, they are both conductors of an emerging organizational spirit.

> Without each other the firm would never have developed. My mother was the engine, and my father the brain. (Jim Haupner)

However, the difference in the roles they played is not the important issue here. A more fruitful explanation for the creative success is achieved by appreciating the unity of spirit between Anton and Bella.

> As a wife she helped, supported, built up my ego as a man. Bella appreciated what I am doing and translated it into practice. (Anton)

Far more significant than their 'compatible personalities' was their spiritual affinity. Their spirits were travelling together, so closely intwined, that they may be treated as one.

Martin Buber, in his book *I and Thou* said: 'I become I only in significant relationships with an other, a thou.'

In this way the spirits of Bella and Anton appeared strong and influential. Their spirit was much of the Transcriba spirit at the creation phase.

Our evenings were filled with assorted visitors, ponderous chess players, the Russian trade delegation, and an assortment of neighbours, friends and translators. We still stuck to the rule that cooking of the evening meal was done by two and two in turn. Thus it was the lot of the Israelis to prepare a particular Friday's evening meal. Candles shone, the table was decorated with a white cloth and the meal was spread in great magnificence. There was a variety of salads, chopped liver decorated with red and green vegetables, soup with bits floating in it, chicken, half boiled, half baked, wine and coffee.

The development of the corporate spirit, however, demanded more than the spiritual interaction of Anton and Bella. Other people – their first employees, their children – all contributed their own spiritual characteristics.

The strength of the spirit makes it easily sensed, and identified by the employees. Those not compatible find out early on. For those who are compatible, the spirit becomes a lifelong joy in which they develop and on which they themselves have an influence.

I started working with Bella and Anton more than twenty years ago as a part time secretary. Later after having two children, I rejoined the company, this time on a full time basis. We were underpaid, but it did not really matter. We socialised a lot, had many parties, and enjoyed evenings out together. We used to celebrate other staff members' birthdays here in the library room, and we used to make lunches here together. It was a great place to work in. (Jean Creswell)

Surrounded by its conductors the spirit was eventually able to grow larger than its source. It influenced more people, and its initial dependence on two conductors evolved into a creation of conductors.

An individual becomes an individual in relationship to a group. Either by identification with the spirit of the group, or by distinction from it, the individual comes to understand what he or she is or is not. (Harrison Owen)

The creation of the powerful Transcriba spirit was made possible not only because employees were compatible with one another, but also because they were able to feed from and nourish the organizational spirit in a process of mutual strengthening.

However, in the early 1980s, Anton suddenly died. Six months later Bella had also gone, having died of a broken heart. Two years earlier, the Haupners' eldest son, Jim, had taken over the managing directorship of the business. As a trained accountant, and amateur musician, he had attempted to introduce more control into the business.

To help him along the way he merged Transcriba with Firma, a publishing company with more formal structures, and a stronger British base. Transcriba's geographical strengths lay in Continental Europe, in America and the Far East.

The merger took place in 1984 between an efficient, centralized and rigidly run Firma, and the decentralized Transcriba.

CHAOS

'Tohu Vavohu'

The forms and modes of Transcriba have changed significantly since those days of the company's creation. The differences of being tells us that the spirit has moved on.

In this section we take a closer look at the actual passage, when form dissolves and spirit transforms.

We chose to use the term 'Chaos' to describe the period 1978-1988 as we felt that 'death' is inappropriate given its association with terminability. In its ordinary usage it is only applied to the ultimate situation when a body ceases to function. As spirit is eternal, and hence never ceases to exist, a description of standstill would be essentially wrong.

'Chaos' on the other hand implies a certain level of activity, unfocused and erratic. It is associated with disaffection, disharmony, imbalance – almost a battlefield of colliding sources of energy.

An appropriate term for this state of chaos can be found in the Hebrew word 'Tohu Vavohu', taken from the Old Testament. People in a state of 'Tohu Vavohu' have lost all faith. Their world has been shaken by an almighty power; the earth and the sky turn into one, fire and water will rise from the deep. This is a time of destruction, but only for the purpose of further transformation into a better, new life. Through its resurrection, the spirit of mankind will become a source of renewed belief, a new, purer faith.

At the stage of Transcriba/Firma's existence in 1987, its transformation in spirit had resulted in misunderstanding, disorder, communication problems, destructive contradictions and disagreements and a general feeling of disbelief.

> My parents never envisaged what has happend so far, no way. They were always more family orientated and they treated their staff like family too. My father would come down in his pyjamas and kiss all the girls hello in the morning. It was hilarious . . . people coming in could not believe their eyes. They were actually very upset about the merger. They had already retired when it took place, but I think they felt the control was getting out of their hands. (Irene Haupner)

A simple analogy could be made with a large orchestra, with that time in between two pieces when the players tune up their instruments. The sound could be ear piercing, very disharmonious, chaotic. Yet seconds before and again seconds after, the spirit of the orchestra is transformed into its new and harmonious manifestations.

Returning to our analogy of the Transcriba spirit as a strong religion, we see how this faith weakens as the spirit, in its journey of transformation, dissolves in order to transform. This leads to the state which Harrison Owen calls 'open space', a period of suspended animation.

Open space

It is important, in acknowledging this 'open space', to remind ourselves of what made the Transcriba spirit develop and radiate during creation. Strong sources, that is Bella, Anton and early employees, fed the spirit, as well as receiving strength in return. What may be termed 'insulators' or sceptics of the Transcriba faith, were neither strong nor influential.

After Anton's heart attack the Transcriba spirit began to deflate for two reasons. First, the nourishment that it received from its founders declined. However, this may not be the main cause of spiritual loss, for in the late 1970s the spirit was still being replenished by employees who were compatible with, and conductors of, a Transcriba in which they had a strong faith.

The deflating of the spirit and the implanting of the first seeds of chaos arose through atheism. Insulation and incompatibility detracted from the mythos through which the Transcriba spirit had previously manifested itself.

> Until this very day the merger has not been fully integrated between the two companies. There are two separate identities, Firma and Transcriba. A feeling of 'us' and 'them', specifically in a geographical sense. (Jean Creswell)

This atheism was reflected in the indifference towards the faith of communal and loving success, the faith of Transcriba. It came first in the form of Jim Haupner, unemotional and rational in his attitude towards the company. This was the atheism of a personally disbelieving spirit. The sterile organizational spirit of Firma was the second source of atheism, contrasting sharply with the strength of faith in Transcriba.

The Transcriba religion, which drew very heavily on Jewish culture, began to be choked by the atheism of those running the newly merged company and also the organizational spirit of Firma.

The resultant chaos emerged through the isolation of the remaining Transcriba spirit. There was no spiritual faith in Firma that could enable a transformation of the Transcriba spirit into a new and effective form. There was no renewal. Nothing was generated out of the open space, and so the transformative process remained incomplete.

Physical and emotional manifestations

A spirit, though unseen and indefinable as we have shown, is reflected at times through physical manifestations. When the spirit is in chaos, when its strength is receding, then those physical manifestations result in disturbance and disharmony among the personal spirits in the organization.

This chaos is recognized by many, but most meaningfully by those most compatible with the spirit in its creation phase.

> Why not have everybody move to St Albans? Once the company moves out of this place it will be the final death of Transcriba. That would definitely be the end of it all.
> It is sad on the one hand (I have lovely memories of the Anton and

Bella days), but then again, times have changed and we need to move on . . . (Jenny Mack)

Recognition is not always expressed in sorrow. Others regard the decay as necessary, and there is a desire to move on.

There is a need for someone to transform what we have, and I feel I am not the right person. (Lena Shultz)

I think we are at a transition phase really. We are at that size where it hurts to grow, but if we don't, then we will start to drop back. (Christine Morrow)

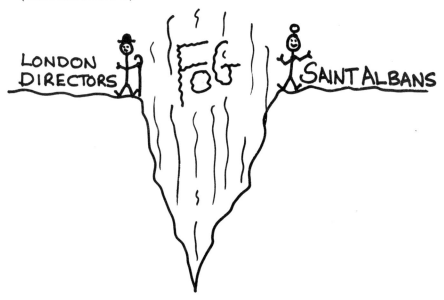

There is a tremendous divide between the offices in London and the St Albans branch.

The Transcriba spirit, in the 1950s and 60s, had flowed with love and compassion. In this chaotic phase in the eighties however, insulators of the spirit became more and more dominant.

I was not emotionally involved with the company, but I felt I had a responsibility to run it when my father became ill.
    We must see where the business is going and make the people fit. We cannot do it the other way around. (Jim)

The mutual understanding that nourished individual and organizational spirits is not there any more.

Firma London have been rather insensitive to our own needs here in St Albans. I don't think they know anything about the history of Transcriba. It would be very positive if they did know something. I don't know much about Firma either. (Jenny)

There is no longer a unifying spirit. Instead there are competing wills, and their intermittent combat results in further weakness.

They introduced new rules of a rigid, inflexible nature. There is now a new hierarchy of authorities in the London office, and to be able to make a major decision authorization is required. This lengthy process slows us down tremendously and by the time the final OK is given, it may be too late to take action, or the whole set of conditions has altered. (Jenny)

I think Transcriba worked on a fundamentally different basis from Firma. Firma were very structured. They had top management, middle management and minions. Transcriba did not work like that. We were a family. (Molly Singh)

The Sales department is going out for dinner and a show. Other departments don't do anything. They were all furious when I was booking up Chess last week, and they were not invited. (Christine)

There is a conflict between the two cultures, whether it is acknowledged or not, and just because we are physically separated means that it is diluted to a certain degree. (Lena)

Direction and leadership, lacking spiritual guidance becomes uncommitted.

Jim does not run the company. It is his weakness. He is also not interested in running the company, as it happens. He is weak. His weakness is in dealing with the nitty gritty. He does not like telling people what to do. (Lena)

Finally, we find that the present chaos becomes a betrayal of the past.

My parents never envisaged what has happened so far, no way. They were always more family orientated and they treated their staff like family too. (Lena)

Denial and resistance to change

Most people possess an understandable and problematic fear of death. In the corporate context we shall describe this phenomenon

as the fear of change. A change in the company objectives, procedures, covenant, language, and key people – all manifestations of
a change in the direction and momentum of the spirit's journey of
transformation.

As people are afraid of change, they exert maximum effort to
delay death as long as possible.

Many of the employees of Transcriba/Firma resisted the changes
introduced after the merger; the introduction of new procedures,
new authorizations and the like. There was a strong resistance to
the realization that the end of a particular path had been reached,
and that there was no going backwards. Clearly, those who
assiduously avoided the fact of this 'end' are effectively evading the
possibility of a new future, in all its richness.

As Harrison Owen says:

> There is another way of looking at things which has many advan-
> tages. That way is to see death as the natural concomitant of life,
> present on a daily basis, and necessary for the orderly progression
> and fulfilment of the human spirit, otherwise known as transforma-
> tion.

It is from this point that the new beginning emerges. Therefore, the
old company employees have to let go, acknowledging that what
was in the old days of Bella and Anton should be revered, but is no
longer, and that the journey of the spirit must now take a leap
forward into the unknown.

This is the stage when the resurrection of the company spirit
begins. A new vision is about to appear.

RESURRECTION

In Spring 1988 the merged Transcriba/Firma was taken over by a
much larger, French publishing company, Montagne. At that point
Transcriba, and the Haupner family, effectively disappeared from
the publishing scene.

Montagne, in fact, had its own sense of mission, having been
created by a staunchly Catholic family in Lyons during the 1920s.
The company was currently engaged in diversifying out of books
into electronic publications on a global scale.

Creating the conditions for a new corporate spirit

In our description of the resurrection we need to be clear about what is being given new life. The old Transcriba spirit has dissolved, but it is immortal. It no longer exists, but it has not died. It is eternal. It must now transform itself into the new spirit that will be created from the fusion with Montagne.

Montagne symbolizes height and purpose, and from this we also envisage strength and expansiveness, open space in which transformation is possible. Its family origins in the Catholic Church is a clear indication that faith is present in strength.

The important point to note is that a religion, a faith, exists in the company. The particular faith, however, is a secondary feature and not the crucial issue in itself.

The presence of such a powerful faith is necessary if the Transcriba spirit is to transform and renew itself. Its existence is the linking factor between the old and the new. The important point is that the faith and spirit that is the essence of Montagne can, and indeed must, be the source from which the Transcriba spirit renews itself.

At the same time, the Montagne spirit cannot and should not remain unaffected by its association with Transcriba/Firma. If success is to be achieved then the Montagne spirit, while retaining its essence, must provide sufficient open space into which the personal spirits of Transcriba/Firma can enter.

There are three essential stages through which the spirit of the resurrected company must pass, in order to transform:

- griefwork
- the new story telling
- celebration

Griefwork

This is the process through which an organization passes from the mourning of the past to the acceptance of the new.

To achieve this there must first be 'shock and anger', when employees of Transcriba express the dissatisfaction they feel for the passing of the spirit with which they once felt so comfortable.

This expression of pain must be followed by some form of 'denial' which provides employees with the breathing space to let the new reality sink in. It is here, under the protection of denial, that the reconfiguration of the corporate spirit must begin.

This reconfiguration may be accelerated by recalling past memories, which in time will provide the seeds ideas for the future.

If management is sensitive then this critical passage from memory to hope may be enhanced and directed in a manner that is compatible with the needs of the organization.

The new story telling

A new story (tale) is needed from the company; it is a new story that, once told, will assist in the process of the spirit's transformation. This story ought to be told by the top management of the new company.

This tale needs to be created through a carefully planned entwining of the visions of the company, with the visions, stories and heroes of Transcriba/Firma's past.

The new general managers may start with a new 'story line': for example, the globalization of publishing as it has never been done previously.

This global vision, for instance, could be linked and tied in with Anton Haupner's vision of a global network, facilitating better communication between mankind.

The new combined story will need to be flexible enough to be changed several times as the newly merged company's spirit grows and strengthens.

In order to give the new story a depth of reality in time and space, it will be important to use all possible modes of communication available. The story must be believed, so that listeners (the company employees) can smell it, touch it and sense it. If it is told in this way, it may stimulate the imagination of the employees and give rise to new additions and creations from their own imaginations.

Most importantly this story needs to become the organization's story, a story that all employees recognize as theirs.

Celebration

Celebrating the new turning point in Transcriba/Firma's corporate life is no less critical than the griefwork undertaken over the company's past.

The takeover by Montagne provides an excellent opportunity to concentrate upon the company's future. It is therefore most important that the first encounters of the Transcriba/Firma employees with the spirit of Montagne are positive and optimistic.

In celebrating this company milestone, an element of fun and joy can be introduced into an otherwise long and painful transformation process.

This joyful attitude can be linked back to the founders of Transcriba. Bella had always believed in an optimistic philosophy towards life – doing what feels good and enjoying every moment of it.

The celebration can be executed in many different ways, such as a company party to greet the new and honour the leaving employees. Heroes of the past need not be ignored, but should rather be honoured and 'enshrined'.

The fusion, transformation and growth of a combined new corporate spirit must then occur. Management must ensure that there is sufficient open space in which a spirit that encompasses, and allows for, the roots of all can be formed.

The mythograph, illustrated and analysed in this chapter, is a technique that management may utilize to identify and release corporate spirit. Resurrection will not be successful if management fails in its tasks of identifying and comprehending the journey of the spirit.

Constructing the mythograph

The objective of the mythograph is to arrange the stories gathered in a form that will enable management to identify and cohere the corporate spirit. It is a formalized representation of the organization onto which the elements of myth and ritual may be plotted.

It can help to show the cohesiveness between stories as well as elements of conflict and dissonance. Thus the mythograph plays an important role in the transformation of the spirit, by guiding the creation of a new story.

We have developed two mythographs: one illustrates the Transcriba spirit of the past, the other the chaos of the Transcriba/Firma spirit in its recent manifestation.

Under ideal circumstances, when the metaphysical management of the organization is functioning effectively, all cells should show the same seminal story, with minor and due variations, according to level and sector. That sort of coherent picture would represent a 'one-pointed' spirit, creating the potential for an uninhibited powerful flow of physical and human energy.

In this situation not only is the culture coherent, but the spirit remains free and flexible – free to develop and transform.

Table 10.1   Mythograph _A_ – creation

	Company	Customers	Community
Directors	1 The telex	2 The Concorde contract	3 The orphanage
Family	4 Pioneering a kibbutz	5 Chocolate box	6 Music shop
Staff	7 International gastronomy	8 Anton's return	9 Sunbathing

As can be seen from mythograph *A* (see Table 10.1), the company, the employees and the community are all in harmony. One story reinforces the other, and the corporate spirit is manifested in a visible, coherent manner. There is a general theme present between the cell, with stories exemplifying the strong family atmosphere and an optimistic approach to life.

Analysis of mythograph A

1	The telex	It was Anton's idea to install a new telex machine so that text could be received and returned at high speed. This was reported in many national newspapers and the publicity resulted in a big step forward for the company.
2	The Concorde contract	On winning an important contract with Concorde, there was an urgent need to register as a company, and thus the name Transcriba was born.
3	The orphanage	Bella and Anton ran a summer boarding-house which catered for orphan children.
4	Pioneering a kibbutz	The Haupner children, following their parents' strong link with Israel, were part of a pioneering group of kibbutzniks in Northern Israel.
5	Chocolate box	A translation job for Rowntrees was typed by one of Bella's daughters throughout the night. Bella's letter of apology explaining the typing errors was answered with a huge box of chocolates sent by Rowntrees to the Haupner children.
6	Music shop	Jim Haupner ventured into the local business by opening the first music shop in the locality.
7	International gastronomy	The varied international background of the employees became a daily ritual when they took turns in preparing large meals for all.
8	Anton's return	Whilst awaiting for the outcome of Anton's perusal of a very large contract, Anton's thumbs up sign on return led to a loud cheer from the translators who were waiting nervously at the windows.
9	Sunbathing	A reporter who came to write an article on Transcriba was shocked when he came across pretty girls sunbathing on the lawn as they translated.

Table 10.2 Mythograph *B* – chaos

	Directors	Staff
Eichners	1 Jim is weak	2 Who's Bella?
Company	3 Whispers	4 Them and us
Environment	5 Georgian chairs	6 Moving house

Analysis of mythograph B

1	Jim is weak	There are complaints from different levels of the company in respect of the lack of leadership qualities required from the chairman.
2	Who's Bella?	Both Transcriba's and Firma's employees are unaware of the history of their respective companies.
3	Whispers	There is a real concern amongst the directors not to reveal important information to employees; a high degree of confidentiality prevails behind closed doors.
4	Them and us	Ever since the merger of the two companies the separation of the two identities has been maintained.
5	Georgian chairs	When an American branch ran into cash flow problems, the need to generate money led to management placing price tags on a set of Georgian chairs which had been previously bought for the office.
6	Moving house	The current lease on the London offices is about to expire, and a new location is eagerly awaited by many of the employees.

Mythograph *B* exemplifies the current dissonance within the company. There is no coherent spirit reflected from the story cells.

However, there is evidence of open space present; as illustrated, there is a strong need for both leadership and clear future direction. The arrival of Montagne as a spiritual force is essential for a new corporate leadership and vision. This is where our role in the recognition and resurrection of the company spirit is handed over to the new management.

Appendix 1   Methodology

The methodology used to identify the corporate spirit has been developed by Harrison Owen and involves the following four steps:

Step 1   Desk research. Obtaining a general knowledge and understanding of Transcriba/Firma by analysing the company.
Step 2   Qualitative research. This stage entails in-depth interviews with the corporate leader. The aim is to reveal corporate culture, and the leader's aspirations for the future of the company.
Step 3   Systemwide qualitative research. This stage entails in-depth interviews with personnel from all levels of the organization with similar objectives to those in step 2. It is through the gathering of stories from these interviews that the culture of the firm, and the state of the corporate spirit, will be identified.
Step 4   Presentation. There is no one uniform way of presenting the newly created corporate story to the organization. We suggest one possible form in Appendix 2.

Appendix 2   Presenting a metaphysical concept

The following is a script of a presentation aimed at describing the journey of the Transcriba/Firma spirit and the metaphysical approach to corporate culture.

Needless to say, there are numerous alternative approaches and the chosen one will depend mainly on the researcher's imagination, the nature of the subject matter (i.e. the company spirit) and the active participants.

Transcriba/Firma – the dream

Narrator: 'On the 31st March 1988 Transcriba/Firma was taken over by the French Publishing conglomerate, Montagne.

Montagne is an international company with headquarters in Lyons, France, and is run by a staunch Catholic family.

M. Jean Prideau is the chairman of the company and is currently troubled by the recurrence of a powerful dream. He decided to call on his Catholic priest and seek his advice.'

[Scene location: at the Catholic priest's home.
Participants: Jean Prideau, the Catholic priest]

Priest: 'Hello Jean.'
Jean: 'Hello François. Look, I've been having this very powerful dream which I feel I need to talk to someone about. I think I

understand it, but I am not quite sure how exactly I should be using it. It feels very spiritual, almost religious. This is why I thought that perhaps you may understand.'

Priest: 'Sounds very interesting Jean, tell me more about it.'

Jean: 'Well, in this dream, three young figures, students perhaps, appear like three prophets and take me on a journey to an unknown land.'

Priest: 'Why not try and relive the dream. It might help us, understand it better.'

Jean: 'OK, let me see if I can . . .'

[The dream: new location – a garden.
Participants: three young prophets; Jean, now narrating, is played each time by a different member]

Jean (played by prophet 1): 'Three young people, let us call them prophets, came to take me away on a long journey to an unknown place.

[Background music: Beethoven 6th Symphony (*Pastoral*)]

It was a garden, or maybe a field, covered with yellow daffodils.

It looked like paradise. The three prophets were talking to me, saying sweet things; it was spellbinding . . .'

The three prophets (in turn):

summer	birth	flower
dove	tender	breast
yellow	orange	daffodils
harmony	Garden of Eden	party
laughter	joy	husband ·
Anton	idea	kiss
wife	Bella	little feet
home	language	world
brainwave	tomatoes	creation
candles	family	chickens
warmth	love	butterfly
music	Jewish	spirit

Jean (played by prophet 2): 'I was in the most beautiful state of mind. I would have stayed there for ever, but things began to change.

[Music stops]

A man entered the garden and started building a stone wall. Flowers began to die as the wall grew higher.

[Background music slowly increasing: Brian Eno and David Byrne, from the album *My life in the bush of ghosts*]

The light was fading, a storm was about to begin. I remember I could feel it in my bones and it was all becoming unpleasant, almost like a nightmare. The prophets now made me feel unpleasant.'

[Music increases]

The three prophets (in turn):

grey	unpleasant	barbed wire
hammer	destruction	blind
stone wall	rigid	their fault
judge	clash	who's Bella?
tank	chaos	them and us
noise	conflict	sterile

Prophet 1: 'It's still and quiet, no feeling, no senses at all, just numbness, floating, drifting, no direction. It's dark and cold, but there seems to be no way out, just eternal nothingness.'
Prophet 2: 'No, no, not at all. It's like an invasion, an army marching into town. Tanks; the sound of shooting, nobody wants to know what the people want. An occupation, our voices are small, timid and unheard.'
Prophet 3: 'No, it's a fire on your tongue, and steam on your feet, and hell-dark creatures tormenting you by spitting ash into your open eyes.'

[Music dies out]

Jean (played by prophet 3): 'And then the earth began to shake, hot lava was erupting from below; the trees caught fire which spread across the garden. The wall was falling, caving down.

[Silence]

. . . Later, there was nothing left, just ash rubble and dust. The three prophets were standing there and pointing to me – they were reciting this poem, I can still hear it in my ears . . .'

[Music from the *Rite of spring*, Stravinsky]

The three prophets:

'Are you willing to be sponged out, erased, cancelled, made nothing?
Are you willing to be made nothing?
dipped into oblivion?

If not you will never really change.
The Phoenix renews her youth
only when she is burnt, burnt alive, burnt down,
to hot and flocculent ash.

Then the stirring of a new small bulb in the nest
with strands of down like floating ash
shows that she is renewing her youth like the eagle,
Immortal bird.'

[Music stops. New location. Back to Jean and the priest]

Priest: 'Well Jean, it sounds very religious, spiritual – the link with creation, death and resurrection. But you are the dreamer after all; it is up to you to find your own meaning from it. Can you see how it might relate to you in any way in your personal life?'
Jean: 'Well, I received a report from three researchers in London who have provided me with a new insight into corporate culture, in particular in relation to Transcriba/Firma, a firm I have just taken over.

Maybe the dream is suggesting that I have an active role in the, shall we say, resurrection of the corporate spirit of Transcriba. I think I shall go and read their report once again . . .'

END

11 Managing Cultural Change

INTRODUCTION

In the concluding chapter to this book I want to draw together all the cultural threads, thereby providing you with an overall perspective on the management of cultural change.

Approaches to cultural change

Firstly, as has become apparent, there are four distinctively different approaches to managing cultural change, which are summarized in Table 11.1.

Table 11.1 Approaches to cultural change

Approach	Managerial input	Process elements		Organizational ouput
Primal (JMS Seed Co.)	Instinct	Cultural values	Cultural network	Enterprise and community
Rational (ACS)	Intelligence	Underlying assumption	Attitudes and beliefs	Freedom and order
Developmental (Psion)	Insight	Technological evolution	Historical roots	Adaptability and harmony
Metaphysical (Transcriba)	Imagination	Myth and ritual	Journey of the spirit	Energy and vision

In all likelihood, as an agent of change you will apply a mix of all of these in bringing about cultural evolution. The particular emphasis you adopt will need to depend on:

215

- Your *individual personality*. If you are a highly rational individual, who is rather switched off by matters meta-physical, there is not much point in focusing on 'the journey of the spirit'. You will inevitably distort the process of cultural transformation.
- Your *national culture*. If the country in which you operate, for example, is strongly primal in its business orientation, the place to start is with the 'cultural' network, and with the fostering of shared values.
- The *stage of development* that your organization has reached. A youthful enterprise lends itself to primal treatment. An established organization yields, most naturally, to the rational way. A company in midlife, and in need of organizational renewal, will benefit most from a developmental approach. Finally, a large and mature corporation may be in need of fundamental, and metaphysically based, cultural transformation.
- The *corporate culture*. Finally, and inevitably, your own corporate culture will impinge on your approach. In fact the four cultural approaches we have identified can also be viewed as a typology of corporate cultures, or cultural domains. Your organization will be more advanced in some cultural respects than others.

The example cited in Figure 11.1 is that of Psion.

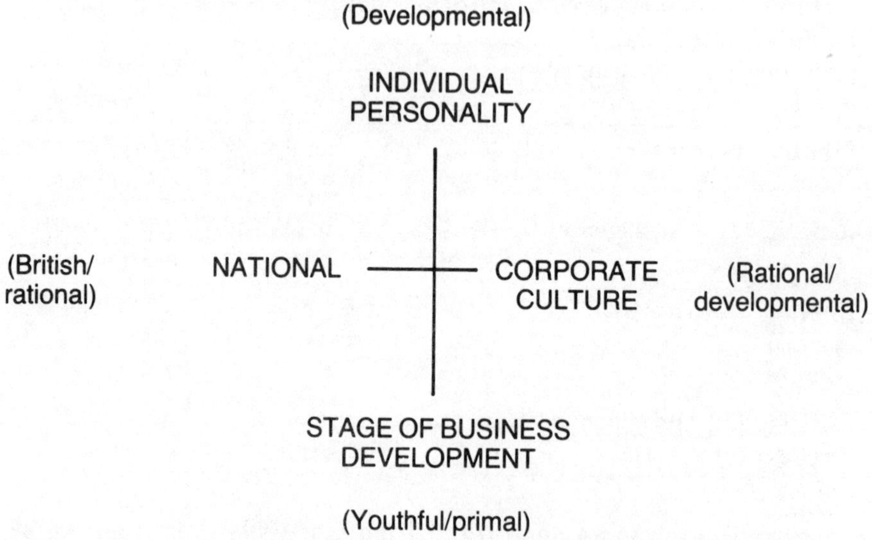

(Developmental)

INDIVIDUAL
PERSONALITY

(British/   NATIONAL ——— CORPORATE   (Rational/
rational)   CULTURE   developmental)

STAGE OF BUSINESS
DEVELOPMENT

(Youthful/primal)

Figure 11.1 A contingent approach to cultural change (rational/ developmental)

APPLYING A CULTURAL INVENTORY

The four cultures

There are, then, basically four kinds of organizational culture, each of which is represented particularly strongly at one stage of the organization's development. These 'cultures' which pervade both the organization's attitudes and beliefs, and its products and markets, are also influenced by the part of the globe in which it is based.

The *primal* culture is characteristic of the pioneering enterprise, and of the American West. JMS Seed Company is a case in point. The *rational* culture is characteristic of the established organization, and of the European North. ARK Computer Services is typical of such. The *developmental* culture is characteristic of the transnational enterprise and of the Japanese East. Psion is such a corporate culture. Finally, the *metaphysical* culture is characteristic of the truly global corporation and of, potentially, the developing South. Transcriba, albeit subconsciously and embryonically, is an example.

The eight subcultures

People and enterprise

Each of the four cultures has both hard and soft variations. The hard primal culture is 'enterprise' based. The symbol is a spider's web. The soft one is 'people' based. Its symbol is a circle.

Network and hierarchy

The hard rational culture is 'hierarchical'. Its symbol is the family tree. The soft one operates as a 'network'. Its symbol is a net.

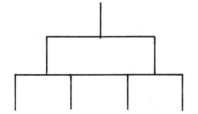 

Enabling and harmonic

The hard developmental culture is 'harmonic'. Its symbol is a molecular structure. The soft one is 'enabling'. Its symbol is a river course.

Naturebound and nuclear

The hard metaphysical culture is 'nuclear'. Its symbol is the nucleus of an atomic structure. The soft one is 'naturebound'. Its symbol is a spiral.

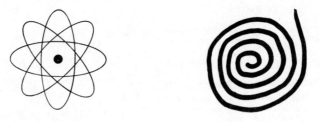

The organizational spectrum

Finally, each of the four cultures – and eight subcultures – differ across a spectrum of physical, social, intellectual, economic, organizational, environmental and creative attributes (see Table 11.2).

The aspirations inventory

Please rank each of the attributes, listed below, in terms of your personal feelings about the aims of your organization.

Rank (R) order the four statements, in each case, from 1 (least) to 4 (most). This ranking indicates what you feel your organization presently aspires to be. In other words a ranking of 4 reflects the most appropriate goal, and a ranking of 1 the least appropriate. Finally, the ranking must always proceed from 4 to 1, with no equal scores. Read all four statements, therefore, before you decide on your rank order.

Table 11.2 The organizational spectrum (high and low)

Corporate culture	Performance attribute						
	Physical	Social	Intellectual	Economic	Organization	Environmental	Creative
Primal							
Rational							
Developmental							
Metaphysical							

PHYSICAL GOALS	R

1 We're encouraged to work hard

2 Productivity is what we're after in this organization

3 Our aim is to interact with one another very intensively

4 We assess our performance according to the rate and velocity of our human energy flow

SOCIAL GOALS	R

1 Enthusiasm is what we're after

2 We need to operate in highly effective teams

3 Quality of life is our performance gauge, both within and without the organization

4 Our aim is to establish a richly cohesive corporate culture

INTELLECTUAL GOALS	R

1 We need to keep our wits about us wherever we go

2 We require both very finely tuned and highly adaptable controls

3 Our aim is to establish and maintain a genuine learning environment

4 We need, consciously, to acknowledge and to flow with, a world of flux and change

ECONOMIC GOALS	R

1 Our will to win has to be very strong

2 We need an aggressive business strategy that will outdo and outlast all our rivals

3 We require a cooperative strategy designed to develop fully our technical and commercial potential

4 We need to be so strongly intertwined with our clients and associates that we become a joint personality

ORGANIZATION GOALS   *R*

1 Our organization must be able to handle all possible manoeuvres that might be required   _____

2 We must structure our organization efficiently and effectively, taking in all functions and contingencies   _____

3 We have to establish an intricate corporate architecture, harmonizing our constituent organizations   _____

4 A natural form of management, modelled on the laws of nature, needs to be established and maintained here   _____

ENVIRONMENTAL GOALS   *R*

1 We have to have a feel for the market   _____

2 Our powers of market analysis and response need to be highly developed   _____

3 We need to plan the evolution of our business through intimately formed links with our stakeholders   _____

4 We need to be able to recognize unlimited possibilities by developing insight and farsightedness   _____

CREATIVE GOALS   *R*

1 We need enough imagination to be able to see round tight corners   _____

2 We must be able to manage innovation systematically and successfully   _____

3 We require the creative capacity continually to develop and renew our people and our businesses   _____

4 We need the vision to transform the spirit of our organization, and the resources of the globe   _____

Now add up your rankings for each category, and divide your answer by 7. This gives the mean ranking which you can chart in Table 11.3, together with the corresponding rank orders.

Table 11.3 Cultural aspirations

	Ranking total	Mean ranking	Rank order
Primal	–	–	–
Rational	–	–	–
Developmental	–	–	–
Metaphysical	–	–	–

The performance inventory

The above inventory, and assessment, covers your organization's aspirations; we now turn to performance. You need to rate your organization, on a scoring (S) of 1 (low) to 4 (high). Looking at each statement, independently, assess the extent to which you agree with a particular one. For example, if you feel people in your organization work extremely hard, but that the productivity rate is not particularly high, you may score 4 on the first count, and 2 on the second.

PHYSICAL PERFORMANCE S

1 We work very, very hard _____

2 Our productivity, that is the ratio of output to
   input, is second to none _____

3 We interact with one another constantly and
   intensively _____

4 The rate and velocity of our human energy flow
   is probably unsurpassed in the industry _____
   Sub total: _____

SOCIAL PERFORMANCE S

1 We're an incredibly enthusiastic bunch of people _____

2 We operate in highly effective teams _____

3 The quality of our relationships, both within the
   organization and without, is superb _____

4 Our corporate culture is richly cohesive _____
   Sub total: _____

INTELLECTUAL PERFORMANCE | *S*

1 We're very shrewd operators _____

2 Our management systems and controls are both finely tuned and highly adaptable _____

3 Our organization offers a superb learning environment _____

4 We consciously acknowledge, and perpetually flow with, a world of flux and change _____

Sub total: _____

ECONOMIC GOALS | *S*

1 Our will to win is absolute _____

2 Our aggressive business strategy will outdo and outlast all our rivals _____

3 We have a cooperative strategy designed to develop fully our technical and commercial potential _____

4 We are so strongly interlinked with our clients and associates that we have formed a joint personality _____

Sub total: _____

ORGANIZATIONAL PERFORMANCE | *S*

1 Our organization is able to handle all possible manoeuvres that might be required immediately _____

2 We have structured our organization effectively, taking in all functions and contingencies _____

3 We have established an intricate corporate architecture, harmonizing our constituent organizations _____

4 A natural form of management, modelled on the laws of nature, has been established and is being maintained _____

Sub total: _____

ENVIRONMENTAL PERFORMANCE	S
1 We have a very good feel for the market	_____
2 Our powers of market analysis and response are very highly developed	_____
3 We intuitively plan the evolution of our business through intimately formed links with our stakeholders	_____
4 We are able to recognize unlimited possibilities through our unique insight and farsightedness	_____
Sub total:	_____

CREATIVE PERFORMANCE	S
1 We have enough imagination to be able to see round most tight corners	_____
2 We are able to manage innovation systematically and successfully	_____
3 We have the creative capacity to develop and renew our people and our businesses continually	_____
4 We have the vision to transform the spirit of our organization and the resources of the globe	_____
Sub total:	_____

Now you can plot each of the sub totals in the Figure. Connect each performance rating with a graph line. This will provide an indication of your organization's overall development across the spectrum of cultural attributes.

Cultural performance spectrum

Performance

Physical   Social   Intellectual   Economic   Organizational   Environmental   Creative

Next, you need to total all your scores for questions 1, 2, 3 and 4, in turn. This provides a performance score on each of the primal, rational, developmental and metaphysical domains.

If you have scored:

24-28 you are very strong in that domain
19-28 that domain is reasonably strong
14-18 you are of moderate strength there
11-13 you are rather weak in that domain
7-10 that domain is totally underdeveloped.

Cultural performance domains

Total score

Primal   _____

Rational   _____

Developmental   _____

Metaphysical   _____

CONCLUSION

Managing cultural change in Great Britain

In Great Britain, which naturally lends itself towards a rational approach to management and organization, there has been a recent reversion to primal or 'enterprise' culture. For that reason both primal and rational approaches are relatively easy to access.

As an agent of cultural change, in the UK, you will therefore find it easier to tap underlying assumptions and to work with attitudes and beliefs than anything else. The job of instilling shared values, and creating or resurrecting a cultural network might be less easy than in the United States, but certainly will not be beyond the bounds of possibility. It is therefore the developmental and metaphysical approaches which will prove to be most difficult.

If you are operating within a middle-sized company, based predominantly in Western Europe and in America, the primal and rational approaches are likely to stand you in good stead. However, if your operations extend East and South, and if you are working within a large and mature corporation, you are likely to have problems.

The people of the East and South are more receptive, generally, to the developmental and metaphysical approach to cultural change than those of us in the West and North. Moreover, if you are to effect fundamental transformation, as opposed to modest cultural change, you will need to redirect the spirit of your organization.

Managing cultural change across the globe

With the advent of 1992, not to mention the progressive globalization of business, the promotion of shared values and an enterprise culture, at a primal level, will not be enough. Similarly, a rational attempt to change attitudes and beliefs will prove inadequate.

If, as an agent of cultural change, you wish to turn your organization from a nationally- to an internationally-based institution, you will need to develop its people and technology, and transform its spirit. In that context the Psion and Transcriba case studies are more appropriate than those of JMS and ARK.

However, and in the final analysis, many of you will manage to make great cultural strides by merely applying, rigorously and appropriately, the primal and rational approaches that have worked for JMS Seed Company and for ARK Computer Services.

I wish you well on your way.

Index

action and activity
    as cultural attributes, 13–14
    human, 69, 72, 160
    metaphysical, 133–4
actuality (reality)
    creation of, 123–6
    organizational, 69, 70–1, 155–7
adaptability, 13, 124
'Aha' experience, 119–20, 192
amateur, cult of, 22–3
analysis of cultures, 65–73, 129–33,
    217–25
    see also case studies; models
anthropology, 5
Apollo, 56, 59–60, 61–5 passim
Apple Computers, 86, 89
ARK Computer Services (ACS)
    case study of, 149–66
art and creativity, 24–8
assumptions, cultural, 69–73,
    154–62
AT & T, 91
Athena, 57, 60, 61–5 passim
Athos, A., 6–7, 8, 9, 32–3, 82–3
atomization, organizational, 43–4
Austin, N., 35–7

Babbage, Charles, 28
Bayley, Stephen, 27
balance, cultural, 61-3
Bank of Credit and Commerce
    (BCC), 89–90, 92, 95
Bauhaus School of Design, 27
behaviour, organizational, 47, 49,
    65–76
    case study (ARK), 149–66
behavioural sciences, 3–4, 46

Bennis, Warren, 4
Blake, William, 105
Bodyshop International, 95, 102,
    103
born heroes, 38–9, 141–2
Branson, Richard, 83, 91
Britain
    cultural attributes of, 28–31, 83
        disorder, 20
        love of recreation, 20–4
        pursuit of quality, 14–16, 28–9
        spirit of creativity, 24–8
        spirit of tolerance, 16–20, 29
    history of, 17–20
    managing cultural change in,
        225–6
Buber, Martin, 198
businesses see corporate culture

capitalism, rise of, 16
Cartwright, Edmund, 22–3
case studies
    ARK Computer Services, 149–66
    JMS Seed Co, 137–46
    Karanga Mininc Co, 119–26
    Psion Computers, 173–90
    Sony, 111–19
    Transcriba, 191–214
Caxton, William, 22
ceremonies see mythos
Chandler, Alfred, 86
change, cultural, 41–2, 76
    approaches to, 215–16, 225–6
    and cultural inventory, 217–25
    managed and unmanaged, 73–5
character, corporate, 50, 52, 96–100
community, corporate, 50, 51–2

compass heroes, 38–9, 142–3
computers, 28, 30
  see also ARK; Psion
Conran Foundation, 27
Conran, Terence, 91
consolidation phase of
  development, 84–5
corporate culture
  definitions of, 2
  evolution of idea of, 3–11, 46
  see also developmental;
      metaphysical; primal *and*
      rational approaches
cottage industry, 15–16
covenant, organizational, 118–19
creation of an organization, 74, 84,
  119–21, 191–200
creativity, 24–8
culture
  definitions of, 1, 3, 5, 6–7, 8, 46–7
  see also corporate culture
Curie, Pierre, 108
customs, 51–2
  see also mythos

Data General, 105
Deal, T., 6, 33, 34–5, 37–44, 75
design
  industrial, 26–7, 29–30, 87
  organizational, 63–5
developing countries
  cultural attributes of, 13–14, 83
  see also Zimbabwe
developmental approach to
  corporate culture, 8
  case study of, 173–90
  and character types, 96–100
  and cultural change, 215–18
  evolutionary idea of, 78–9, 105
  laws of, 79–81
  and national characteristics, 81–3
  process of, 84–90, 105–6
  and products and services, 100–5
  roots of, 90–2
  and types of organization, 92–6
diagnosis of corporate culture, 40–1
  see also analysis
Dionysius, 58, 61, 62–5 *passim*

disorder, 20
diversity, cultural, 54–65, 76
Drucker, Peter, 98
Dube, James, 122–3, 126

eccentricity, 29
'enabling' company, 94, 96
enterprise, 13, 85–6, 92–3
environment, organizational,
  69–70, 154–5
ethics *see* values
Eurotunnel Group, 91
evolution, 73, 76
  see also developmental approach
excellence, 34–7
'existential' (people) culture, 57–8,
  61, 62–5 *passim*

F International, 119
family form, 118, 138–9
Fayol, Henri, 4
Ford, Henry, 85–6, 102
freedom, 14
  and creativity, 24–8
  and order, 30–1
  and recreation, 20–4

Gabor, Denis, 28
gardening, 20, 23–4
General Motors, 86–7, 102
Global Business, The, (Lessem), 13
Glyn, Anthony, 19–21, 23, 24–5
gossips, 39–40, 141, 145
Great Britain *see* Britain
griefwork, 206
Gropius, Walter, 27
guilds, 15–16

Habitat, 91
Handy, Charles, 22, 47, 48–9, 54–65,
  76, 78
'hard' cultural attributes, 32–3
Harrison, Roger, 48, 54, 76
health, organizational, 4
Heilbronner, Robert, 88

heroes, 38–9, 92–3, 94
    examples of, 140, 141–3, 157–8
Hewlett Packard, 33, 34
history
    of Britain, 17–20
    corporate, 50–1, 128–9
Hobson, J.A., 15
humanity
    action of, 69, 72, 160
    and management, 3–5
    nature of, 69, 71–2, 157–9
    and relationships, 69, 72–3, 160–2

Iacocca, Lee, 76
IBM, 33
ICI, 109
identity, corporate, 90–1
ideology, organizational, 47, 48–9,
    66
individualism, 21–2
industry, development of, 15–16,
    25–8
institutionalization of culture, 52–4
interactions, 51–2, 125
invention, 22–3, 27–8, 29
inventory, cultural, 217–25

Japan
    cultural attributes of, 13, 82–3
    management style of, 7–8, 32–3,
        87–8
    example of (Sony), 111–19
JMS Seed Company
    cultural network in, 140–6
    cultural style of, 137–9, 147–8
    rituals in, 139–40
Jobs, Steve, 86, 89, 91

Karanga Mining Company, 119–26,
    127, 129–33
Kennedy, A., 6, 33, 34–5, 37–44, 75
Kidder, Tracy, 105

Land, Edwin, 120

Lawrence, T.E., 20
laws of development, 79–81
leadership, styles of, 74–5
    examples of see case studies
Lievegoed, Bernard, 76, 80
liturgy, 117–18, 127–8, 134–5
Lovelace, Ada, 28
Lunar Society, 23, 26, 29

McCoy, Charles, 48, 50–4, 76
managed cultural change, 74–5
management
    basics of, 5–10
    see also developmental;
        metaphysical; primal and
        rational approaches
Marks, Michael, 10
Marks and Spencer, 10, 184–6
Marshall, A.H., 15
Marx, Karl, 30–1
Maslow, Abraham, 88
Masuda, Yonedi, 21
mavericks, 40, 145–6
MBWA (management by walking
    about), 36
meaning, 6–8, 53–4
    see also mythos
metaphysical approach to corporate
        culture, 9–10, 108
    case study of, 191–214
    and cultural change, 215–18
    and cultural evolution, 88–90,
        104–5
    process of, 109–11
        facilitation of, 126–35
        in Karanga Mining Co, 119–26
        in Sony, 111–19
models of cultures
    Harrison/Handy, 54–65
    Schein's, 68–73
        case study of, 149–66
Mond, Ludwig, 109
Morita, Akio, 111–19, 127, 135
mythos (myth and ritual)
    and covenant, 118–19
    creation of, 133–4, 207–8
    examples of see case studies
    function of, 113–14, 127

mythos (myth and ritual) – *contd*
  importance of, 2, 8–10, 36, 43,
    51–2
  life cycle of, 114–17
  and liturgy, 117–18, 127–8, 134–5
  mythographs, 128–33, 208–10
  nature of, 111–12
  tellers of, 39, 141, 144

Nehanda, Mbuya, 132, 134, 135
Newton, Isaac, 26, 29, 31
Nobel, Alfred, 109
Nossiter, Bernard, 14–15, 21
'nuclear' company, 95, 96

Olivetti, 91
operations, metaphysical, 111,
    128–34
order
  and disorder, 20
  and freedom, 30–1
  and quality, 14–16
  and tolerance, 16–20
organization *see* corporate culture
outlaws (mavericks), 40, 145–6
Owen, Harrison, 9–10, 108–35
    passim, 192, 199, 201, 205

Pascale, R., 6–7, 8, 9, 32–3, 82–3
'person' (existential) culture, 57–8,
    61, 62–5 *passim*
personal identity, 90–1
Peters, T., 1, 2, 5–6, 34–7, 81–2, 108
phenomenology of religion, 9
pioneering phase of development,
    84, 95–6, 97–8
policy making, metaphysical, 110,
    111–119, 126
potentiality
  and actuality, 123–6
  creation of, 119–23
Potter, David, 28–9, 168–73
  and Psion Computers, 173–90
'power' culture, 55–6, 58–9, 61–5
    passim

'priest' role in corporate culture, 39,
    117, 140–1, 144–5
primal approach to corporate
    culture, 6, 75
  attributes of, 32–3, 34–7, 43–4,
    137–9, 147–8
  and corporate evolution, 78,
    85–6, 99, 101–2
  and cultural change, 41–2, 215–18
  and cultural diagnosis, 40–1
  and cultural network, 38–40,
    42–3, 139–46
proactive organizations, 125
Proctor and Gamble, 34
products and services, 100–5
propriety, cultural, theory of, 48–9,
    61–5
Psion Computers, 29
  case study of, 173–90
public companies, 93, 96

quality, pursuit of, 14–16, 28–29, 87

rational approach to corporate
    culture, 4–5
  attributes of, 50–4
  basis of, 47–9
  case study of, 149–66
  and corporate evolution, 78,
    86–7, 99, 102–3
  and cultural analysis, 65–73
  and cultural change, 73–5, 76,
    215–18
  and cultural diversity, 54–65, 76
  scope of, 46–7, 75–6
reality *see* actuality
recreation and leisure, 20–4
relationships, human, 72–3, 160–2
religion *see* metaphysical approach;
    mythos
renewal, 85, 98–9
responsible character, 98
Rhodes, Cecil, 133–4, 135
Rhodesia (Zimbabwe), 20, 119–26,
    129–35
rituals *see* mythos

'role' culture, 56–7, 59–60, 61–5
   passim
Roots of Excellence, The, (Lessem),
   8, 79
Rostow, Walt, 25–6, 29
Ruskin, John, 15

Schein, Edgar, 4, 47, 49, 65–76, 149,
   166–7
Schultz, Frances, 144–5
Schultz, John H., 142, 143
Schultz, John M., 137, 139, 141–2,
   147–8
Schultz, John M. II, 142–3
Schumacher, E.F. 23, 31
scientific revolution, 25–6
Scott Bader Commonwealth, 94
self-development, 88, 105–6
Selznick, Philip, 4, 47–8
senses, utilization of, 35–6
services and products, 100–5
Shirley, Steve, 119
Shockley, William, 113
show business, management as,
   36–7
Sinclair, Clive, 28, 89, 91
   and Psion Computers, 176,
       178–9, 181, 182, 189, 190
Sloane, Alfred, 86–7
Smith, Adam, 30–1
social evolution, 81
'soft' cultural attributes, 32–3
Sony Corporation, 111–19, 127, 135
spies, 40, 141, 145
spirituality *see* metaphysical
   approach; mythos
stories *see* mythos
strategy, organizational, 86–7,
   110–11, 119–26, 127
symbolic management, 37–43,
   139–46
synergy, 87–8

'task' culture, 57, 60, 61–5 *passim*
Teague, Walter, 103
3M, 33, 119
tolerance, 16–20, 29

Toynbee, P., 17, 29
trademarks, 117–18
transcendence *see* metaphysical
   approach
transcorporate identity, 91
Transcriba, case study of, 191–214
transformation stage of
   development, 85, 99–100,
   109–10
tree of life, concept of, 79, 84
   'branches', 96–100
   'fruit', 100–5
   'roots', 90–2
   'stem', 92–6
Trevelyan, G.M., 16, 22–3

United States of America
   cultural attributes of, 13, 81–2,
      225
   management styles in, 32–3
universal identity, 91–2
unmanaged cultural change, 73–4

values
   and rational approach, 47–8, 50–4
   shared *see* corporate culture
Virgin, 91
vision, 13–14, 121, 129

Waterman, R., 1, 2, 5–6, 34–5, 81–2,
   108
Watson, T.J., 2
whisperers, 40, 141, 146
whistle blowers, 40, 145–6

Yoishi, Yokoi, 116

Zeus, 56, 58–9, 61–5 *passim*
Zimbabwe (Rhodesia), 20, 119–26,
   129–35

Dr Lessem's other publications include

The Roots of Excellence, 1986
Intrapreneurship, 1987
Global Business, 1987
Heroic Management, 1988
Global Management Principles, 1989
Development Management, 1990
Towards the Learning Organisation (forthcoming 1991)